The Money Noose

Noose

—Jon Corzine and the Collapse of MF Global

Brick Tower Press
Habent Sua Fata Libelli

Brick Tower Press
1230 Park Avenue
New York, New York 10128
Tel: 212-427-7139
bricktower@aol.com • www.BrickTowerPress.com

Library of Congress Cataloging-in-Publication Data
Skyrm, Scott E.D.
The Money Noose, The Rise and Fall of MF Global
ISBN 978-1-883283-35-3

1. Business—Economics 2. Business—Corporate History
3. Business—Business Leaders 4. Panic of 2008 5. Business—Capital
Markets

Copyright © 2013 by Scott E.D. Skyrm
Trade Paper, Nonfiction

First Printing, June 2013

The Money Noose

Noose

—Jon Corzine and the Collapse
of MF Global

Scott E.D. Skyrm

TO MY FAMILY

ACKNOWLEDGEMENTS

I wish to thank the following people: Andrew Spencer, who worked tirelessly helping me with the writing of this book, consolidating my technical expertise with his literary creativity and without whom I could never have completed the work. I also wish to thank: my wife, Jennifer Skyrm, who edited many chapters, and Stan Jonas, Peter Buckley, Bill Blain, Antoine Carle, James K. Broder, Leonard Teifeld, and Ruth Engelke for help proofreading.

Contents

Preface 9

Introduction 13

Chapter One, Man Financial 19

Chapter Two, Refco 29

Chapter Three, Raising Capital 41

Chapter Four, Going Rogue 51

Chapter Five, Enter Roseman 65

Chapter Six, Jon Corzine 75

Chapter Seven, Changes 91

Chapter Eight, The European Debt Crisis 105

Chapter Nine, Repo-to-Maturity 119

Chapter Ten, Managing Risk Management 131

Chapter Eleven, Over-Leveraging 143

Chapter Twelve, Downfall 155

Chapter Thirteen, Bankruptcy Week 171

Chapter Fourteen, Interactive Brokers 191

Chapter Fifteen, Liquidation 201

Chapter Sixteen, The Money Noose 217

Chapter Seventeen, Finding the Money 227

Chapter Eighteen, After 239

PREFACE

It seems that you can't turn on a television, open a newspaper, or even log on to the Internet today without finding news about the current state of the economy. Whether it's jobs numbers or the national deficit, economic news has become commonplace. And since the beginning of the financial crisis in 2008, much of that news has focused on the banking industry, specifically investment banks.

There has been a great deal of negative sentiment concerning the banks coming from upset Americans. And quite frankly, much of that anger is justified. It's easy to lash out at those faceless entities when you see your own retirement fund tanking while a CEO's annual bonus eclipses the GNP of many small countries.

Compounding the bad news that so many of us are seeing are the all-too-frequent news stories about companies accused of misusing clients' funds or otherwise bilking their own customers for money. It's bad enough that many large banks contributed to the economic downturn, but nothing can incite angry investors and government officials more than the criminal mischief in the industry.

In 2010, President Barack Obama signed into law the Dodd-Frank Wall Street Reform and Consumer Protection Act. The scope of that law is tremendous, and to fully dissect it would require a book of its own. Suffice it to say, though, that the new law tightened banking restrictions and increased the government's oversight into the goings-on of investment banks and other financial institutions.

But just like any law, Dodd-Frank was only as good as its enforcement. And in the case of Wall Street, it's next to impossible to watch out for every investment firm at every hour of every day. Case in point: despite the new restrictions imposed by the law, MF Global was bankrupt less than a year after the law's passage.

That event was precipitated by the firm's misuse of customers' money, specifically the "seg funds" that were supposed to be sacrosanct and untouchable by a brokerage firm. When news of the bankruptcy became public, many average investors greeted the news of MF Global's demise with a shrug. It didn't affect them in any way, so it was just another case of greedy bankers getting their just reward.

And that is, more often than not, one problem with the business news. Articles frequently use business-specific jargon like "seg funds" or "central clearing counterparties" or "repo-to-maturity," and those without a Wall Street background often have no idea what the terms mean. The common reaction is one of blissful ignorance; if I don't know what it means, it must not have anything to do with me.

But it does.

And not just to the thousands of customers of the failed futures broker whose missing segregated funds became an important reality. Any customer of a brokerage firm – be it an online account that you manage yourself or a traditional brick-and-mortar investment bank – needs to understand the importance of seg funds. Any cash that is not directly tied up in a specific investment that is in the customer's account is technically part of the "seg fund" pool. And that money – the seg part is short for "segregated" – is kept separately, and is legally untouchable by the brokerage firm. So if you're giving an institution a good chunk of your personal property to hold and to invest, you rest easy in the knowledge that they won't misuse your funds.

But as the case of MF Global has shown, sometimes those seg funds aren't quite as segregated as an investor might hope. Sometimes those funds are used by the firm for its own gain. And sometimes, as in the case of MF Global, those funds are used by the firm for its own loss. And in the most extreme of those cases, those losses become the individual customer's losses.

It is comforting, to be sure, to believe that governmental regulations are enough to prevent the sort of fraudulent activity that brought down MF Global. But again, those activities occurred despite the fact that the regulations were already in place. The security blanket was very painfully torn away, and MF Global customers were major losers in the end.

How, then, can investors protect themselves from this outcome? The best answer is education. Investors need to be fully aware of what is involved in the investment process, and that includes an understanding of seg funds. It is, after all, their money. This book is designed tell the story of MF Global, what went wrong and how things came to an abrupt end. In those regards, it's an incredible story. However, the story will also provide you with the fundamental education you need in order to protect yourself. And while there is no guarantee that financial institutions won't repeat the mistakes made by MF Global, an educated investor will know the questions to ask before it's too late.

Introduction

"All things are subject to interpretation.
Whichever interpretation prevails at a given time is a function of power
and not truth."

                                             -Frederich Nietzsche

        When explaining or remembering an event or situation, there
are generally two ways of looking at it. There's the simple way, the
description that goes on for a few words or a single sentence. It makes
thinking of the event tidy and easy. You can sum it up quickly, then
remember it that way for the future. It's a by-product of the culture we
live in, where politicians and news reporters talk in sound bites and
headlines.
        Then, of course, there's the more complicated version. It has a
more complex explanation. There are inter-relations among events and
different people have different interpretations of what occurred. It is an
example of what is referred to as Chaos Theory. The oft-cited
explanation of Chaos Theory involves a butterfly somewhere in
equatorial Africa. That butterfly flaps its wings, causing a microscopic
disturbance in the air around it. That disturbance joins with others, and
eventually they all add up to a hurricane. Without that initial butterfly's
wings flapping, the argument goes, there would be no hurricane.
        Regardless of which type of explanation you prefer, there is the
issue of interpretation of that information, as posited by Nietzsche in the
above quote. If you prefer the shorter version of stories, it is up to you

to fill in the blanks regarding how the action moved from the beginning
to the end. What happened between that initial butterfly moving and
the eventual hurricane? Alternatively, the longer style of the description
will better fill in the blanks, but can leave just as many questions as
someone gets deeper into the story. Both types of storytelling involve
interpretation by the one who reads them. What caused the second
butterfly to suddenly flap its wings at that exact moment?

Today's news is filled with a seemingly endless supply of
corporate scandals, ranging from the relatively ho-hum events of
individuals operating outside the lines of federal regulations to firms
literally stealing billions of dollars from investors. Names like Kenneth
Lay and Dennis Kozwloski. Firms like AIG, Tyco, and Enron. These are
names that many of us are familiar with, though our familiarity is usually
tinged with what is only a basic understanding of the events.

Our understanding of those stories is, like all stories, predicated
on our interpretation of whatever source of news where we got the
original information. There are those who have labored intensively over
the story of such firms as Bear Stearns and Lehman Brothers, seeking to
better understand what disastrous sequence of events led to their
respective demises. There are those, too, who are content to simply
know that there once were two investment banks that went by the
name of Bear Stearns and Lehman Brothers, and both collapsed several
years ago.

Another name that made headlines is MF Global, and its story
shares many of the same characteristics of those that came before it. We
know what happened. At least we know what the headlines told us. The
firm was forced into bankruptcy after committing fraudulent acts.

On the surface – in the condensed version of the story – MF
Global will be remembered as a highly leveraged firm that used
customer money to hide a loss. That single-sentence description of the
firm's downfall is a tidy package that sums up the basic outcome. It's a
headline, albeit a somewhat long one.

But as Chaos Theory tells us, there's much more to the story
than can be contained in that single-sentence description. The full
truth of what happened is incredibly complicated. So complicated, in
fact, that it's too long for even a book to describe all the events that
contributed to the MF Global collapse. That said, I am going to give my
best attempt at explaining it.

In one way, an obscure trading strategy known as repo-to-maturity (RTM) brought down MF Global. Again, that's too simple of an explanation. Because in another way, those same trades did not. The RTMs created the liquidity squeeze on the company, which caused the capital deficiency, ultimately setting events in motion that would doom the firm. The RTM trades impacted MF Global in many other ways too. By September, the margin required to support the RTM trades was reducing capital allocated to other businesses. Their mortgage group and prime brokerage groups did not have enough capital, and were actually asking clients to reduce their trading positions to free up margin just for LCH.Clearnet. Any business could not survive under such circumstances.

On the other hand, MF Global was making money on the RTM trades and they did not lose money on any of them – none of the European securities they owned defaulted or had been restructured. Former MF Global Chief Risk Officer Michael Stockman even added in his testimony before Congress that all of the securities "that reached maturity have been paid in full." The bankruptcy was not due to a loss on the RTM trading position. If the trades could have been held to maturity, MF Global would have received their entire margin, their entire principal, and all their interest back. MF Global's bankruptcy was sparked because of a liquidity crunch following their earnings announcement and disclosures of controversial sovereign-debt trades, not because they booked a giant loss. In reality, their liquidity squeeze was not really about margin and leverage, it was more the perception of leverage that became the reality.

The reality MF Global existed in was an unfortunate one at best. The world had just experienced a severe banking crisis three years earlier. After the collapse of Bear Stearns, Fannie Mae, Freddie Mac, Lehman Brothers, AIG, and Washington Mutual, it was no surprise MF Global's counterparties and creditors were quick to cut off their funding lines and stopped doing business with them. A senior member of the MF fixed income management team summed it up best by saying, "MF Global had the wrong business model and the wrong people, at precisely the wrong time in the market. We did not deal with our central problem of unprofitable core business operations and out-of-control overheads, choosing instead to embark on a difficult path of recreating an investment banking business into what is widely recognized as historically one of the most challenging times in financial markets' history."

But plenty of companies survived the same period in history, so what was it that doomed MF Global when other firms came out battered, but still kicking? The short answer goes back to the idea of perception versus reality. There was a perception of a liquidity crisis within the firm, a rumor that created a new reality. But, of course, there's more to the story.

The story begins, though, with a noose. As a noose tightens around the neck of its victim, the airway is cut off. The victim struggles to breathe as the tension increases from all sides. The airway is cut off, the body is deprived of life-giving oxygen, the victim lapses into unconsciousness and eventually death.

The same phenomenon happened to MF Global. As the perception became reality, there was a noose tightening around the neck of the firm, cutting off the financial lifelines that it normally could have drawn on for survival. And like any human fighting to stay alive trying anything to ease the burning in his lungs as his airway is constricted, the executives of MF Global felt their own survival instincts kicking in. They did things that they shouldn't have done, things that were illegal. As the Reverend Jesse Jackson once said, "In tough economic times, desperate people do desperate things." MF Global was facing some of the toughest economic times in modern history. In turn, they did what can only be described as desperate things.

Chief among those desperate things is an act that is, ironically enough, still somewhat shrouded in mystery. The end fact – absolute reality that it is – is that someone from the firm authorized the illegal use of customer funds to help keep the dying firm afloat. But who authorized it – or whether anyone authorized, for that matter – is a matter of debate, and one that has resulted in much finger-pointing. And it worked, if only for a few days. It was an action that, although illegal, was done with arguably the best of intentions and an arguable lack of malicious forethought.

Does that serve as a defense for those who allowed the illegal act? It again comes back to your own interpretation. Is the beggar who steals a loaf of bread to feed his family guilty of theft? The same moral implications are present in this story, though MF Global lacks the sentimental humanity associated with a homeless person trying to provide food for his starving children.

What follows is a general accounting of the facts that led to MF Global's collapse, as well as the story of the major players involved. It is a chaotic story, one in which individual actions taken in and of themselves are relatively minor. But the sum of those individual actions equal the same end result. In math, two plus two always equals four. There's no room for interpretation. But in the larger world – even a world in which math plays a significant role – there is room for interpretation of how, exactly, two and two added up to four. But even though the facts of the story are open to interpretation, the reality, just like in math, is concrete.

CHAPTER ONE

Man Financial

The place was known as the home of the less-desirables, the dregs of society. It was given that designation because it sat outside the protective walls of its larger neighbor to the west, the City of London. Whitechapel, England, was home to tanneries, breweries, and other sorts of businesses that were shrouded in less-than-pleasant aromas. In turn, those businesses employed that segment of society willing to work in such horrible conditions, oftentimes for minimal pay.

As businesses in Whitechapel grew and the population of social outcasts ballooned, a faction of entrepreneurial-minded women sprang up in the hamlet, pedaling the services of the world's oldest profession. The town resembled something out of a Charles Dickens novel – overcrowded, polluted, and crime-ridden. It was so deplorable that American author Jack London wrote a book about the village, called *People of the Abyss*.

But Whitechapel was not without its would-be saints, men and women set on protecting and saving the population's collective soul. One such man was William Booth, a Methodist missionary born to moderately wealthy parents. When he was a child, Booth's family sank into abject poverty and his father became an alcoholic. By the mid-1800s, Booth had become a robust lay minister for the Christian faith, and in 1852, he became a full-time Methodist minister. After a rift with the governing body of the Methodist Church, Booth broke away to form his own Christian mission in Whitechapel, the Christian Revival Society. After two decades of effort, he decided a more forceful approach was needed. He fashioned himself into a religious soldier, fighting the good fight to rid the world of poverty by encouraging and empowering those less fortunate. In 1878, in a small building on Whitechapel Road, the Salvation Army was established.

It wasn't just the do-gooders trying to elevate the image of Whitechapel above the bottom rungs of the societal ladder. There were others with similar motives, though their actions were less aligned with religion. One such person was a man who, according to one of his letters to the authorities, was "down on whores." His personal remedy for cleansing Whitechapel was through murder and dismemberment. He signed that letter with his trade name, Jack the Ripper.

It is, on some level, appropriate that the same village that bore the likes of Jack the Ripper and other "people of the abyss" also served as the home of a man who would form what was to become MF Global. After all, if history has taught us anything, it is those who truly exceed the status quo that are remembered by historians. If you want to commit financial fraud and be remembered, follow the lead of MF Global and make sure you're one of the largest financial bankruptcies ever. In other words, swing for the fence.

Of course, James Man had no way of knowing what would happen 250 years after the founding of his business. He was just a kid from Whitechapel and wasn't so inclined to be remembered by historians as either the saver or the murderer of social miscreants. Rather, he fancied himself a businessman. His business training was rudimentary at best. As a young boy, Man was apprenticed to a Whitechapel cooper named William Humphrey, from whom Man was to learn the business of barrel making. Man finished his period of apprenticeship in 1776 and began paid employment for Humphrey, a position he held until 1783, when Man was 29-years old.

After leaving Humphrey's employment, Man started his own sugar cooperage and brokerage. His plan was to broker the sugar itself in addition to making the casks to store it. Within a year, the lucrative nature of sugar brokerage made the cooper business seem less important, until it disappeared altogether in 1784. At that time, the British Royal Navy contracted with Man to supply the sailors with rum, a contract that the Man Group would hold and continue to service for nearly 200 years.

The business made Man very wealthy. Though he died in 1823, the firm he'd built continued to grow and today remains one of the United Kingdom's largest investment groups. After his death, the business offered gainful – and lucrative – employment to many generations of his offspring. In 1869, the company became E.D.F. Man, named after his three grandsons who expanded the business into coffee and other physical commodities. While E.D.F. Man grew at a relatively good clip through the nineteenth and early twentieth centuries, it wasn't until the late 1970s that things really accelerated in terms of the firm's expansion. Moving away from solely physical commodities brokerage, they added a division specializing in commodity futures and then into futures brokering.

By 2000, the overall business was becoming too large to manage as one entity, so in March 2000, they separated into three separate businesses. ED&F Man was the name ascribed to the division that handled the business of agricultural commodities. The arm that handled funds management became Man Group PLC. And the futures brokerage business became ED&F Man International, which later changed its name to Man Financial, with Kevin Davis named the new firm's CEO.

Davis was born in London, England, the son of a menswear store owner and his homemaker wife. As he grew up, Davis worked in his father's store on Saturdays and school holidays. The young man's professional ambitions went well beyond just selling clothes to London's fashionable male population, and he enrolled at the University of Kent at Canterbury, where he earned a bachelor's degree in politics and government.

After graduation, since he didn't want to work for his father, nor take over his father's business, like so many kids both before and after him, he used his father's professional network to search for gainful employment. The senior Davis knew a clothing supplier in Chicago with connections to the American financial markets through Henry Shatkin, a well-known Chicago futures trader with a legendary reputation. Shatkin was a professional futures trader, well established in the industry and during his 50-plus years of work served as a director at the Chicago Board of Trade.

Davis got a job working for the Henry Shatkin Trading Company in 1982, where he started as a runner on the floor of the

Chicago Board of Trade. Davis was charged with taking pit cards, getting lunch for the traders, and generally running errands. It wasn't glamorous, to say the least, but it was the first rung on the ladder to becoming a trader.

He did what he was told, paid close attention to the action around him, and learned a lot about the business. When Prebon Yamane bought out Shatkin's firm the following year, Davis had a chance to return to London to work for the new parent company. By this time, Davis had proven himself on the floor, and had been promoted to the position of desk broker. He left Prebon Yamane to accept a job with Balfour Maclaine in 1983, and later that year was hired by ED&F Man International to start the firm's European interest rate futures business.

In 1994, Davis was named global head of interest rates at ED&F Man, a position he held for five years, until 1999, when he became the global head of brokerage activities. He'd certainly come a long way since his days running pit cards in Chicago, but he wasn't done climbing just yet. Within a year, Davis was named chief executive officer, where his future and the future of the newly-created Man Financial seemed bright.

* * *

Under Davis' leadership, Man Financial developed a specialized business on what was called "block trading" in the European financial markets. Block trades are privately negotiated trades in futures and options that are negotiated off the exchange. The reason block trades must be relegated to private settings away from the official exchange is because of the size of the trades and liquidity of those particular contracts. The trades typically involve numbers of contracts large enough to move the market dramatically if the transaction occurs publicly. They are kept out of the public view by the broker in order to preserve the liquidity and price levels for the client.

For example, if an investor wants to sell a large number of contracts – say 100,000 – he can do one of two things. One, he can send it to the exchange where the contract is traded. The result, however, would be that the price of the contract plummets dramatically due to the sheer volume of the sale in a thinly traded contract. The other option – a block trade via the futures broker – would be a much better option for both parties. For the seller, they would get a much better price than if they were to unload the contracts publically on the exchange just by letting the futures broker find a buyer or buyers for the entire size of the transaction. And the buyer would typically be able to negotiate a better purchase price than what the current market dictates.

Running concurrent with the concept of block trading is the concept of liquidity in the back-months of futures contracts. Back-month contracts are those contracts that settle further in the future than the "front-month," which is generally where most trades in the contract occur. Typically, the further the contract away from the front-month, the less liquidity it has. Depending on the particular futures contracts, back-months can lose liquidity after just a few months or after a few years. There was a great deal of money to be made in back-month contracts, which was historically captured by the floor traders in the exchange pits. But when the futures exchanges moved from open outcry in the trading pits to electronic trading from desks, liquidity that had been provided by the pit traders for the back-month contracts evaporated.

Open outcry is the name given to the communication methods employed by traders on the floor of futures exchanges. As its name suggests, open outcry is associated with brokers yelling back and forth to one another while executing trades. The noise can be deafening, and it's commonplace to see brokers use hand signs as an alternative method of communication. With the dawn of electronic trading, open outcry increasingly gave way to computers, though there are still some contracts traded via the old-fashioned method. Proponents of open outcry point out that a trading pit is a lot like a poker table, and actually being able to see your adversary's face can help you determine his moves. However, as other markets became more electronic, speed and efficiency made computerized trading the preferred method.

That move to electronic trading – and the corresponding removal of the element of direct human interaction – killed the liquidity of back-month contracts. When the open outcry system was in place, the brokers on the floor served as market makers. In addition to taking orders, they'd provide both the bid and offer prices, thus taking the risk of buying and selling, which provided liquidity to execute client orders. But when they moved out of the pits and were forced to sit at desks staring at computer screens, they were no longer in the thick of things, seeing the other traders on the floor, and monitoring other contract prices. In other words, they'd were taken from the poker table and forced to play online, which made it that much harder to read their opponents' faces and follow the depth of the market. Electronic trading created more volume and liquidity in the front-months, but created a void in the least liquid and hardest months to trade.

Man Financial and its new CEO saw a business opportunity to allow them to exploit the situation. Their new business model was built on the development of electronic screen execution for back-months contracts traded on European futures exchanges. The key was to have enough buyers and sellers in the back-months; if a firm could provide both, they could create the requisite liquidity themselves. Once the parties were assembled, it was just a matter of pairing them off like kids at a dance, then sending the orders to the floor. And that is exactly what Man Financial did.

Because they had created what was nearly a monopoly, Man Financial was able to charge huge commissions to trade the back-months because they were able to get trades done, whereas other firms could not. So they got what they wanted. In the early 2000s, in fact, anyone trading back-months of Euribor (the Euro Interbank Offered Rate) or Short Sterling in futures or options would be running at least part of that trade through Man Financial. It was a brilliant business move that made a lot of money for Man Financial, but it had one major limitation: it didn't travel well.

As an international firm, Man Financial wanted to expand its operations across borders, and especially across the Atlantic Ocean to the large markets of North America. Chief among the expansion goals was to bring back-month futures trading to the American market, but there was a major obstacle, namely that American futures exchanges had much stricter rules governing block trades.

For starters, the U.S. trading rules prohibited futures brokers from internalizing order flow, so all transactions had to be reported and traded on the exchange. That meant those orders that defined block trades couldn't be out of the public view, which also meant block trades would directly affect the contract prices. From the brokers' perspective, that wasn't necessarily a bad thing, because it meant they received nice commissions, since futures commissions were still higher in the back-months in the U.S. But the clients – and they are, after all, the *raison d'être* for the brokers – didn't get the best prices after paying those huge commissions. And while some of these rules have been relaxed in recent years, the U.S. still has the world's strictest rules governing block trading.

And so it seemed a flaw in Man Financial's plan for expansion since they weren't able to grow their business organically. That, however, was a small hurdle that was easily cleared; it just meant that they'd have to purchase other firms to expand their reach.

Man Financial's expansion-through-acquisition plan had two phases. First, they planned to expand their futures brokerage business, and grow it beyond physical commodities and back-month contracts. Second, they wanted to expand their operations into the United States. There were two major acquisitions that would set the stage for their future dramatics: London-based GNI and the American firm, Refco. These acquisitions would allow Man Financial to grow into other financial areas as well as expanding their reach in existing businesses.

The first major acquisition Davis oversaw was the November 2002 purchase of GNI Limited, a financial services firm based in London that offered brokerage services for futures, equity derivatives, and options. They also provided clients with investment research and advice, as well as the facilitation of online investing. A successor to the old London money brokerage firm Gerrard & National, GNI was a perfect complement to Man Financial's existing business. Whereas Man Financial was stronger in commodities, GNI offered the benefits of specializing in financial and energy futures and options. GNI also brought to the table a strong resume in equity derivatives and foreign exchange.

Just as important, however, was the fact that GNI had invested heavily in technology. They had established an online component to their business, and Davis knew that online transactions were the future of investing. Man Financial's policy wasn't so much that of trailblazer when it came to technology; rather, they took a more "acquire and adapt" approach. Davis said of the firm, "As a rule, we're a buyer of technology, not a developer. We buy other peoples' systems and then customize them to our needs."

A significant innovation that GNI brought to the Man Financial fold was the equity derivatives business called contract-for-difference (CFD). Invented by English traders in the early 1990s, CFDs were initially embraced by institutional traders in the United Kingdom. By the late 1990s, however, GNI had brought CFD contracts to the individual investor. It was, for lack of a better comparison, like the introduction of off-track betting to horse racing fans.

Off-track betting is a way for those wishing to bet on horse racing to do so without having to actually be at the horse race. So when you can't come up with the money to actually get to Saratoga or Belmont or Churchill Downs to play the ponies in person, you can always go to your local OTB betting parlor and experience the next-best thing. A CFD is much the same concept. You can place your bet and, if you bet right, collect your winnings, all without a major outlay of cash.

Playing the stock market – or any investment product, for that matter – typically involves the upfront cost associated with purchasing the actual product itself. So if you want to buy a thousand shares of XYZ and it happens to be selling at $10 a share, you're going to cough up $10,000 in order to purchase those shares. Of course, if the price of the stock goes up and you sell, you make back that initial outlay plus the profit on top of that. On the other hand, if it goes down and you sell, you're not going to make back your initial investment. But to have the opportunity to make or lose, you need that $10,000, or about half that amount, in a securities margin account.

Wouldn't it be nice if you could somehow reap the benefits of a rise in a stock price without spending a ton of money to get into the stock? That's exactly what a contract-for-difference allows investors to do. You don't buy shares of a stock; rather, you pretend to buy them, but it's just like you did. It's a single-stock futures contract or swap for the individual investor. If the stock goes up, you collect your profit; if the stock goes down, you pay the difference. In order to keep accounts current, the parties involved exchange money at the end of each day to settle the difference, just like in a futures contract or swap.

CFDs have, to be sure, gotten their fair share of criticism. Often the option to invest in a CFD is marketed toward new or otherwise inexperienced investors, who typically don't understand the risks involved. Given that the customers aren't paying to own the stock, the argument goes, they don't feel they're risking as much money, when in fact they are risking significantly more. For the same amount of investment in CFDs, an individual can leverage themselves much more than in real stocks. That criticism led regulators to make sure that the risks associated with CFDs are very clear to potential clients.

The CFD business is reminiscent of the "bucket shops" that were common in the U.S. a hundred years ago, though the term originated in England in the 1820s where homeless children would find near-empty kegs that were discarded from local drinking establishments and drain what was left into a bucket. They would then take the buckets to an abandoned shop and drink the literal bottom of the barrel. This practice became known as "bucketing," and the places where the children hid out to drink their pilfered beer came to be known as bucket houses. The term later morphed into a descriptor of illegal brokers who sought to make a profit from quasi-legal practices.

Bucket shops flourished in the U.S. in lower-class neighborhoods in the late 1800s. Back then, anyone could walk into a bucket shop – which were effectively gambling casinos – and place bets on stock and commodity prices without actually buying or selling the instrument, very much like a CFD. The bets at the bucket shop were purely wagers on the price of the security, since no actual shares were transacted on the exchange. Bucket shops offered low margin – as little as one percent – and often took the other side of the trade. The bucket shop charged the customers interest on the margin loan as well as a commission on the transaction, making the business very profitable.

During the Panic of 1907, bucket shops were demonized as contributing to the panic by running what was, more often than not, a fixed game. Because so many "investors" at the bucket shops were betting and trading on margin, they were not just subject to the risks associated with leverage, oftentimes they had no chance because the bucket shop could manipulate the price of the instrument.

Many of the stocks that bucket shops allowed were stocks that the shop traded in real life. So whereas the client of the bucket shop was simply betting on the price, the bucket shop had a much more vested interest in the performance of the stock in question. It wasn't uncommon for the bucket shop to buy or sell the shares on the exchange, causing the price to rise or fall. Once the price moved enough, the shop could declare the bet lost and collect their money. They bucket shop pulled in money on many fronts – the trading of the stock, the margin account, and from the manipulation of the poor sap that got suckered into what he thought was a fair game. The term is still used today to identify less-than-scrupulous brokerage houses, and laws banning them and their practices were enacted thereafter, effectively eliminating them by 1920.

On one level, the CFD business is the same thing as the bucket shops. They allow people to play the market without having to commit to the initial outlay of cash in order to buy their way in. They can drain the bank account of a novice investor who gets himself in too deep before he knows what he's done. For that matter, they can drain the bank account of an experienced investor for the same reason.

CFDs have a litany of benefits as far as the financial firm is concerned. The CFD business allows the firm to make markets in investments without actually owning and settling them, which means there is less capital outlay and no balance sheet considerations for the company. For the customers, a CFD enables them to speculate on securities without owning them, enabling them to speculate on products they otherwise could not, or be able to short sell stocks without all the rules associated with it. And with margin requirements significantly less for CFD trades, just like the "bucket shops," customers leverage their investments much more than possible with a traditional purchase.

GNI was heavily involved with CFD products, and the market was very lucrative for them. And what's more, they effectively had a monopoly on the business, which meant that Man Financial would inherit a true cash pipeline with the purchase of GNI. That market, paired with their repo and stock loan matched-book business, made the acquisition of GNI by Man Financial amazingly lucrative. Insofar as exporting the CFD business to the U.S., that was another non-starter due to U.S. regulatory concerns once again. Man Financial now had two solidly profitable and original businesses – back-month futures trading and CFDs – but neither could be exported to the U.S.

So once the GNI purchase was completed in November 2002, Davis set his sights on acquiring the next financial firm, this one based in New York City. They needed a futures and commodities brokerage firm that would give Man Financial a foothold in the American markets. That opportunity came along just two years later with the collapse of a firm called Refco.

CHAPTER TWO

Refco

It was in 2005 that Man Financial made its largest acquisition, the $323 million purchase of the client assets from a struggling financial firm called Refco. "Struggling" is perhaps not an accurate representation of the situation in which Refco found itself. "Bankrupt" or "completely insolvent" are better descriptors. Regardless of the semantics, however, for Man Financial it was an acquisition that proved again that failure to learn from history dooms one to repeat it.

Refco was a futures broker that listed among its distinctions as that of the largest broker, at the time, on the Chicago Mercantile Exchange, with over $4 billion in client assets and approximately 200,000 accounts. As a global firm, they had operations in 14 countries with over 2,400 employees. Refco was well known for providing futures trading, clearing, prime brokerage and financing to small hedge funds and professional trading groups, and they were especially well known for doing business with marginal accounts. For four consecutive years – 2001 to 2005 – Refco showed annual earnings gains of 33%, so when the company went public in 2005, for many investors it looked like a sure thing.

With Refco's financial state, the fact that Man Financial was still willing to spend a third of a billion dollars to buy it seems odd. If you were to buy a used car, and the description said the car was "held together with rust and duct tape" or that it had been "torched by a scorned ex-girlfriend," you'd probably move on to another option. But the management at Man Financial saw something in Refco that made them want it. Badly.

Refco was formed by a man named Ray E. Friedman and his stepson, Thomas Dittmer. During the Vietnam War, Dittmer had served as a White House social liaison, a post that introduced him to some of the country's most powerful politicians. His stepfather, on the contrary, had been on the other end of governmental power, having been convicted of selling substandard chickens to the United States Army during the Korean War, an offense that landed him in federal prison. Dittmer felt his stepfather deserved a second chance and leveraged his White House connections to obtain a presidential pardon from Lyndon Johnson on behalf of Friedman.

With a clean record, Friedman was off and running again, this time trading cattle futures on the Chicago Mercantile Exchange. As one of the first traders to enter the new market, he was, for all intents and purposes, printing his own money. In 1966, he invited his stepson to join him in the business, and in 1969, the pair formed Ray Friedman & Co. As the firm outgrew its Chicago headquarters – and, for that matter, the Chicago futures markets – they moved to New York City and changed the name to Refco. In 1974, Friedman sold his stake in the firm to his stepson, making Dittmer the chief executive officer of Refco, though Friedman continued to trade futures through his own account at the firm.

By 1998, the CEO's desk was filled by an Englishman by the name of Phillip R. Bennett, who had joined Refco in 1981 after working in lending at Chase Manhattan Bank. Bennett worked his way up the corporate ladder, gaining the rung of chief financial officer at Refco in 1983 and took over as chief executive officer 15 years later, though at the time Dittmer remained chairman of the board. The year after being named CEO, Bennett faced his first major obstacle in the form of a $6 million fine from the CFTC. A fine levied after an audit discovered a company-wide failure to keep accurate records and lax internal controls. Thomas Dittmer resigned as chairman and Bennett assumed that title in addition his role as CEO. Soon after, Dittmer would leave the firm altogether. At the time he assumed full control, Bennett owned about 50% of Refco, and over the next few years, under his tutelage, Refco added 16 smaller futures brokers to its stables, pushing the firm into new markets and new businesses.

Perhaps not surprisingly, given the firm's questionable moral compass, in addition to that $6 million, there were plenty of violations to go around. In fact, the *Wall Street Journal* listed Refco as "among the most cited brokers in the business, according to data provided by the [National Futures Association]." In 1983, Refco was fined $525,000 and Thomas Dittmer suspended from trading futures for four months for trying to corner various agricultural commodities. And in 2001, there was an incident involving a broker using fake order tickets to clear trades, a serious action that resulted in the National Futures Association ordering Refco to pay $43 million to 13 different investors. Then, in 2006, well after the bankruptcy, it was revealed that Refco had offshore accounts housing as much as $525 million in bonds that, it turned out, were actually fake. Over the years, the CFTC and NFA reported punitive action against Refco over 100 times. Given that Refco was founded in 1969 and dissolved in 2005, over the course of 36 years Refco was the target of federal investigations approximately once every four months.

Refco's corporate officers weren't the only ones participating in shady dealings. The firm was known to have accounts that were, to be kind, of questionable character. There was no semblance of customer standards at Refco; as long as the clients brought in money, the firm didn't care who they were or where their money came from. And with few barriers of internal controls to ensure legal standards were maintained, when a client could not get an account at a larger futures broker, they went to Refco. It was the mythical Wild West of the industry.

Despite its renegade nature, Refco was very much the beneficiary of good timing. Friedman founded the firm just as the cattle-futures business was taking off, which meant he was in on the ground floor and rode the swelling market all the way up. Dittmer's timing was pretty good, too; he managed to take over control of Refco just as foreign exchange and interest rate contracts were added to the futures markets. Interestingly enough, Bennett was able to continue the trend by building the firm and expanding into many other business lines. But it wasn't just the corporate officers who had Midas luck in terms of timing. At least one client – perhaps with a little help from a Refco broker or two – seemed to have equally impeccable timing.

In 1978, a female Refco client decided to invest a relatively modest sum in cattle futures. She handed $1,000 to a Refco broker and a very short time later, that $1,000 investment had turned a profit of $99,000. You read that right. When she cashed out her holdings, the client in question took home a cool hundred grand. The chances of making a return of that magnitude – even with the best financial minds advising you – are astronomical, unless there is some reason a firm would help that customer walk away with $100,000. Nothing was ever proven, however, and no criminal charges were filed, but there was always a cloud of suspicion hanging over the woman's head, however; a cloud that would later threaten her husband's presidential bid, though Bill Clinton still managed to get past the questions about his wife's financial luck.

Refco's successes, regardless of blind luck, relied heavily on acquiring client assets and adding brokers and traders, continually leveraging the firm by acquiring new talent and getting into new markets. It's a great business model, assuming the capital base continues to grow to support the asset levels. However, the risks associated with leverage are numerous. If the firm, for example, loses partner capital or funding – or if they take losses on specific trades – then they're looking at a major problem. First the firm loses the capital, and has to sell off positions to cover their margin calls. That leads to higher margin rates, which in turn can trigger more margin calls, which in turn leads to more financial losses. And the more leveraged the firm, the bigger the problem. It is like s snowball rolling downhill.

Ironically, losing funding while being overleveraged is surprisingly common in the financial markets. Examples of the danger of overleveraging are rampant in the annals of modern financial history: Bear Stearns, Lehman Brothers, and Sentinel Capital Management were all victims of this potential trap. And, as we shall soon see, the firm known as MF Global wasn't spared in the leverage noose. That's what happens when you get caught with too much leverage and the market loses confidence. Customers flee and counterparties desert the firm.

Refco bet on the markets and, at the end of the day, won more often than they lost. It was a profitable business model, and it was a business – which came with the accompanying personnel and problems associated with it – that was effectively imported into Man Financial when they bought the company. Refco wasn't the financial peach of the orchard when Man Financial acquired them in 2005. They were, to be more precise, bankrupt. How does a firm on the metaphorical top of the financial world fall so far so fast? In a word: fraud. In two words: *massive* fraud.

* * *

The downfall that Phillip Bennett oversaw can be traced to the year prior to his taking over. It began with a client error, which led to the decision to hide the loss, the origin of which was never fully explained. That loss, however, came directly from the collapse of Asian markets in 1997 and Russian default the following year. Beginning in July 1997, Asia was wracked with a financial apocalypse that began with the collapse of the Thai currency, the Baht, a collapse that was fueled by the Thai government's acquisition of foreign debt. The debt crisis in Thailand triggered an avalanche that spread across Asia, resulting in the International Monetary Fund being forced to step in with a $40 billion financial-aid package to help stabilize the region. But like a tsunami triggered by a distant earthquake, the damage was done, and the reverberations would reach far across the Pacific, to Refco in New York.

Many Refco clients were highly leveraged in Asian futures positions and securities, which tanked during the crisis. One such client was legendary hedge-fund manager Victor Niederhoffer, who racked up a $35 million loss trading short-put spreads. When the Dow Jones Industrial Average dropped 550 points on October 27, 1997, Refco immediately liquidated Niederhoffer's entire account and Refco was stuck with the loss. Other losses were generated from many customer financing positions that Bennett – at this point the CEO – had green-lighted in Asian and Russian securities that were experiencing financial distress during the crisis in Asia. When both the Asian and Russian markets collapsed, the clients were unable to repay the loans, and Refco was left with huge losses. By 1999, the losses topped $250 million, and occurred just at the time Dittmer was cashing out his Refco ownership. Whether or not that qualified as an insider fleeing a dying company is open to interpretation, but it concretely meant that capital was flowing out of the already strained Refco business. A loss at that moment would mean a loss of confidence by customers and counterparties of the firm, who would surely begin pulling their money out of Refco. It was, in short, a perfect storm of financial disasters. Bennett decidedly did not want to disclose the loss and chose to hide it, which, in the end, only delayed the inevitable collapse for several years.

It was, to be sure, a nightmare for the newly minted CEO, who flailed helplessly to preserve what was left of Refco. Bennett decided that the easiest way to cover the losses – the only immediate solution to curtail the crisis engulfing the firm – was to create phantom receivables to offset the losses. The scam was, in essence, the embodiment of a snake eating its own tail. Capitalizing on the legitimate business that Refco had relied on for so long to be profitable, Bennett set up a scheme with multiple Refco subsidiaries, fully utilizing the repo and clearing businesses.

Bennett arranged phantom money movements between a series of companies that ended up at Refco, which meant the customer losses were offset by money – albeit non-existent money – that magically showed up on the balance sheet. An affiliate called Refco Capital Markets (RCM) was the head of the snake. It originated cash loans to a hedge fund called Liberty Corner Capital Strategy (LCCS). LCCS then, in turn, loaned that money to Refco Group Holdings, Inc. (RGHI), an offshore entity maintained by Phillip Bennett with no actual legal connections to Refco. Refco Group Holdings, then, and seemingly benignly, appeared to owe the money to Refco Group (the parent company).

The scheme was called "round-trip loans" because the cash effectively moved around in a circle, from one Refco entity to a third party, to another Refco entity, and back to the last Refco entity. In the end, Liberty Corner Capital Strategy showed up as the group that had borrowed the money from one Refco entity and loaned it back to a different Refco entity, and it's still not entirely clear as to what, if anything, Liberty knew about the financial scheme they were facilitating. Many Refco officers knew what was going on, according to internal documents and emails, and assisted in the creation of fraudulent documents and transactions to help cover the fraud.

As Dittmer and other long-time Refco partners continued to cash out and leave the firm, all while Bennett was dancing frantically to keep the losses hidden, Refco desperately needed to raise capital to support the continued growth of their business, not to mention to keep themselves financially afloat.

In 1999, BAWAG, an Austrian bank, purchased a 10% stake in Refco. That helped the situation for the short term, to be sure. Five years later, in August 2004, Thomas H. Lee Partners, L.P., purchased a majority interest in Refco for $1.9 billion through a leveraged buyout; $500 million of that purchase price was financed through cash from Thomas H. Lee Partners, $600 million through notes sold to private investors, with the remaining $800 million borrowed from various banks. The result of the LBO was that the company went from $616 million in equity and $330 million in debt in 2004 to $152 million in equity and $1.2 billion in debt in 2005. It was a huge amount of leverage to support such a business, especially with a giant fraudulent hole in its capital base.

The change in ownership activity in Refco led to an initial public offering for its shares, underwritten by Goldman Sachs and Credit Suisse First Boston. Through the IPO, Refco raised an additional $583 million. The company's history of profitability and growth – paired with what seemed like optimism on the part of those willing to invest in Refco – triggered a buying spree on the first day of trading, August 11, 2005, and the stock price for RFX went from an initial offering price of $22 up to more than $27 a share by the end of the day's trading. It would hit its highest price on September 7 of that year, when the price hit $30.55. The financial euphoria associated with RFX, however, was short lived. On Monday, October 10, about two months later, the announcement came down that Refco's CEO was engaged in behavior that gave investors real reason to worry.

On that Columbus Day, all of the executives involved in the fraud had taken a vacation and were out of the office. The third-quarter end had just passed on September 30 and the round-trip loans booked at the end of September came due. Someone was supposed to move the funds back to Refco Capital Markets, but never did. That created a hole in the balance sheet that day and that led to the surprise disclosure being made public that a Refco company, controlled by the CEO, owed

$430 million to Refco. The receivable that the firm reported on its balance sheet was being hidden by phantom transactions each quarter-end to hide the missing funds. The next day, the company provided more information on how Bennett hid the debt. Bennett immediately repaid the money by obtaining a $390 million overdraft loan through BAWAG bank, Refco's early outside investor. Bennett used his Refco stock as collateral for the loan, which was certainly a bad judgment call on the part of BAWAG, which tried to halt the money transfer after the news reports of problems at Refco emerged and they could see Refco's stock price collapsing.

The events continued fast and furious after more details of Bennett's actions came to light. The story was initially reported in the press as, at its core, a simple pyramid scheme. Refco had lost money on loans several years earlier, and was not in the position to write them off as bad debts since it would hurt their capital base. Bennett didn't want to tarnish the firm's image, so he took it upon himself to buy the bad debts from Refco. One of the numerous problems, which would surface later, was that he used money from one Refco subsidiary to buy Refco's own bad debts instead of using his own funds.

With the deluge of negative press, investors began to panic. The CEO's name began a slow and lengthy trip through the mud, but it wasn't the usual dredge that seems to dog public figures so often in today's world. Philip R. Bennett, chairman and CEO of Refco, hadn't been engaged in an extramarital affair and he hadn't been arrested for driving under the influence. No, it wasn't Bennett's personal life that caused investors to panic. Rather, it was the revelation that Bennett had hidden approximately $430 million in debts from financial auditors and investors. The cherry on top of that sundae was the announcement that Bennett would be taking a leave of absence from his duties for an undetermined length of time. Presumably that departure was intended to shore up investor confidence and minimize the damage. It was hoped the scandal would then go away.

It didn't work.

Legal requirements state that any relationship between a corporation and its top officers involving company funds must be made public in various filing documents available to investors, auditors, and anyone else interested in the firm. The fact that Bennett was siphoning money through a chain of various financial transactions and that Refco had lost hundreds of millions of dollars isn't something a CEO generally wants to advertise, so Bennett opted not to disclose that information in the IPO.

Bennett's failure to make public his internal Ponzi scheme to prop up the firm's financial reputation forced the Refco board of directors to issue a statement to shareholders, in which they acknowledged that the firm's financial statements "as of, and for the periods ended; February 28, 2002; February 28, 2003; February 28, 2004; February 28, 2005; and May 31, 2005, taken as a whole, for each of Refco Inc., Refco Group Ltd. LLC and Refco Finance Inc. should no longer be relied upon." In other words, the esteemed financial history and amazing returns that the firm had showed – the numbers that sent the stock price skyrocketing in the first place – were entirely bogus and not to be trusted. The stock price, predictably enough, fell in as spectacular a fashion as it had risen, slumping down to $10.85 per share at the close of trading that day, less than 50 percent of the original IPO price. But in a refrain that was to become something of a pattern for Refco, things would get worse.

Two days after the announcement, on October 12, Phillip Bennett was quickly arrested by federal authorities and charged with securities fraud. It was, to be sure, a rapid series of events. Federal authorities cited a taped conversation between Bennett and an unnamed person in which Bennett said he would be leaving for Europe in 48 hours. The threat of imminent departure to a foreign land by a man who was the target of a federal investigation was enough to set things in motion, and Bennett was taken into custody by federal authorities with no incident.

In an interesting twist, at Bennett's bail hearing, the defense attorney told the judge that Bennett had actually repaid the $430 million deficit that was unaccounted for when he'd pledged all of his shares of Refco stock as collateral. There's a saying about teaching an old dog new tricks that applies here. Just as Bennett had done before, he argued he borrowed money to save the company from bankruptcy, thereby keeping the stock price afloat. He used his shares of the stock as collateral, so if he failed to repay the loan – that would inevitably send the shares plummeting again – the lender would be left holding worthless shares of Refco stock. Somehow he reasoned he was doing good by committing fraud, perhaps something that some MF Global employees would do several years later.

As the days passed, the situation became increasingly worse, both for Refco and for those unfortunate enough to call themselves Refco shareholders. Refco was forced to shut down Refco Capital Markets, Ltd., the Bermuda-based non-regulated securities business they owned. They had lost all liquidity for the firm, since no counterparties would trade with them nor fund their trading. That single tremor triggered the leverage avalanche that would bury the firm.

News like that can't be kept quiet, and clients – both existing and potential – soon found out what was happening with Refco. Those with accounts at the firm pulled their money, and would-be new clients steered clear of the troubled firm. With customers fleeing and no way to continue booking transactions, Refco Capital Markets had no choice but to close its doors.

That in and of itself was disastrous enough to Refco, but the bad news was to continue. It also came to light that Refco had failed to disclose transactions involving its own executives and the debt owed to the company. That news would add to the existing fraud charges the corporate officers were facing. The avalanche was burying Refco, and there was no end in sight to the fallout.

Despite everything that pointed to the contrary, Refco Securities, the futures broker, still had enough capital to operate as a firm. It remained effectively open and was not placed in bankruptcy. It had been operating on $530 million less capital before the IPO, just two months before. But the scandal and negative publicity had killed the business. Once counterparties and clients stop doing business, they experienced what amounted to a "run on the bank." While they were still effectively solvent, they were effectively dead in the water because nobody would do business with them. They began winding down the firm in an orderly manner, while they searched for a buyer. By the time the firm was sold, $4.1 billion in client assets had been transferred out of Refco's holdings, and all their counterparties stopped trading with them and funding them. Refco was stuck in quicksand.

It's a good lesson in the financial markets for financial firms and something of a foreshadowing seven years later for the firm that assumed control of Refco: once counterparties and customers lose confidence, the company is doomed to failure. When the funding counterparties, clearing banks, and central clearing counterparties begin increasing margin and stop doing business, there's no turning back. The firm sinks.

On October 17, Refco Holdings sought Chapter 11 bankruptcy protection, initially declaring assets of $49 billion. That staggering figure would have made the Refco bankruptcy the fourth largest financial bankruptcy in United States history, a title that would be held by MF Global just seven years later. But the size of the bankruptcy would be revised a few days later, putting the company's assets at $16.5 billion, a number offset by the $16.9 billion in debt after the collapse.

On October 19, the New York Stock Exchange ceased trading Refco shares. At the end of the trading session on that day, Refco shares were trading on the "pink sheets." The price per share had dropped to $0.80. No doubt BAWAG bank, that had given Phillip Bennett the $430 million loan to make good on his own financial mismanagement, still had their fingers crossed, hoping that Bennett would repay the loan out of some hidden bank account reserved for just that purpose.

The only recourse left for the dying firm was to find a buyer. After some searching, three buyers emerged. One was a group of investors led by J.C. Flowers, a New York and London-based private equity firm. They made a bid for all the stock of the futures and commodities trading entities owned by the firm, including the Refco name, of $768 million. Interactive Brokers, a lesser-know online investment business, topped the Flowers bid by offering $790 million, but neither of the two were declared the winner in the auction.

The winning bid went to Man Financial, which offered only $323 million in cash, but assumed all of Refco's debt as part of the purchase. The deal was made official in November 2005, with Man Financial acquiring all of the assets of Refco, Inc., and its affiliates. The transfer took place through Chapter 7 bankruptcy, which better protects the buyer than the more common Chapter 11, which is more a liquidation. Man Financial received Refco's exchange seats, customer accounts, and employees. The tangible assets were, at the time of acquisition, valued at $115 million. From Man Financial's perspective, the purchase had immediate benefits: new customer accounts, new businesses and a full quorum of employees to support it, even giving them an immediate presence in India, Canada, Taiwan, and Korea, countries that had been, up to that time, off their professional radar.

The dissolution of Refco was not the final insult for disgraced CEO Phillip Bennett. Man Financial had acquired the Refco clients and businesses that Bennett had worked so hard to build, but it was to get worse for him. Insofar as Bennett's business life was concerned, the end had arrived, but he still had some semblance of freedom, at least, in his personal life. That last shred of happiness dissolved, however, and the final death knell came on July 3, 2008: Bennett was sentenced to 18 years in federal prison, having pled guilty to 20 criminal charges, including securities fraud.

CHAPTER THREE

Raising Capital

When Man Financial finalized the acquisition of Refco in 2005, the firm's status within the world of financial wheeling and dealing was elevated, as Man was suddenly a much larger player in the realm of both retail and institutional futures brokerage businesses. The increased status also meant an increase in business activity, so with the absorption of the Refco businesses and personnel, the overall company, which beforehand was relatively small, also became much larger.

The brokerage unit – now a significant player in the U.S. futures markets – employed approximately 2,800 people in various capacities. The company was issued an investment grade rating by all three rating agencies, including A3 by Moody's and BBB+ by both Standard & Poor's and Fitch.

But a significant drawback was that the business was severely undercapitalized. Before the Refco purchase, Man Securities, Inc., the U.S. brokerage operation, had only $50 million in equity capital, which was extremely small by today's standards. After adding the entire Refco operation, given they had purchased the business and personnel without receiving any extra operating capital, they were even more undercapitalized. At first, they obtained a subordinated loan from their parent company for $60 million, which brought their capital up to $110 million, though it still left them capital-deficient given the size and reach of their businesses. That left Man Financial management with the challenge of figuring out new ways to bring more working capital into the company. If the plan was to keep growing their business – and that was very much the plan – then the firm would need more capital.

It was at this point that the decision was made by Man Group that the brokerage unit should be separated from the other two affiliates. The brokerage group Man Financial would be renamed MF Global after the spin-off, and much of the needed capital could be raised through an IPO. However, that capital would still not be enough to fully operate the business they imagined. So at the same time the company looked for other, more unconventional means to raise capital elsewhere.

And while MF Global had all the outward appearances of being an investment bank, it was strictly a brokerage firm with a brokerage mentality. Most of the traders and salespeople had a brokerage background; it was the business model they knew and were comfortable with. But conspicuously absent was any kind of investment banking-associated activities. There was no mergers-and-acquisitions group, no asset management, and no retail investment advisory business. They were in the brokerage business, period.

MF Global was what was affectionately referred to as an "eat-what-you-kill shop." In other words, it had a commission-based compensation system, where the salespeople were paid based on the revenues they brought in. There were no large bonuses to be anticipated at the end of the year, with questions swirling around the offices about who might get paid well and who would not. The brokers at MF Global got paid for every trade they completed, as the firm calculated the profit and loss and immediately credited the broker's account.

A compensation system like this was necessary because MF Global was still on the smaller side of investment firms, so they had to offer higher commission percentages than their bigger New York counterparts if they wanted to compete for the best talent. Top brokers at MF Global would be pulling in 35% to 50% of their net revenues, which was an extremely good living for many of them.

As a smaller firm, MF Global also faced the obstacle of not being a well-known name brand, which made attracting and retaining brokers and clients more difficult. That hindrance meant they needed to hire personable brokers who could go out and undertake the huge marketing efforts in order to develop relationships with clients to foster loyalty. This effort was now concentrated on both sides of the Atlantic.

Before the Refco purchase, most of the firm was London-based. Now, with the Refco personnel, the firm was almost equally split between Europe and the U.S., with approximately half of the revenues being generated in Europe, about 40% of the total made up in the U.S., and the remaining 10% percent coming from the Asia-Pacific region.

The futures business was the main contributor to the firm's bottom line, and a typical futures broker generates income in three different ways. The first two were, predictably enough, the two mainstays of a futures brokerage firm: execution and clearing. Execution commissions are the transactions that involve a broker's placing an order on behalf of a client at the futures exchange, and then collecting a commission for that service. In the case of institutional clients and asset managers, a pure execution broker is only involved in buying or selling the futures contract. And that's where the commitment ends. If the client doesn't have a clearing account with the executing broker, that broker relinquishes control of the contract to the client's clearing firm.

In the case of clearing commissions, these are the fees charged by the broker to cover the clearing and maintenance of the futures trade. If the client has a clearing account with a broker – in this case, MF Global – the broker holds the contract in their account at the exchange, which means the broker is required to maintain the contract, including all the margin and the regulatory requirements.

While an investment firm is generally assumed to be in the business of helping make money for its clients, the firm is also in the business of making as much money as it can for itself. But one of the best businesses ever invented was making money from the customer's money. One of the greatest sources of revenues generation at MF Global, like all futures brokers, was from making money from its clients, namely the revenues generated by holding the clients' cash.

The interest revenues a futures broker is able to earn comes from the margin deposits, which are customer funds held by the broker to offset potential market losses. The broker assumes the risk of holding the futures contracts, and that cash margin is used to make sure that the broker isn't going to suffer from losses based on a client's holdings. And as an added benefit to the broker, the investing rules allow the broker to invest the client's margin cash and make a mark-up on the income that cash generates.

The amount of income the broker can make depends on the return on the investments and the interest spread negotiated with the client, but in the case of MF Global, the typical client received a rate equivalent to the federal funds rate less 25 basis points. So if the federal funds rate is 5.25%, MF Global would typically pay its clients 5% interest and keep the .25%; but the spread MF Global charged could also be much larger.

The futures broker then takes the cash margin and invests it in accordance with rules established by the United States Commodity Futures Trading Commission (CFTC) as well as those investment policies set by the company. Depending on the brokers' willingness to take risks on those investments, they could make a great deal of money on their clients' funds. Or they could stick to conservative investments and generate a lower return. In general, though, the typical broker could expect to make about 15 basis points above the federal funds rate.

Investment income from customer margin was one of the most profitable businesses at a futures brokerage company. By investing the cash about 15 basis points above the fed funds rate and paying the clients about 25 basis points below the funds rate, MF Global assumed an income of 40 basis points above whatever the base level was after paying interest to their clients. With large enough client margin deposits and a willingness to take on risk, it meant the firm was able to generate over $1 billion in interest income annually. It's important to remember, though, that the lower the fed's target interest rate, the lower the income level the spread the brokerage firm could expect to make. If interest rates shrunk, so would their spread on the investments.

Another major source of MF Global's business was in the realm of principal transactions. Principal transactions are really a formal name for a wide spectrum of brokerage activities – bringing a buyer and a seller together in a transaction – but in general, they are transactions where the firm buys a security from one counterparty and sells it to another. In essence, the broker is merely a go-between, serving as a liaison between the two counterparties facilitating the purchase and the sale.

The counterparties involved in a typical principal transaction may be banks, dealers, other brokers, or customers, and the pairing of different counterparties can be any combination. One client might have a corporate bond to sell, so MF Global would find a buyer for that bond. The broker in the transaction, MF Global, would make money off the mark-up difference between the purchase price paid by MF Global when they bought the bonds from the customer and the sale price the firm was able to command when they sold the bonds to another firm. Typical financial products traded in this type of transaction include foreign exchange, equities, fixed income, equities, and even physical commodities.

Rounding out their revenues stream, MF Global had a well-developed financing business called repurchase agreements, known simply as repo. Like so many financial firms, the repo desk was an integral part of the overall MF Global business. On a typical repo desk, the traders would handle the specific cash and securities borrowing and lending needs for their customers. Any customer of a bank or broker-dealer will have excess cash or need to borrow cash, and the repo trading desk provides the means for their clients to receive daily funding or to invest their excess cash.

Repo desks have trading strategies that not only generate a spread from the interest rates they charge their customers, but also that bring additional cash into the firm, and that cash can be used as capital to fund the overall business. These capital-generating businesses allow firms like MF Global the luxury of relying less on the firm's own equity and bank funding. In mortgage-backed securities, the margin spread that they could earn is less, but the size of the trades can be much larger. One example of a mortgage-backed security type of financing transaction is what is commonly referred to by traders as an REIT trade.

REIT is the acronym that stands for real estate investment trust, and there are many different REIT companies available to investors. Briefly, REITs are a specific type of corporation that is set up with the sole purpose of owning real estate. The types of holdings vary, but can include commercial and residential properties, as well as real estate-related securities like commercial mortgage-backed securities (CMBS), residential mortgage-backed securities (RMBS), or federal agency securities like the bonds issued by both Freddie Mac and Fannie Mae. REITs enjoy special standing in the tax code because they are required to distribute 90% of their taxable income to their investors. Whereas

REITs are a good source of investment income for their shareholders, they are also a lucrative source of revenues for a firm like MF Global.

Many REITs are leveraged, so they need to borrow funds to pay for many of their real-estate purchases, and when a company needs leverage, they often go to Wall Street. A dealer bank finances the mortgage-backed securities for the REIT by lending cash to the corporation in exchange for the security, which serves as collateral. In other words, it's a typical repo transaction. By loaning out some of their mortgage-backed securities through repo transactions to firms like MF Global, the REIT gets the funding they need.

The primary purpose of many customer trades is, like any investment-related transaction, to generate revenues for the firm. However, in the case of an REIT customer, the overwhelming purpose is to generate capital for the broker-dealer, whereas the profit from the interest rate spread comes secondary.

Here's how it works in a typical repo transaction. The repo dealer will generally charge 5% margin on the trade, which the REIT pays. The dealer loans the securities they're holding as collateral to another customer, so that they can borrow cash in order to finance the position. Typically, the dealer is able to borrow the financing money and pledge only 2% margin, which means that they're pocketing the 3% difference in margin.

And while that might not seem like a significant amount of money, if the trade in question is worth $1 billion, the REIT trade generates $30 million in working capital for the firm. When that number is combined with the profit associated with the 15- to 20-point basis point spread on the interest rate, it's easy to see how these trades can be so lucrative. In the case of MF Global, REIT trades were an important cash-generating strategy. The firm's REIT book was much larger than $1 billion – it was reported, in fact, that the firm had about $6 billion in REIT trades on their book – and they were generating about $180 million in capital alone.

By 2007, the decision had been made to take MF Global public, which meant an initial public offering (IPO). IPOs gained a lot of notoriety during the infancy of the Internet and the tech companies that seemed to multiply like rabbits as that industry blossomed. When the market was constantly climbing, announcing an IPO equated, in the minds of a lot of investors, as printing money. The theory was that if you were able to get in on the ground floor, you could ride the wave of the stock as it went up, up, up.

But the unfortunate reality of an IPO is that there is no guarantee that the stock price will go up. Many IPOs end up losing money in their first days of public trading – the well-publicized IPO of the social networking website Facebook is a prime example – and those early adopters who jump on the IPO price end up riding the financial wave in the wrong direction, and losing a lot of money in the process.

When management first planned to take MF Global's stock public – trading under the ticker symbol MF – they expected the opening price to be in the $36 to $39 range, and the plan was to sell 97 million shares. By the first day of trading, the stock opened with something of a sigh, where underwriters could only generate an initial offering price of $30 a share. Thirty dollars a share, well below the predicted $36-to-$39 range most analysts had expected. Hindsight being what it is, it's easy to look back at the lackluster opening as a foreshadowing event. But hindsight is one of many luxuries not afforded to those in the investment world.

The IPO raised approximately $2.9 billion in operating capital for MF Global, which was to be their seed money to finance the brokerage business's operations. But following the IPO, things went south in a hurry. Within the first three months of its existence as a publicly traded company, MF Global lost $90 million. And while at the time nobody could have predicted what disastrous realities the future held for the new firm, many MF Global employees would look back at the IPO as the beginning of the firm's downfall because of the fact that it put new pressure on the firm to generate quarterly profits, as opposed to affording them time to build the business with a more long-term view.

Additional problems associated with the IPO included the fact that MF Global was no longer under the protection of the financial umbrella afforded by the Man Group. Whereas prior to the IPO, Man Financial could have gone to its parent company to seek financial assistance if needed, now since the firm was a public entity, that door was closed. They were on their own, and it was up to them to determine whether they'd sink or swim.

Another issue that arose as a result of the IPO was the increased reporting requirements that came along with being a public company. Investing rules require public companies to make public a great deal of information, including all financial documents related to the firm's liquidity. Those financial documents had a direct impact on the firm's ability to borrow money and the interest rates they'd pay on loans. They also had a direct impact on the confidence both customers and stockholders had in the firm's ability to remain profitable.

* * *

When Man Financial acquired Refco, they immediately got a much larger share of the financial services markets in the United States and expanded their presence in the U.S. futures market. It also launched them into the fixed-income business, including a fixed-income prime brokerage and repo financing. Something else Man Financial inherited was an accounting method that they had never used before, known as the Alternative Method for calculating futures client seg funds, which had been in wide use at Refco.

The CFTC views customer margin deposits as sacrosanct customer property; the money belongs to the customer, and the brokerage firm must hold that money safely and account for it all times. It must be "segregated" from the firm's own money, thus the money is colloquially called "seg funds."

It's important to understand that rules allow a certain amount of comingling of customer money and company money, but only under very limited circumstances. Brokers can, for example, deposit their own money in the customer seg fund accounts to protect against adverse price movements in the market, thereby assuring that the customer account will never dip below the required levels set by federal regulations. By the same token, brokers can withdraw their own funds that they'd previously deposited in the customer seg fund account, but again, there are very clear and strict rules governing withdrawals. The broker is never to withdraw customer money from the account.

That sounds pretty cut-and-dried, and most of the time it is. But there is a potential loophole within the rule. Because the accounts are reconciled at the end of the day, there are those who argue that so long as the account balance is correct at the end of the day, it's not a problem if a broker dips into the customer funds for a very short period of time during the day. The CFTC has spoken on this issue, and the answer is a resounding no. Under no circumstances can a brokerage withdraw customer seg funds. However, intra-day borrowing of customer money remained a practice in the futures industry, especially at MF Global. It was assumed that money could be removed from the customer seg fund accounts as long as it was back, safe and sound, by the end of the day.

That said, there still was another loophole in the protection of customer seg funds because not all kinds of customer deposits were treated equally. There is a regulatory difference between foreign and domestic margin deposits, and brokers are required to hold those two different categories separately. Domestic client funds are called 1.25 funds, named after the CFTC rule regulating how those funds can be invested. Foreign client funds are called 30.7 funds, which are separated and specifically used to buy or sell futures on non-U.S. futures exchanges, and are, again, named after the corresponding rule regarding their use.

For 1.25 funds, regulations stipulate that those client funds can be invested in U.S. Treasury bonds, federal agency bonds, municipal bonds, bank CDs, commercial paper, sovereign-debt securities, and corporate bonds. The 30.7 funds generally have the same investment rules; however each category does require the money be held in separate accounts, so a typical futures broker manages a pool of money for domestic customers, the 1.25 funds, and for foreign futures customers, the 30.7 funds.

Like approximately 90% of the industry, Man Financial had used the much more conservative Net Liquidating Method to determine how much of their clients' funds had to be segregated from Man Financial's own funds. In this accounting method, you add up the liquidation value of the total customer accounts plus any customer securities. It's a very simple and straightforward process from there. If the futures broker had to sell the long positions and buy back all of the short positions for all their customers' futures positions and then added back all the cash and securities held in the accounts, that final number would be the amount of money they needed to have segregated from the firm's own money.

However, the seg fund landscape changed dramatically when the Alternative Method came into existence in 1987. The new method for accounting for seg funds allowed new rules for foreign futures accounts. Before the adoption of the new rule, participation by U.S. firms in the foreign futures markets was just beginning, and only a few firms were offering access to foreign futures exchanges at the time. The sentiment in the futures industry was that it didn't make sense to apply the domestic accounting rules to foreign futures exchanges, because the rules would be too much of a burden, given the limited computerization for calculating seg funds at the time.

So the CFTC cut the industry some slack and allowed the Alternative Method to come into existence. Again, hindsight is 20/20 and in the case of MF Global, this was yet another watershed moment that would determine the company's future, but nobody could have predicted it. In order to determine seg fund requirements under the Alternative Method, you add up the maintenance margin requirement, any open trade equity, and the value of securities and net options. In other words, you're only adding up the values of all futures and options positions in the customer accounts. If the customers have any excess cash or securities, the futures firm did not count those assets toward the total. That meant that the futures broker was able to use any excess funds – money that belonged to the customers – for their own internal purposes.

Because of the fact that the Alternative Method provides a firm with the chance to leverage client funds legally, it's perhaps surprising to realize that only about 10% of futures firms used it. On the other hand, given the risky nature associated with leverage, it's also something of a relief to know there were so few were using it, as the Alternative Method meant more client money was being used by the firm instead of being kept safely in the customer's own account. And it should come as no surprise that Refco was using the Alternative Method in order to account for their customer seg funds. Refco, whose numerous run-ins with regulators made them "among the most cited brokers in the business," passed on the Alternative Method to MF Global when their personnel arrived at the offices.

And as we shall see, this became be a very important consideration when things started to go wrong.

CHAPTER FOUR

Going Rogue

Any sailor who has spent time on the ocean has heard the stories of monster waves – "freaks," as they're known to old salts – that have no apparent cause. Typically encountered far from land in the deepest water, these waves have been known to damage the strongest offshore deep-water drilling platforms and have sent freight ships to the bottom of the ocean. Their destructive power is awesome; their predictability is elusive. For those reasons, scientists and mariners alike refer to these colossal walls of water as "rogue waves."

For years, rogue waves were relegated to the ranks of mermaids and sea monsters and weren't officially declared to exist until 1995, when an offshore drilling platform in the North Sea was damaged by a rogue wave on New Year's Day. Once science confirmed their existence, oceanographers worked to identify what caused the phenomenon.

In the strictly clinical sense, a rogue wave is defined as a wave having at least twice the height of what is called the significant wave height. A rogue wave itself does not have to be a towering wall that crashes down on top of an ocean liner; it is simply a wave that is twice as large as the biggest waves in a series. So if that series is composed of waves maxing out at two feet, a four-foot wave would, by definition, be considered a rogue.

But a four-foot wave isn't going to make headlines. No, the rogue waves that make the news tend to be much larger. While on a research vessel, British oceanographers once measured a rogue wave off the west coast of Scotland at 84 feet tall. European scientists, using satellite imagery in 2004, discovered 10 separate rogue waves, all measuring over

82 feet. To put the destructive capability of a wave that size into perspective, consider the tsunami that struck Japan in 2011. Scientists put that wave's height at 77 feet. That wave killed more than 15,000 people and caused damage into the hundreds of billions of dollars.

The difference between rogue waves and tsunamis, however, is that a tsunami typically has a preceding cause – usually an earthquake, as was the case in Japan. And while an earthquake is basically impossible to predict, a tsunami can be, to a degree, foretold by such seismic events. A rogue wave, however, has no trigger that science has yet discovered. They just happen. And for that reason, they can be exponentially more dangerous.

Rogue waves are characterized by an unpredictable nature and massively destructive potential. But at the risk of personifying forces of nature too much, there are plenty of "rogue waves" in the human world, too. There are people who live and work amongst us and seem to be regular, status-quo professionals, but suddenly, without any sort of warning or trigger, snap and do destructive things. These actions are not always destructive in terms of human life, but can cause monumental amounts of damage other ways. One such individual was a 40-year-old man named Evan Dooley who worked as a futures broker for MF Global. And one night, Mr. Dooley just went rogue.

By all appearances, Evan – Brent, to his friends – was straight out of central casting for the typical Wall Street broker. Short-cropped hair and chiseled features gave him the look of one of Tom Wolfe's "Masters of the Universe" that populate the Financial District of lower Manhattan. But Dooley lived far from that world, choosing instead a life of relative quiet in the more pastoral settings of his home state of Tennessee.

He was, by all accounts, an all-American boy. He was raised in a middle-class family in small-town Tennessee. He would later go on to the University of Memphis, where he studied finance, was active in intramural sports and held multiple leadership positions in university organizations until his graduation in 1991. A former employer referred to him as "just an average kind of kid." A friend described him as "the guy next door." A family man, a church-goer, the kind of guy you would want your daughter to marry. In short, the exact opposite of the sort of person you'd expect to find at the epicenter of a massive trading scandal brought about by his own actions.

After graduation, Dooley worked for a collection of various financial companies, eventually landing a commission-based job at MF Global's Memphis office in 2005. It was there that this all-American boy, about whom nobody had a disparaging comment, wrought one of the most sensational trading losses in recent financial history. When the final numbers were tallied, Evan Dooley had lost MF Global $141 million in the space of several hours, and, according to the firm, had done so after a long night of unauthorized trading. In other words, Dooley had gone rogue. And just like a rogue wave, this rogue trader gave no warning as to the extent of the destruction that would follow in his path.

* * *

According to the company's own records, Dooley reported his net worth at approximately $250,000 at the time of his hiring, so they assumed he was accustomed to being around money, knew how to handle it and how to invest it. That gave Dooley not only a job at MF Global as a futures broker, but also gave him a personal futures trading account. Through that personal trading account, Dooley traded in the volatile wheat futures market at night from his laptop computer at home using the Chicago Mercantile Exchange's Globex electronic trading platform.

Futures contracts are legally binding agreements to make or take delivery of a specified quantity of a commodity at a specified date in the future. They provide a mechanism for commodities consumers and producers to lock in the prices of their products. And unlike stocks, it is just as easy to have a short position as having a long position in the futures markets.

A short position in a futures contract is an agreement to sell a commodity at some point in the future. When someone is carrying a short futures position, they have one of two options before the expiration date: they can buy it back, or deliver the agreed-upon commodity to the buyer. A wheat farmer would be a typical futures client with a short position. He likes the price of late-season wheat contracts and knows he's going to have a harvest coming in. When he locks in his selling price today, he has pre-sold a given amount of wheat, requiring him to either deliver it to a pre-determined warehouse or buy it back before the contract expires. He might be worried the price of wheat might fall by the end of the year, so he wants to make sure his harvest is sold at the current market price.

A long position is the other side of the equation, namely the agreement to buy the agreed-upon commodity at a set date in the future. After the contract's expiration, the buyer will either receive that commodity on the agreed-upon date or have sold the futures contract prior. For example, a futures customer might purchase wheat in July to be delivered in December. In this example, a consumer – a bread maker, for instance, who wants to lock in his profit margins – is looking at the wheat prices at the end of the year, and worried that the prices might go up. So he would agree to the wheat price in July and take delivery of the actual wheat in December. That way he doesn't have to worry about the prices moving higher over the next six months.

In the futures markets, buyers and sellers of a commodity can agree on the price now, rather than being forced to wait months later to make the purchase or sale. The benefit to both parties is that the price is locked in; because of that, it's also a risk to both parties. The price could go up or down depending on production levels – which are themselves susceptible to a variety of factors – so in the futures market, somebody is getting a good deal and somebody isn't getting as good deal as they could have had they waited.

For example, in the wheat market, you've got a farmer who grows the wheat and buyers who purchase it from him. If the farmer sells his wheat at $10 a bushel on the futures market, he knows exactly what he's getting. Of course, if the price goes to $20 a bushel at the time of harvest, he doesn't get quite the profit he could have had he waited. But if the price goes down at harvest, then he's made a bigger profit than he would have. Futures markets offer ways for market participants to hedge and offset the risks inherent in their businesses by reducing the risk of price fluctuations and thus achieve better planning for their businesses.

Outside the Main Street benefits of the futures markets, there is a Wall Street trading arena in the futures pits where these transactions take place. There, it boils down to one side having guessed right, and the other having guessed wrong. And when you trade futures contracts for a living, you want to find yourself on the side of guessing right.

Wheat was the original futures contract traded on the Chicago Board of Trade – now a subsidiary of the Chicago Mercantile Exchange – beginning in 1877. Wheat futures are the single-most-liquid commodity traded on any exchange in the world, with more than 13 million metric tons of wheat changing hands daily. To put that in perspective, a single futures contract is for 5,000 bushels of wheat; that volume is equivalent to 136 metric tons and over 95,000 wheat futures contracts are traded on an average business day. For the buyers and sellers of wheat futures contracts, they are, on average, trading 12.9 million metric tons of wheat on any given day. That's quite a lot of wheat!

Participants in this huge market include wheat producers, processors, millers, and exporters, as well as the traders and speculators who treat futures like any other money-making opportunity. And while there are some futures contracts that are traded in the pits in Chicago with the open outcry system, the vast majority of futures contracts are traded electronically through the CME's Globex system. Wheat is somewhat of a hybrid trading contract, traded in the Chicago trading pits during the day and electronically on Globex at night. Most futures brokerages have their own software system for accessing Globex; in MF Global's case, the software was called OrderXpress. It's that last category of futures market participant that Brent Dooley fell into as a late-night trader and speculator. He was a 40-something Memphis broker who thought he knew the overnight market better than anyone else and expected to reap wild profits from that knowledge.

Late in the evening of January 27, 2008, Dooley logged onto his laptop and accessed MF Global's OrderXpress trading platform. Throughout the night and well into the wee hours of the morning, Dooley executed a series of buy and sell orders in wheat futures. The overnight futures markets have fewer participants, so trading is typically thinner and less liquid, that is, much lower-volume trades. Dooley plowed straight ahead anyway; by the time he'd logged off, Dooley had traded approximately 1,500 contracts, representing a total of 7.5 million bushels of wheat.

At one point during the session, Dooley was long 673 contracts on March 2008 wheat futures, with a total value of about $32 million. That is a lot of contracts for an individual to trade in a single setting; but what was even more staggering was the fact that Dooley had started his session with only $482 in his MF Global trading account. When Dooley finally closed out his trades for the session, he netting a profit of $37,000. Not bad for a night's work.

And while Dooley might have been patting himself on the back for turning $482 into $37,000 – obviously leverage can be very lucrative when it's used properly – his superiors at MF Global were neither impressed nor amused. When his activity was discovered on the morning of January 28, Dooley was immediately contacted and given a harsh reprimand. He was told that his trading activity had been "out of line" and had far exceeded his risk limits, which were based on the amount of money in his personal trading account. In other words, somehow Dooley had circumvented the risk constraints in the system, if there were any, allowing him to trade with money he didn't have. In fact, it was a great deal of money he didn't have.

Dooley, for his part, was contrite. He apologized for his actions, telling the powers-that-be at MF Global that it was an unfortunate "trading error." Though he never publicly elaborated on how, exactly, several hours' worth of trading tens of millions of dollars in futures contracts with little money in his account was a trading error, MF Global personnel somehow accepted his explanation and his apology. No further action was taken. One can only assume that no one at MF Global wanted the public embarrassment associated with the news, so they let it die. And after all, the kid had made $37,000 by being on the right side of the market. Maybe he really was a pretty talented trader after all.

It was about a month later when Evan Dooley jumped back into the late-night trading arena. On the night of February 26, 2008 Dooley fired up his laptop and logged on to MF Global's OrderXpress system once again. There is no explanation for how Dooley was allowed to circumvent the MF Global rules, let alone do it twice, but in retrospect, there did seem to be a pattern developing, a pattern that pointed to Dooley's having an uncanny ability to get around the rules when trading the electronic overnight session.

What was going through his mind at that time is anybody's guess, and Dooley has never offered an explanation. Perhaps he was buoyed by his success the previous month and was swinging to top his profit of $37,000. Maybe he had run down his money from the previous month and needed to replenish his account. Maybe he thought that because it was the overnight session, MF Global wasn't paying close attention to what he was doing. Whatever his thought process, not only was he about to violate the internal MF Global trading rules again, but this time the rules of the Chicago Mercantile Exchange as well. Dooley was about to go rogue.

This time, however, he started the session with a negative balance in his account. One might expect a firm to deny a customer with a negative balance of $3,000 the ability to leverage that balance hundreds of millions of times, but for whatever the reason, Dooley managed to do just that. He set his sights on wheat futures for March, May, July, and December; though he occasionally bought some contracts, he was a heavy short-seller the whole night. In total, he bought and sold a total of 31,964 contracts over the course of the evening.

During the winter of 2008, agricultural commodity prices had been experiencing large price swings. Winter droughts killed off many crops, which was suppressing the available supply. Meanwhile, demand for wheat continued to rise, a condition that, when paired with low supply levels, is typical for rising prices. Dooley was not following the upward market trend, he was selling wheat futures into this rally, thinking the market had peaked and would begin to decline. In some ways, trading commodities futures is just like farming the wheat, where there are many factors beyond an individual's control. In the case of farmers, they find themselves at the mercy of the elements. Too much rain or too much sun can mean a disastrous harvest. Just like the wheat farmer, no matter how good a trader and how thorough the analysis, a trader's position can be swept away by the markets.

During the course of the night, Dooley was consistently selling more and more wheat, trying to push the market lower. If he could sell enough contracts, he could move the market lower and then buy the contracts back at a cheaper price, but this market was deeper than he expected and price did not move so easily. He continued to sell more contracts to the all-night traders and was finally able to drive down the price, but at a cost: he amassed a huge short position in the process. By sunrise, the price of May 2008 wheat futures reached the price of

$12.295, also known as "limit down," which was the lowest price that futures contract was allowed to trade during that session.

Between midnight and 6 a.m. on February 27, Dooley had amassed a 16,174-contract short position in the various wheat futures delivery months. In other words, he had sold contracts for 2.8 million metric tons of wheat worth approximately $872 million. That's right, close to a billion dollars worth of wheat with a negative balance of $3,000 in his trading account. That meant he personally controlled about 10% of the entire open interest of wheat futures and at that moment, he was the largest single participant of the night's trading session, being three times over the position size limit allowed by the Chicago Mercantile Exchange.

Given that Dooley wasn't in the position to deliver the actual wheat – he wasn't really a farmer, after all – by holding such a large a short position, he was making a commitment to deliver the wheat, or, to buy back the contracts before the contract expired. He had sold at the higher prices earlier and now the price was "limit down," as low as it could go. He successfully drove the price of wheat to the lowest level possible that session, working the markets all night long. Had he been able to quit at that moment, he would have turned a monumental profit. He most likely would have received another reprimand from his bosses at MF Global, the whole situation forgotten, and walked away with tens of millions of dollars. Since MF Global did not allow him to carry open positions in his account, especially not of that magnitude, his account had to be flat by the end of the trading session. The profit he was sitting on was just a "mark-to-market" gain, he was still short the contracts and had to cover them back

At this point in the morning he began to buy the contracts back and close some of his short position. Given that the price was limit down, he assumed he was going to make a killing, probably calculating the profit every few minutes. But as he attempted to buy back so many contracts, the price started to creep up again, a fact that cut well into his profits. In order to keep the price from moving any higher, he had to sell more contracts to keep the market "limit down." So even though he was still trying to buy, he had to sell more and more contracts to keep the price from rising. Traders call that "painting the tape," and regulators call it "spoofing." If the market "looks" like there are more sellers than buyers, other traders are more likely to sell, potentially making it easier for Dooley to buy. That's exactly what Dooley was trying to do, but this time it didn't quite work. Like an unexpected flood, market forces can move against you, just like they did for Dooley. So as Dooley sold more contracts to try to keep the price down, it just increased the size of his short.

Then another factor beyond Dooley's control kicked in. Other smart traders following the market smelled something wrong. Most likely, those traders had bought many of the contracts Dooley had sold and knew someone had to buy them back before the end of the session. Dooley found himself in a situation called a "short squeeze."

A short squeeze occurs when there is a limited supply and high demand for a specific investment, most often because of an abundance of shorts in that security. In the squeeze, the traders with short positions are forced to buy at prices that are constantly – and rapidly – going up. Though short-squeezes are mostly associated with stocks, they are also common in the bond market, physical commodities, and futures. Sitting there with a massive short position and a limited time to buy it back, Brent Dooley found himself in a classic short squeeze.

The Internet has made communication a light-speed practice, and the discussion of Dooley's activities didn't go unnoticed that night. On one web-based chat room dedicated to commodities trading, a user posted the news that, "there is quite a huge battle on WK08 tonight. Two institutions have been buying/selling to each other for two hours before the shorter/profit taker dumped real shitloads of WK08 showing 500/100 lots." Other users chimed in, as Dooley's implosion became something of a virtual spectator sport: "The guy is going down with 245 lots in front of 1-to-5 lots…LOL…There are about 20 lots to buy in the whole book…LOL."

The intrigue grew over the course of the night, and another chatter opined, "At the beginning, I was thinking that the guy was in 'scogen' mode, basically taking every buyer and moving his size lower to liquidate. But maybe he wanted to short everything he can, manipulate the thin overnight session to reach the limit and settle it there for the regular session. Now he is short large and perhaps the session will stay limit down."

These anonymous chatters knew exactly what was happening, so it stands to reason that many traders involved understood the dynamics of the market that night. In other words, the traders with skin in the game probably knew exactly what was going on. And just as Dooley thought he was punting around enough contracts to manipulate the market, other traders at the poker table were moving to manipulate the price against Dooley.

Wheat futures prices began to rise even though Dooley was selling more contracts in his failed attempt to keep the price low. The other traders who knew there was a big short were doing their best to push prices higher, Dooley now found himself short 17,181 contracts for May 2008 wheat just after 10:00 a.m. and by 10:30 a.m., the price for those contracts had gone "limit up," meaning the price for Dooley to buy a single bushel of wheat was $13.495. And just as the contract was "limit down" earlier that morning, when a contract goes "limit up" it has reached the highest price at which it could trade. Astonishingly, price fluctuations from "limit down" to "limit up" are rarely seen over the course of an overnight session, let alone a daytime session. To see such a dramatic shift from "limit down" to "limit up" in such a short time was unprecedented.

That said, it demonstrates how much of a poker game the practice of trading can be. As any good poker player knows, at every card table there's always one sucker, and if you don't know who it is, you're it. If a trader has the skills and unlimited money to manipulate the market, he can generate huge profits. But that trader needs to be sure other players at the table don't know what he's doing. If he's trying to bluff his way to victory, he hopes they don't catch on. And that's where Dooley fell down.

The futures market – just like the stock market – is basically a large auction block. While trading in the market, the buyers and sellers who bid and offer contracts see the prices and the size of the transactions displayed. Savvy traders are good at "reading the tape" and pay attention to when large players are trying to move the market. In the case of Dooley's misadventures, it was pretty obvious to those traders that Dooley was trying to push the market lower. When it came time for Dooley to buy the contracts back, in order to squeeze him, they outbid him, placing bids higher than Dooley's bid, driving the price up and forcing Dooley to bid higher and higher.

Futures trading is a zero-sum game, so the amount of long positions will always match the amount of short positions. Dooley had to cover his short position by buying back contracts from traders he had sold them to earlier that morning. Because the other traders knew they had a sucker at the table, they kept working to drive the price up, forcing Dooley to pay more and more. It was simply a game they were playing to make Dooley lose money, and his loss was their gain. As his buying was driving the wheat price up, they were able to sell their contracts at progressively higher prices.

When he finally managed to close his positions, Brent Dooley found himself in the unfortunate financial position of being down $141 million. But because futures are a zero-sum game, by losing $141 million, Dooley made it possible for the other traders in that session to make the same amount of money. MF Global's loss was other people's gains. In other words, in the futures market, when somebody loses a dollar, somebody else gains a dollar. So for every dollar Dooley lost, somebody else made it. Just like with the wheat example, somebody is always getting a good deal, and somebody else isn't getting as good a deal as he could. The trick is to make sure you're on the right side of that equation.

* * *

On the morning of February 27, 2008 there was no sign from anyone inside MF Global's headquarters that anything was amiss. However, by about noon that day, someone discovered a horrific line entry on the position reports. Somehow, the firm was showing a $141 million loss in wheat futures contracts. They located the delinquent account and immediately closed it. They liquidated his positions, and calculated the damage. Dooley had lost $141,021,489.00.

MF Global was required to cover those losses because it was a clearing member of the exchange, and the exchange's rules dictated that it had to cover the loss. Fortunately enough for the firm, though, they had insurance that was designed to cover such losses. They filed a claim with their insurance company – Fidelity Bond Insurance – with the full expectation that they'd recover their losses. They were wrong. Fidelity Bond Insurance declined to pay the claim.

Not surprisingly, Dooley was immediately fired. MF Global made the announcement, without a trace of irony, that Dooley had "substantially exceeded his authorized trading limit." That much was obvious to even the least knowledgeable of observers. What was perhaps less obvious, though, was the fact that Dooley had somehow managed to exceed the Commodity Futures Trading Commission's own limits. The CFTC prohibits any individual from "controlling a contract," meaning that no single investor can own or have sold short more than 5,000 contracts in a single month or 6,500 in all months combined. Dooley exceeded the size limit by almost three times in a single night's trading.

CEO Kevin Davis told investors on a conference call that what Dooley had done was "an absolutely awful event, but we believe it was an aberration in our risk control. We are deeply, deeply upset that this has happened, but we believe we've fixed it and it will never happen again." His optimism wasn't contagious.

Dooley's transgressions were just the prelude to the looming storm that was brewing on MF Global's horizon. The Dooley incident was symptomatic of a larger cancer that had taken root at MF Global; the firm had grown so much that, like the colossus that was the Holy Roman Empire, it was overwhelmed by its own size. It was less than a year after the company had gone public, and they were already on the cusp of financial Armageddon. How was a mid-level broker working from his home laptop after business hours able to lose over $141 million without triggering any sort of alarms until it was too late?

The answer to that question would become clear in time, and it was not the answer that MF Global investors were happy to hear. The incident had exposed massive weaknesses in MF Global's risk-management systems, as well as the overall management of the firm. Additionally, the loss wiped out a significant portion of MF Global's profits for the year and led to two rating-agency downgrades. And just to add insult to financial injury, the Commodities Futures Trading Commission fined MF Global a staggering $10 million as punishment for their poor risk management.

The loss was significant, the breakdown in controls was monumental, but the firm was still solvent. The larger problem, however, was the possibility that the news, once public, would cause investor and customer panic. Investors and customers of MF Global might lose any faith they still retained in the firm, and begin to sell their shares or close their accounts en masse. To salvage their client base, management needed a plan.

Though explanations weren't forthcoming from MF Global as to how an individual with a negative bank balance had been able to lose $141 million, the situation did illuminate the less savory side of the financial world. First of all, it demonstrated how easy it is for a trader with seemingly unlimited resources to manipulate prices of futures contracts on a short-term basis. If you have the financial wherewithal to buy and sell massive quantities, you can control the price.

The poker-table metaphor is apt insofar as Dooley was concerned. As news outlets learned more about this rogue trader, a picture emerged of a man who wasn't quite the person that he and others claimed he was. He had declared bankruptcy as recently as 2002, and had lost both his car and his home to repossession. His wife had divorced him, citing her husband's gambling addiction as one of the causes of the failed marriage. It even came out that Dooley was reportedly $10,000 behind in alimony and child-support payments going back to 2006. All these negative reports were just a drop in the bucket of the financial avalanche that buried the "broker turned trader" from Tennessee.

So it makes sense, perhaps, that Dooley took the risk that he did that night. He thought he was in a position to erase his money problems in a single night. He could make a huge fortune, retire from his job, pay off his debts, and still have plenty of money to live a life of luxury. His legacy would be cemented as a legendary trader, a legacy he probably could have parlayed into a spot on a financial television program after writing several books showing other traders how the game was played by the winners. But it didn't work out quite that way, as we know by now.

In April 2010, Dooley was indicted by a federal grand jury in the Northern District of Illinois. The 18-count indictment included two counts of violating the Commodities Exchange Act's position limits and 16 individual counts of wire fraud. Each of the counts carried a potential of five years in prison, meaning that Dooley's sentence could effectively be 90 years in federal prison.

CHAPTER FIVE

Enter Roseman

Every kid out there has, at some point in their lives, spent what seems like an eternity setting up a complex array of dominoes, carefully positioning each one just so. The end result is a tangled maze of black rectangles, all precariously balanced in such a way that they're close to one another without touching. And then, at the moment of truth, the first one in the sequence gets a little nudge towards the one closest to it and the whole project comes toppling down in an unequivocally satisfying cascade of clicks, as each successive domino falls into the next, sending it toppling into the one next to it.

And this is not just a child's pastime. There are countless examples of adults – very intelligent adults, at that – who spend hours creating exotic and oftentimes impossibly complex arrangements of thousands of dominoes, sending them splitting off in different directions only to have them converge at a later point. But the end result is the same, regardless of the age of the creator or level of complexity of the creation. In the end, all the dominoes end up falling down neatly, leaning or lying flat on the ground. It's as if they collectively committed some sort of ritualistic mass suicide, their now-dead bodies the only evidence of what once was.

This "domino effect," as it is known colloquially, has been applied to many other real-life settings, including the financial markets. One little nudge can send markets into a free-fall, contagion in one market spreads to the next as history as proven time and again. Perhaps the most significant example is the stock market crash of 1929, which was triggered by a series of market sell-offs at the peak of a speculative bubble, which wrongly led to tight Federal Reserve monetary policy and high interest rates, which led to bank failures causing a banking panic, and it kept going and going. The end result was, of course, the Great Depression, a period of economic collapse that profoundly changed the landscape of the American financial system forever. So disastrous was the financial ruin that federal legislation was instituted, including the Securities Act of 1933, Securities Exchange Act of 1934, and the Banking Act of 1933, better known as Glass-Steagall, to prevent such events from ever happening again. At least that was the hope.

It didn't work out quite that way, as recent historical events have illustrated all too well, but the new system remained relatively stable for over 70 years. The 2008 collapse of the venerable Wall Street investment bank Bear Stearns is an example of how fast a firm can go out of business and how the dominos of financial panic can continue to fall. It took the space of a single week – five working days – for Bear to go from being the fifth-largest investment bank in the world to becoming a historical footnote, a warning of what can happen to the complex array of dominoes with just a little tap in the right place.

March 10, 2008 was a Monday. It wasn't unlike most Mondays in the offices at 383 Madison Avenue in midtown Manhattan. Bear Stearns traders were at their desks, the ubiquitous sounds of the cable financial news channel droning in the background, coming from several television monitors situated throughout the floor. The noise went mostly unnoticed, until the name Bear Stearns was mentioned. Suddenly ears pricked up. Something was in the air.

Rumors of liquidity problems at the investment bank were circulating, according to the news reporter. Traders around the Street knew that the bank was heavily leveraged and that the Bear was deep into subprime mortgages. And there was the crashing real-estate market that had fueled a few losses – including the spectacular collapse of two Bear-run hedge funds the year before – but liquidity problems? Those were worries that other banks had. Certainly not Bear Stearns.

But as the day progressed, the news continued to report the problems. Frantic phone calls to various personnel at the firm's headquarters reassured traders that there were no problems with the bank's liquid assets. The numbers were fine, traders were told, so they should reassure their clients that all was well and life would go on. But the rumors refused to die. Clients grew increasingly nervous, and began pulling their funds. Suddenly, those rumors were becoming true, as if by their own divine creation. Just as the Bible tells of God literally speaking the world into existence, Bear's liquidity problems were magnified by the fact that somebody said they had them.

Ironically enough, though, the larger world outside the financial district didn't seem to notice. Over the next few days, Bear was facing the very real prospect of imminent collapse, but when the Reuters news agency issued its list of the day's most newsworthy stories, Bear's teetering on the edge of bankruptcy ranked third and the top two stories were, in fact, unrelated to finance at all. But as the news gathered speed, more and more clients began to pull their money out; next Bear's financing lines were pulled, and by the end of the week, clients just stopped doing business with them. Within days, the firm's stock price went from trading at a high of over $170 per share in 2007 to just over $3 the following Monday.

When it came Bear's turn to face its own mortality, the New York Fed was noticeably reticent in terms of extending lifelines to the rapidly dissolving investment bank. There was no direct bailout organized to save the dying firm; instead, a deal was brokered whereby JP Morgan acquired Bear at a price that would make even the most bargain-basement of fire-sale prices blush. It took five days for Bear Stearns to go from being the fifth-largest investment bank in the country to utter bankruptcy, and few tears were shed at other firms in the financial district when the firm was sold for $2 a share.

What made the issue of Bear Stearns' meltdown all the more poetic – and perhaps controversial – was what many saw as coincidental timing on the part of the Federal Reserve. When Bear Stearns was going under, it was clear that the firm needed a financial lifeline, most likely in the form of government dollars. But due to the legalities imposed by the Glass-Steagall Act, Bear wasn't allowed to borrow money via the Federal Reserve's discount window; they needed some kind of federal bailout to stay in business. Hank Paulson, then-secretary of the treasury, was the man who could potentially make the call, but there was nothing the man could do to save Bear Stearns. And just to add insult to injury, soon after Bear Stearns had been declared dead, the Fed opened the discount window to investment banks, as a precaution against another collapse. As the collapse of Lehman Brothers a few months later showed, again, legislation wasn't enough to keep the dominoes from falling.

It wasn't just Bear Stearns stock that had taken a beating. The Monday after the Bear avalanche had begun, MF Global's stock felt the sting of investors across the board pulling money out of financial stocks. The drop was explained as a knee-jerk reaction by investors to the Bear Stearns collapse. If Bear had liquidity problems, it seemed logical on some level that other financial firms, like Lehman and MF Global, could be experiencing the same issues. But MF Global didn't seem to be in that negative financial territory. They issued press releases telling the world that their repo lines were not affected and that they'd not drawn on their $1.4 billion revolving credit facility. And just as an added reassurance, they told their investors that they had no exposure to the subprime mortgage market, which meant that they should be safe from the fluctuations in that incredibly volatile market.

And while all that news was aimed at assuaging fears, it didn't help many major Bear Stearns investors who suffered huge financial hits. One such investor was legendary billionaire Joe Lewis, who had made billions by trading currencies. He was a major stakeholder in Bear Stearns, with his shares representing approximately 10% of company ownership. When the shares were trading above $100, Lewis looked like a financial genius. When the shares dropped to $5, he looked like a man who'd just lost a billion dollars of his net worth.

He'd suffered such a loss from his Bear Stearns stock that he was forced to sell off substantial holdings in other firms, and given the cloud that seemed to be permanently stuck over the financial industry, they were the most likely candidates to meet the auction block from Lewis's perspective. He sold off his MF Global stock, sending the stock into a free-fall. The stock on that Monday had opened at a modest $16.10 a share; it would close the day's session at $6.05 after hitting a low of $3.64.

All of this came, of course, weeks after the debacle wrought by Evan Dooley, an event that was serving as something of a frame to an artistic depiction of financial ruin. If MF Global was to survive, they had to mitigate the damage done by Dooley; that much, they could theoretically control. What happened in the rest of the financial market was outside of their sphere of influence. So management set its sights on controlling what they could.

Following the Dooley affair and the subsequent stock collapse, two things became painfully obvious. First and foremost, MF Global needed some kind of cash infusion – an investor – to keep them afloat and show support for the firm. There was the potential for clients to abandon the firm like rats off a sinking ship, as had happened to Refco and Bear Stearns. And that's what began to happen. Whereas after the IPO, MF Global stock had traded solidly between $25 and $30 a share, the price plummeted to $6 following the Dooley and Bear Stearns incidents. It climbed briefly back up to $15, but soon retreated to the sub-$10 range, where it stayed for the next three years.

And hanging out there in the wind like a ragged old flag from a Johnny Cash song was the reality of Bear Stearns, a reality that was made that much more vivid by the Refco disaster that so many MF Global clients had already lived through. The fear was that if it could happen to any firm perceived to be as stable and successful as Bear Stearns had been, it could happen to MF Global, too. All it would take was the right nudge, and the dominoes would come toppling down. MF Global needed to do something – something very public – to offset the pending panic. And they needed to do something fast.

More liquidity was needed and that was obvious. More attention needed to be paid to the firm's finances as a result of the Bear collapse and stock free-fall. MF Global immediately hired J. Randy MacDonald from TD Ameritrade as it new CFO. He immediately negotiated an agreement with an affiliate, Man Investments, to free up $800 million in liquidity. But that wasn't enough. They still desperately needed an injection of operating capital.

In the sort of irony that would be written off in a novel as impossibly unlikely, the investor who came to MF Global's rescue was the same firm that Man Financial had outbid to acquire Refco. The firm J.C. Flowers would, it seemed at the time, have the last laugh insofar as MF Global was concerned.

J. Christopher Flowers, the firm's namesake, had made hundreds of millions in the 1990s by investing in distressed Japanese banks. Prior to that, he'd been a partner with investment banking behemoth

Goldman Sachs, where he'd worked closely with a man named Jon Corzine, who, at the current time, was serving as governor of New Jersey. And once Flowers had gained a foothold in MF Global's inner sanctum, his relationship with Corzine would become of paramount importance.

Flowers said of the investment, "We've taken advantage of their situation to make a good deal for ourselves." In other words, Flowers smelled blood in the water and knew that MF Global was on the financial equivalent of life support, so the firm was ripe for picking. Flowers wasn't interested in complete control or ownership; MF Global was damaged goods, after all. Instead, he settled for a seat on the board of directors and a 10% stake through convertible preferred shares with a high dividend. All of this was in exchange for the relatively paltry sum of $150 million, a true life raft for the drowning MF Global. At its core it was, in layman's terms, more than a "good deal" for Flowers. It was a great deal.

The other thing that was clear following the Dooley debacle was that MF Global was in dire need of better internal risk controls. If the firm's history of lackadaisical risk management was the foundation for the proof, Dooley's misadventures in the wheat futures market was the *quod era demonstrandum*. If nothing else could be drawn from the Dooley scandal, at least MF Global had been forced to confront the reality of its need to monitor, assess, and minimize the firm's risk.

The first step was to show that management was doing everything they could to prevent a repeat performance by another trader, rogue or otherwise. A letter dated March 2, 2008 was the first public attempt to reassure nervous investors. In the letter to MF Global's clients, CEO Kevin Davis wrote that the firm had implemented "necessary adjustments" to its order entry system and went on to explain that "[Dooley's] trades were discovered internally and are no longer possible." He closed by confidently assuring clients that MF Global was "well capitalized." Noticeably absent from this – or any other – communication from the firm was any sort of explanation as to how Dooley had orchestrated the trades so easily with so little money in the first place. None of that apparently mattered as much as the requisite steps had been taken to assure it couldn't happen again.

But just to make sure the firm was doing all they could, management hired two separate consulting firms to analyze the risk-management procedures in place and make recommendations. Not surprisingly, both consulting groups found a lack of internal controls, and highly recommended strengthening the firm's risk management. That would mean, according to both, that MF Global needed to hire a chief risk-management officer, preferably from outside the firm. The argument was that such a hire would serve as a public demonstration of MF Global's commitment to strengthening risk management and to ensure such large trading losses could never happened again. If an area of the firm was ever taking too much risk, the chief risk manager, as a senior-level officer, would prevent it.

The new chief risk officer would need to be somebody outside the MF Global family, somebody with no connection to the past risk management failures. The person needed to have experience at a global futures broker, as well as a spotless reputation within the industry. And from MF Global's perspective, the person needed to be available to start yesterday. Barring that, they needed to be able to start tomorrow.

A little searching led them to Newedge and a man named Mike Roseman. Newedge was the renamed firm created when FIMAT merged with another futures broker, Calyon Financial. FIMAT was a firm that had been involved with the collapse of Sentinel Capital Management in 2007 and Mike Roseman was chief of risk management there at the time. Sentinel, another futures broker, had leveraged a massive CDO portfolio using their clients' seg. fund money. When the subprime and CDO markets turned and began to sell off, they raided their clients' seg funds to hide the losses and meet margin calls. The missing funds went unnoticed for almost two months until the financial panic in August 2007 finally caused their collapse and subsequent bankruptcy. Mike Roseman was instrumental at FIMAT during Sentinel's collapse by prudently cutting risk and the firm's exposure leading up to the bankruptcy. So in other words, the risk-management officer at FIMAT for Sentinel was now going to oversee risk management at MF Global. Suddenly the global financial markets were going to seem very small and interconnected.

Roseman was well qualified for the job as head of risk at FIMAT, no question about it. A graduate of the University of Delaware with an MBA from the University of North Carolina, he'd spent his career in financial risk management. Beginning in 1994, he'd been a part of the risk-assessment team at Sanwa Financial Products, a subsidiary set up by Sanwa Bank that traded swaps, but liked to brag that he was "a mortgage trader" who had moved into risk analysis.

In 2001, he joined Bank of Montreal as head of U.S. risk oversight with a mandate to strengthen the bank's risk-management procedures. Three years later, with the opportunity to head risk at FIMAT, Roseman left the bank. Roseman joined FIMAT as chief risk officer of the Americas in 2004, again operating with the mandate to increase risk-management abilities. At FIMAT, he was an aggressive risk officer, the kind that is generally disliked by traders and salespeople, but always did a thorough job, even if acting overly vivacious sometimes. He was not only the type of risk officer who tried to limit what you did, but liked to be "in your face" about it. If you went over a risk limit, he would go straight to your boss without trying to clarify it with you first.

And contrary to what others might have thought, Roseman was proud to tell people that he'd "saved" FIMAT from being dragged down as a part of Sentinel's bankruptcy, crediting his own risk-management skills as the major factor in that salvation. So within a year after the Sentinel bankruptcy – and despite his advertised heroics of saving FIMAT from a similar fate – Roseman was anxious to leave FIMAT.

When MF Global came calling, Roseman saw it as his golden ticket, and jumped at the chance. He had a few lengthy interviews with members of MF Global's management team, and finally landed in the CEO's office. After talking to Roseman for five minutes, Kevin Davis leaned across the desk and put it very bluntly: "Let's get this deal done now. What's it going to take?"

What it took was a generous signing bonus, a high salary and a guaranteed bonus for several years to come. For starters, Roseman wanted $1 million to leave FIMAT and come to MF Global. Done. Then a $300,000 salary plus an annual bonus of a million a year for three years. Done. Roseman made one concession – he had no problem taking some of his bonus in MF Global stock. By August 2008, Roseman had reported for his first day of work as global chief risk officer at MF Global.

The announcement came from MF Global on September 2, 2008. The firm had "appointed Michael Roseman as its new chief risk officer," calling the new hire a "strong addition to our executive

management team." In addition to being the global chief risk officer –
a title that sounded about as all-encompassing in terms of corporate risk
as one could imagine – Roseman would be overseeing the company's
compliance department for all things legal and regulatory. That was, to
many in management, welcome news, given MF Global's history. Maybe
the Dooley unpleasantness had really opened some eyes in the corner
offices. Maybe they were now seeing they needed tighter rules if they
were to continue in their business and truly succeed.

From a strictly professional perspective, Roseman did what was
asked of him. He instituted a full line of global risk systems for MF
Global, generating reports and measuring the risks, and not just as
simple internal guidelines to be followed only if they suited the business.
He implemented a twenty-four-hour/seven-day-a-week risk-monitoring
system, which would have made it impossible for Evan Dooley to go hog
wild after midnight. And he implemented new and tighter controls
across the organization as a whole. In other words, he did everything
that seemed necessary to reign in any out-of-control activities that were
occurring or would occur at MF Global.

But all those new controls led co-workers to resent and dislike
the firm's equivalent of an elementary school hall monitor. He clashed
with traders about the newly imposed limits, especially the dividend
arbitrage business in London and the limited size of some sovereign
repo-to-maturity trades. For that matter, he felt management knew
about the risks associated with many businesses, though he was the only
one with the spine to stand up to the business heads.

If Roseman was the loudest critic of RTM trades, Peter Forlenza,
the MF Global head of equity, was the loudest critic of Roseman himself.
Forlenza blamed Roseman directly for the poor performance of the
equities division, claiming that Roseman's rules and restrictions
prevented him from getting credit lines to potential customers.
Roseman, in turn, argued that all counterparties needed a limit; he
followed that up by asking Forlenza what size limits he needed to make
his business work. To Roseman, everything had to have a limit and
everything had to be measured. Forlenza never responded to Roseman
with a number, but he continued to blame Roseman for his division's
problems.

Just two months after Roseman joined, Kevin Davis would soon discover the truth about the unease of the head that wears the crown. Davis, who had been CEO of MF Global for nine years and a key figure in the growth of the business, abruptly resigned in October 2008. A few months later, Davis was replaced by Bernie Dan, the former CEO of the Chicago Board of Trade. He would not last long, however, as he followed the steps of his predecessor and resigned, rather suddenly, in March 2010, citing personal reasons. MF Global needed an immediate replacement, and it was then that J. Christopher Flowers stepped in, using what leverage he had to shoehorn his own candidate – his old friend Jon Corzine – into the CEO's office.

CHAPTER SIX

Jon Corzine

On December 7, 1903, President Theodore Roosevelt gave his Third Annual Message to the United States Congress. It was the speech that would eventually become known as the State of the Union Address, and was – as it continues under its current name – an annual speech about how things are going in the country. About a month before the first State of the Union, James Hamilton Peabody, the governor of Colorado, mobilized the State National Guard to break up a strike in the mining town of Cripple Creek. That incident triggered what came to be known as the Colorado Labor Wars, which resulted in violent – and often fatal – clashes between the miners and the mine owners or, in more provincial parlance, between labor and capital.

Although it was never specifically mentioned in his speech, it was clear that Roosevelt was referencing the unpleasantness in Colorado when he addressed Congress on that December evening. "The consistent policy of the national government, so far as it has the power," he told the assembled Congressmen, "is to hold in check the unscrupulous man, whether employer or employee; but to refuse to weaken individual initiative or to hamper or cramp the industrial development of the country." He went on to say, "no man is above the law and no man is below it; nor do we ask any man's permission when we require him to obey it. Obedience to the law is demanded as a right; not asked as a favor." It is considered to be one of Roosevelt's most powerful speeches, and his famous phrase about no man being "above the law" has been referenced many times since then.

Jon Corzine, who would never achieve the public notoriety of Teddy Roosevelt while serving in public office, had plenty of his own detractors accusing him of considering himself "above the law." The first hint came on April 12, 2007 when Corzine was then governor of New Jersey, and travelling from Atlantic City to Princeton, New Jersey. He'd been attending the New Jersey Conference of Mayors, and was riding together with an aide in the back of an SUV driven by a New Jersey state trooper. While travelling up the Garden State Parkway at speeds in excess of 90 miles an hour, the governor's vehicle was side-swiped by another car and slammed into the guard rail. Corzine suffered major injuries in the accident, including 11 broken ribs, a broken leg, a broken sternum, a broken collarbone, a broken vertebrae, and severe facial lacerations.

Corzine was by far the most critically injured of all the passengers; he was also the only passenger not wearing a seatbelt. At the time, friends of Corzine said he was never one to wear a seatbelt. That in and of itself, though, was no crime, as New Jersey hadn't yet adopted a statewide seatbelt law. After his release from the hospital, Corzine paid a self-issued ticket of $46 for speeding, and made a public service announcement that began, "I'm New Jersey Jon Corzine, and I should be dead." It was certainly an admirable admission of guilt, albeit somewhat passive aggressively. For what it's worth, Corzine reportedly started wearing a seatbelt when he drove. But his hubris – perhaps buoyed by the fact that he had, by his own admission, cheated death – still flourished.

Jon Corzine's uneclipsed hubris is a true tragic flaw, that personality flaw that brought about his ultimate demise. Rooted in ancient Greek, the term hubris means pride and arrogance taken to their most extreme. The term – especially in Greek tragedy – is linked closely with an inability to admit fault and a calculated overestimation of one's own abilities. In other words, the hubristic person is convinced that he or she can do no wrong. He or she is, in fact, above the law. In his professional life, it would lead Corzine down an increasingly destructive path.

Corzine was the son of a farmer living in Willey Station, Illinois. He was, by all accounts, the perfect small-town kid. He was the quarterback of his high-school football team and captain of the basketball team. He was a good student, and went on to attend the University of Illinois, graduating as an inducted member of the Phi Beta Kappa academic honors society. He served as a member of the United States Marine Corps Reserve from 1969 to 1975, working his way up to the rank of sergeant. During that time, he attended the Booth School of Business at the University of Chicago, where he earned an MBA in 1973. He clearly had the drive and the brains to be a successful businessman. He put that little farm in Willey Station in his rearview mirror and set his sights on the financial world in New York City.

Corzine was hired by Goldman Sachs in 1975 as a bond trader, which was the start of big things for someone from small-town Illinois. He worked his way up the ladder, from bond trader to head of fixed income. Then, in 1994, came his crowning achievement at Goldman: Jon Corzine was named the senior partner of the most prestigious investment bank in the world. In more ways than one, Jon Corzine is the epitome of the American success story. A farmer's son who got an education and served his country, married his high school sweetheart, had a family, and worked hard to provide for them. And he made a lot of money in the process. Several hundred million dollars, in fact. But unlike all good clichés, the fairy tale life of Jon Corzine was not destined for such a happy ending.

* * *

After joining Goldman Sachs in 1975, Corzine began his long and arduous ascent up the trading floor ladder. By the late 1970s, he was working as their "basis" trader, which was the purchase of government bonds that were simultaneously hedged with the sale of futures contracts; in a way, they were not unlike European government bonds with a repo-to-maturity hedge. He was good at his job; other traders described him as a man who loved to work, who loved to trade, who loved to "whip positions around" through aggressive and active trading. Soon Corzine was managing the entire government-bond trading desk, and simultaneously serving as the "long-bond trader," a prestigious designation and being the biggest risk taker on the desk. Five years after that, he'd been named a partner of the firm, the beginning of what can only be called a meteoric rise to the top.

In 1985, Corzine was given a seat on the Goldman Sachs management committee, and in 1988 was made the co-head of fixed income. While acting in senior management of the firm, Corzine continued to trade his own account with the firm's money. He used the account to make large bets on the market, oftentimes holding much larger positions than his peers. He never appeared to lose sleep over losing money, being that he knew he'd make it back and then some. In that same vein, he never lost his temper with traders who lost money, as long as they presented a well-thought-out plan; if the trader could defend his actions with intelligence, it was all right with Corzine.

He was, from all outward appearances, the last person you'd picture as a senior partner at one of Wall Street's most storied firms. He had both a beard and glasses, two things not often associated with financial executives. Rather than a wool pin-striped vest, Corzine opted for a sweater, which often gave the firm a more casual feel. But what most set Corzine apart from the prototypical Wall Street executive was that at his core, he was a genuinely good person. He cared about people and their feelings. He would always say, "thank you" and tipped waiters graciously, showing that he appreciated the work they did. He gave freely to charities and loved to help people. A former employee once said that Corzine could simultaneously deliver bad news to you and make you feel good about it.

Together with his co-head of fixed income, Mark Winkelman, Corzine built the fixed income division into a major player on Wall Street. The pair attracted and cultivated a deep client base and hired the best and the brightest traders and salespeople to support the trading strategies that generated the huge returns for the fixed income group. Such were their successes that in 1992, *International Review Magazine* named Goldman Sachs the International Bond Trading House of the Year.

1993 was a golden year in the history of Goldman Sachs. The firm excelled in both investment banking and trading, achieving a 24.7% market share of mergers and acquisitions, one of the bread-and-butter components of an investment bank. Both Moody's and Standard and Poor's had given the firm the highest credit rating in the industry. Things were good at Goldman, and that was especially true for Fixed Income. The division – which had been one of the worst performing in the early 1990s – became the first in the firm's history to make more than $1 billion in a year. Those eye-popping returns were based, in part, on a huge bull market in bonds, especially in Europe. The division held significant long positions in European debt, and the bond market continued to rise all year. All in all, while the Fixed Income division was providing unbelievable returns, it was Jon Corzine and the traders who were managing those trades that were achieving high regard around the firm.

Though the returns were unprecedented, the risks were also high. One former partner said that the numbers, while impressive, should be discounted for the risks inherent in the trades, which had been equally high. That partner went so far as to say, "If you take into account the amount of risk [Fixed Income] incurred, the firm's performance looked less impressive."

Sour grapes? Perhaps. But there was no question that, at the time, fixed income was a very good business. As both returns and market volatility was increasing, Corzine and the traders at Goldman defied conventional wisdom by increasing their positions, despite the massive price fluctuations. Many seasoned traders would pull back and take their bonuses for the year while waiting for the market storm to clear. But Goldman wasn't interested in conventional wisdom; they were Goldman Sachs and had the resources to ride out any storm. If the market went against them, they could always wait for it to come back their way. It was a philosophy that worked at Goldman because of the advantages they had over other firms. It worked because they had more money to play with.

The good luck didn't last into the following year, when the markets turned ugly. Beginning in February, the Federal Reserve began raising interest rates. The federal funds rate had been hovering at 3% for over a year, but on February 4, 1994, the Fed tightened the rate by one-half-of-one percent. A mere 50 basis points might not seem like a lot, but it sent shockwaves through the market. That increase, as it turned out, was the first of 16 rate hikes by the Fed throughout the course of the year, and sent both the bond market and the fixed income division at Goldman into a tailspin.

It not only triggered one of the worst bear markets in bonds, but resulted in several investments banks, municipalities, and hedge funds collapsing. The most noteworthy collapse was that of long-time Wall Street firm Kidder, Peabody & Co., which took massive losses on mortgage-backed bond positions and was subsequently sold to Paine Webber. Later that year, Orange County, California officially declared bankruptcy, a situation caused by massive losses incurred from leveraged investments in structured agency bonds. And throughout it all, Goldman Sachs remained on the wrong side of the market – just like the others – but still managed to survive. It's good to have extra money when you're in the financial business.

The previous year, Goldman had ridden the bull-market wave, defying more risk-adverse naysayers. They'd made a ton of money, and they assumed that trend would continue, but they were still long when the Fed raised interest rates, an action that immediately caused massive losses. The first major piece of financial news to seep out of the Goldman offices was that the firm had sustained a loss of $80 million from the London office's bad bets on British pounds.

As 1994 continued, at one point Goldman Sachs was losing an estimated $200 million per month. In the end, they were caught taking too much risk. Luckily for Goldman, still being a partnership, they had the wherewithal to ride out the bad market. The partnership structure allowed them to weather the storm since they did not worry about making quarterly earnings estimates and investor scrutiny.

Trading is, by its very nature, a risky endeavor. You buy a security, you take your chances. You try to win more times than you lose, cutting your losses when wrong and riding a profitable position when right. Individual investors are constantly warned about the risks of the market and the potential losses they face. The reason professionals are supposed to be better is because they know how to mitigate the risks. Sometimes bad judgment kicks in and clouds decisions, and traders fail to see that they were wrong. Such was the case at Goldman, as Corzine himself would say, "We developed a pattern of success in macro trading and allowed ourselves to over-concentrate our risk in those areas. That, along with outright poor market judgments, caused the bulk of the 1994 problems."

Stephen Friedman, the senior partner at the time and later chairman of the New York Federal Reserve, adopted a more "I told you so" tone when asked about the losses Goldman sustained. "What happened had been what the models had predicted would happen if the bets went wrong," he said. In the end, 1994 was more or less a wash. Goldman showed a net profit of $508 million at year's end, but that was offset by $522 million that was owed to limited partners and outside investors.

1994 was also a year of management transition at Goldman, with the announcement by Stephen Friedman that he was stepping down as senior partner, which meant the executive committee needed to find a replacement. Friedman's choice to lead the firm was Jon Corzine, and added then-head of investment banking Henry Paulson to create the traditional Goldman Sachs dual-management team. Friedman successfully argued that the two men – Corzine and Paulson – would be a perfect leadership team, representing both the interests of the trading and investment banking sides of the firm. Corzine would lead as senior partner, with Paulson serving as vice chairman. It was a unanimous vote, but despite the one-sided vote, many on the investment banking side were uneasy about having Corzine in the top spot. They thought his vision for Goldman's future with an emphasis on trading was too risky, especially fresh after the losses in 1994. Though with Paulson next in line, they felt assured they had someone who could challenge Corzine enough to keep the trading side in check.

The Corzine and Paulson team first tackled the issue of risk management, and instituted a plan for the firm. Every trader was assigned a loss limit, a specific dollar amount they could lose before having to close all positions. Second, individual trader's mandates were to become more focused; no longer could someone trade any financial instrument. Third, they formed a risk committee, which met weekly to discuss the firm's risk positions and how to mitigate the associated risks, and finally, established a system to monitor the profit-and-loss margins in real-time.

That wasn't enough to satisfy many nervous Goldman partners. The losses incurred in 1994 meant that Corzine and Paulson had effectively inherited a firm in crisis. Partners, clients, and credit-rating agencies were still nervous from the very public losses Goldman had sustained. By October 1994, 23 partners had resigned. Jon Corzine was only 47-years old, and he found himself in charge of the world's most preeminent private financial institution, but it was beginning to crumble beneath him. He needed to do something.

So do something he did. Corzine met with the credit-rating agencies to assure them he had a plan to turn Goldman around. He pointed to the risk-management plan already in place as evidence that the firm could ride out the storm; Goldman had learned from their mistakes, and this would prevent a repeat of 1994's devastating financial losses. He also pointed to the partnership structure employed at Goldman as a way of keeping compensation levels reasonably in-line with other financial firms. In other words, the problems were being staunched; Corzine just needed a little time to prove that Goldman was still on top.

The Corzine and Paulson plan, which targeted a profit of $3.7 billion by getting the firm back on the right side of the profit/loss ledger, began with cutting expenses. By eliminating 10% of the workforce, Corzine and Paulson figured they could save the firm $1 billion annually. They would then hire more traders and bankers to expand the business units, thereby increasing revenues. By the end of 1995, they'd done exactly that. They had laid off 10% of the salaried workforce and cut expenses by $1 billion. They began hiring new traders and bankers and, by the end of the year, the firm posted a profit of $1.37 billion, which was significantly better than the previous year's essentially flat earnings.

As 1996 dawned, there was a push to take Goldman public. Corzine was anxious to bring more capital into the firm to support growing the trading side of the business, but to do so he needed a vast majority of the partners to give their approval. The same idea had been brought up in 1986 and again in 1994. Both times it had been deemed a bad idea, and the third time didn't prove to be a charm. Corzine proposed the idea, and met significant resistance because the valuation of the firm wouldn't be as high as the partners wanted. He decided not to press the issue, and instead shelved it for another day. The fact that he adhered to the partners' wishes and didn't try to push it won him growing support among the partners.

The following year was another record year for Goldman Sachs, with profits topping $3 billion. Trading now accounted for over 40% of the firm's revenues and Goldman was far outpacing its competitors.

Then, in 1998, Corzine initiated the IPO discussion once again. A detailed proposal was again drawn up for the partners, and they were asked to vote on it. On August 10, 1998 the partners voted to take Goldman Sachs public, tentatively scheduling an IPO target date for the fall. The partners stood to gain a great deal of money. The stocks for both Merrill Lynch and Morgan Stanley were trading at more than four times their book value, which meant that Goldman's stock would command at least an equal multiple, making Goldman partners instant multi-millionaires. Individual partners would make between $50 and $70 million each and senior partners over $100 million apiece.

Then crisis hit Wall Street in September 1998, with both the Russian default and the near collapse of Long-Term Capital Management. The former Soviet Union had seen its currency devalued, and was forced to default on its loans. Russia declared it wouldn't make payments on bonds it had issued, which led to further devaluation of the currency and a rampant sell-off in many emerging markets. Back in the U.S., there was a major meltdown beginning, with the potential to spread across the financial community.

The hedge fund Long-Term Capital Management – a name that would become ingrained in Americans' financial lexicon when it lost approximately $4.6 billion of its investors' money – collapsed, threatening to send shockwaves through the American financial markets the likes of which hadn't been seen since the Great Depression. The fund had been created from the bond arbitrage division of Salomon Brothers in the early 1990s, widely considered to be one on the top trading firms in the business. They were so well regarded that even Wall Street investment banks invested with them, and there was a widely held belief amongst financiers that the group could do no wrong. They were the top traders in the industry, bar none.

LTCM began posting bigger and bigger losses over the summer, and the larger financial world that was watching those losses feared panic was gripping the market. Many on Wall Street wanted to stop the bleeding before panic spread to other markets, and thereby calm the jittery nerves of investors everywhere. LTCM was leveraged at one point 100-to-1; in other words, for every $1 in capital, the firm owned $100 in securities.

And while the spread of that ratio might seem to be profoundly risky, the firm made a great deal of money. When you're talking about hedge funds, risk is the name of the game. And just to ratchet up the risk a little bit, consider the fact that much of their positions weren't securities positions, but rather complicated derivatives, which allowed even higher amounts of leverage without the capital requirements. To put it in perspective, Bear Stearns – the firm that many pundits felt got what it deserved when it went bankrupt as a result of over-leveraging itself – was said to be leveraged around 30-to-1 at the time of its collapse.

The primary strategy that LTCM employed in order to get the returns they did was to generate small returns on a large number of what they deemed to be mispriced securities. To accomplish this, the firm utilized the brains of both computer models and those of two Nobel Prize winners employed by LTCM. They created theoretical models of where securities should be priced, then they looked at where those securities were actually trading in the market. They would identify the securities trading at prices higher than their models suggested they should be, and in the cases where they owned them, sell. Then they identified the securities trading at prices lower that their theoretical values, and they would buy those securities. That left them with a short and a long in two related securities, which is, in theory, a relatively low-risk trade. Sometimes it's called "picking up nickels." And when they did it correctly, the brokers at LTCM picked up a lot of nickels.

But the world of hedge funds is a secretive one, and hedge-fund managers do everything they can to camouflage their intentions. In the case of LTCM, in order to hide their trades from competitors at the Wall Street banks they traded with, they spread their trades across many counterparties. As a result, when crisis struck and market spreads widened, LTCM didn't have offsetting trades with the same counterparties, thus grossing their margin requirements. In other words, LTCM had short and long positions, but with different counterparties. One would process a buy order, the other a sell order. In essence, the right hand didn't know what the left was doing. And that was exactly how Long-Term Capital Management wanted things.

But when market spreads widened and the market was in crisis, they didn't have the trades with the same counterparty to offset the margin calls, which meant that they were getting margin calls from both hands. And due to their secretive nature, they couldn't explain away the situation. They were stuck paying both margin calls, and those calls drained their capital reserves.

As more and more counterparties issued margin calls for the firm's outstanding balances, LTCM quickly ran out of capital to meet those margin calls. If word got around that the investment fund couldn't meet margin calls and LTCM was forced to liquidate, it threatened to bring down other financial firms, and potentially lead to a broader financial panic. And that would be disastrous to even the mighty Goldman Sachs, despite their deep pockets and massive reservoirs of capital reserve.

That's how Jon Corzine and many on Wall Street saw it, anyway. LTCM had to be saved, and the only way to do it was to help arrange a massive financial rescue package. The total amount of money needed, according to LTCM, was $1 billion. They cast a wide net in search of potential investors, including some of the biggest names in the history of Wall Street. Names like Warren Buffett and Stanley Druckenmiller were floated, as were firms like Travelers and JP Morgan.

As it turned out, the hedge fund needed more than the previously thought billion dollars. On September 11, 1998 John Meriweather contacted Jon Corzine at Goldman Sachs. Meriweather explained the situation, and asked – perhaps begged is a better descriptor – Corzine to use Goldman's money to save LTCM. Corzine was a trader himself, so he understood both the larger concept of hedge-fund operations and the more micro-level of LTCM's trades. Additionally, Goldman was known to be discrete in their handling of matters like this, and they had the ability to get their hands on a lot of money very quickly. Goldman Sachs was the best hope for LTCM's survival.

Corzine was intrigued by the prospect of partnering with Meriweather. He pledged the embattled firm $1 billion of money using both client funds and Goldman Sachs' own money, with the promise of another billion soon after. But there was a catch. For that much money, Corzine wanted access to LTCM's books, so he knew what he was getting himself in to. It was, in a sense, due diligence on the part of Goldman.

Meriweather agreed to open up the books to Corzine – he didn't have a lot of bargaining room as it was – and that agreement sent teams of Goldman Sachs traders and analysts to the LTCM offices, where they began going over the hedge fund's files. It seemed strange to some of the LTCM personnel who watched the proceedings, prompting one employee to remark afterwards that "it didn't make sense."

If the sight of Goldman Sachs analysts and traders rummaging through the particulars of the Long-Term Capital Management trades "didn't make sense," then it must have confounded the brain when a Goldman trader was caught red-handed downloading LTCM's trading positions onto a laptop computer. As Roger Lowenstein remarked in *When Genius Failed*, "To John Meriweather and his partners, Goldman was raping Long Term in front of their very eyes."

In truth, the access granted to the Goldman employees was mere foreplay, for the true rape was yet to come. In the ensuing days, Long Term partners noticed that the prices of the securities they were holding gradually began dropping. And what's more, those particular securities were seeing price decreases that were not in line with other, similar securities. In other words, there was a mass sell-off of the securities owned by Long-Term Capital Management; the inference was that Goldman traders had used their knowledge of the LTCM strategies to drive the prices of those securities down, so they could short them and turn a quick profit, a strategy that would be especially lucrative if LTCM did collapse. So convinced was Meriweather that there was foul play involved that he filed a formal complaint with the Federal Reserve's Under Secretary Peter Fisher.

When a private rescue package could not be worked out, later that month the largest investment banks banded together and pledged $3.75 billion to LTCM in a bailout organized by the Federal Reserve Bank of New York. In what would become an ironic twist of fate, Bear Stearns was the only investment bank that patently refused to participate. Bear felt they were already overextended as the clearing firm for LTCM's trades, serving just like a clearing bank but for hedge funds. When a clearing client is about to collapse, time has shown, it's best to take as much collateral and margin as possible and not increase exposure to the client.

If Long-Term Capital Management was about to fail, Bear didn't want to increase their exposure by investing directly in them. In addition, it was the philosophy at Bear that in the investment world, you win and you lose. And when you lose, you shouldn't expect anyone to come to your rescue. In an ironic twist of fate, it was Henry Paulson, the number two Goldman partner at the time, who would oversee Bear Stearn's collapse just 10 years later when Paulson was Secretary of the Treasury.

It was at this time that Hank Paulson began setting his sights on the senior partner's office, a position still occupied by Jon Corzine. Paulson, who famously quipped, "I don't want to sound heartless, but in almost every one of our businesses, there are 15 to 20 percent of the people who really add 80 percent of the value," clearly he felt that Corzine wasn't adding enough value to the firm. Goldman contributed $300 million to the LTCM bailout along with the other large Wall Street firms. Corzine's contribution, risking partners' capital to support a counterparty risk originating from the trading side of the business, was not popular with Paulson and other bankers at the firm. Ironically enough, it was reported that Corzine's insistence that Goldman Sachs participate in the rescue of Long-Term Capital Management led to his ultimate demise. According to the report, Paulson was adamantly opposed to Goldman's participation in the bailout, but Corzine insisted on supporting the struggling hedge fund. In the end, Corzine won the battle; Paulson, however, won the war.

Paulson and Corzine were engaged in a war in which the winner would assume sole control of Goldman Sachs. It's been a common scene on Wall Street for years, where bankers and traders battle for control. The side that wins is usually the one that controls the most profitable business at the time. In the end, Paulson's "palace coup" occurred while Corzine was off skiing with his family over the Christmas holiday. In Corzine's absence, Paulson lobbied for support in ousting him, citing Corzine's risk-taking as potentially disastrous for the firm. Paulson convened a meeting of the management committee, which included himself, John Thain, Bob Hurst, and John Thornton. Though Corzine was both a member of the committee and absent, it was assumed he would vote against removing himself from office. The vote to remove Corzine came down to 3-2, with Thain casting the deciding vote. The duty of informing Corzine fell to Thain, who told him in a matter-of-fact tone that the management committee had voted him out.

Corzine took the news in stride. When he next saw Paulson, he said to the new senior partner, "Hank, I didn't know you were such a tough guy." Corzine had worked for Goldman Sachs for 23 years at the time he was forced out. It was, no doubt, a bittersweet moment for him. The blow was softened substantially with a $12 million severance package, and after Goldman went public in 1999, Corzine enjoyed a substantial windfall of approximately $400 million, given that he was senior partner just prior to the IPO.

* * *

Despite having lost the corner office at Goldman, Corzine was not going to stay idle for long. It wasn't another job in high finance he set his sights on; rather, it was the United States Senate. New Jersey Democratic Senator Frank Lautenberg had announced his retirement and Corzine thought his experience in the business world made him the right man to replace the aging New Jersey politician.

Going into the primary, Corzine was trailing by 30 percentage points for the Democratic nomination, but he dipped into to his own personal fortune and spent a record $33 million on his primary campaign. He eventually won the nomination and then spent an additional $30 million of his own money to secure victory in the general election, beating Republican nominee Bob Franks by four percentage points. Once he was in office, it was said of Corzine's presence in the senate that his agenda alone – despite the fact that he'd replace a fellow Democrat – had been liberal enough to shift the political balance of the entire senate to the left.

Five years later in 2005, a year before his senate seat would be up for reelection, Corzine decided to run for governor of New Jersey. He spent heavily from his own bank account again, spending an estimated $33 million on his campaign against Republican Doug Forrester, another businessman with deep personal pockets. Corzine won 54% of the vote, and assumed the position of governor of the State of New Jersey. He appointed Bob Menendez to take over his seat, and Menendez would go on to a successful reelection bid the following year.

Corzine's gubernatorial reign was short lived and marred by negative press. In 2007, the state government effectively shut down due to a budgetary impasse, a shutdown that many blamed on the governor. The following year, he announced plans to privatize the New Jersey Turnpike and raise tolls on the popular commuter thoroughfare, a plan that met strong opposition from the voting public. There was an affair that sparked questions of financial impropriety on the part of the governor, and accusations of abuse of power and ethics violations by Corzine's attorney general, Zulima Farber.

It was the car accident that garnered the most negative attention for Corzine during his time as New Jersey governor. The fact that he was in a car that was speeding while not wearing a seatbelt smacked of entitlement, and reeked of a man who considered himself above the law. That fact, paired with the other political firestorms he'd set off while in office, cemented his fate as a one-term governor. In the 2010 election, Corzine faced Republican Chris Christie, who defeated Corzine by a 4% margin. Corzine was 63-years old and once again looking for a career change.

Just when Jon Corzine was losing his reelection bid for the governor of New Jersey, MF Global had been losing, too. The firm had been losing money since the IPO and for the five most recent consecutive quarters. Add to that the second CEO in less than two years had just departed, and it was clear that the firm needed a shot in the arm to keep investors happy. That shot needed to come quickly, as there was a lot of damage that needed repairing.

J. Christopher Flowers had known Jon Corzine when they'd worked together at Goldman Sachs, and Flowers had already made arrangements for Corzine to join Flowers' firm. But the unexpected departure of Bernie Dan – paired with the unexpected victory by Chris Christie in New Jersey – put those plans on hold. MF Global needed a CEO; Corzine needed a job. It was, at least on the surface, a match made in financial heaven. Flowers approached Corzine with a proposal: would Jon Corzine be willing to take over as interim CEO of MF Global? Just long enough to get the firm back on stable footing and then he could step down when a permanent replacement was found.

Say what you will about Jon Corzine, but understand the man does not do anything halfway. It's all or nothing, and Corzine didn't have any interest in any sort of temporary figurehead position. He'd already declined an offer to join the D.E. Shaw Group – a hedge fund run by David Shaw – as a senior executive. He was intrigued by the idea of taking over a struggling firm and turning it around. It would be, in his mind, a project that would use his abilities and skills, and put them to good use. But he wasn't interested in a semi-permanent gig, if Jon Corzine was going to take over MF Global, it was going to be a permanent assignment.

On March 23, 2010 Jon Corzine was introduced as the new chief executive officer of MF Global. Corzine estimated that he could personally make somewhere in the neighborhood of a billion dollars after turning MF Global around. It was, to be sure, an optimistic outlook. Regardless of that, investors followed suit and apparently shared Corzine's optimism – something that was, at the time, in short supply on Wall Street – and they bought the idea he could right the sinking ship. As a result, MF Global's stock price went up 10% just on the news of Corzine's appointment.

It was the dawning of a new era in MF Global's history. Despite the fact that Corzine had been out of the securities business for 10 years, his reentry was cause for celebration in a market where celebrations were few and far between. He'd risen to the helm of Goldman Sachs, one of the most financially successful investment banks in the world. Clearly he'd learned something from that experience, something that he'd bring to MF Global to turn the tides and stem the losses. That was the prevailing wisdom, that Jon Corzine would be the savior of MF Global.

CHAPTER SEVEN

Changes

In 1966, American psychologist Abraham Maslow famously quipped, "I suppose it is tempting, if the only tool you have is a hammer, to treat everything as if it were a nail." The comment was a paraphrasing of the words of philosopher Abraham Kaplan, who coined the term "the law of the instrument," which he described as: "Give a small boy a hammer, and he will find that everything he encounters needs pounding." While the phrase has been attributed to a variety of sources, it's not the origin that's as important as the philosophy behind the words.

The concept of Maslow's Hammer, as it's been called, suggests that oftentimes human beings approach new problems by looking for similarities to past experiences. If the only tool you have in your toolbox is a hammer, then it's the only solution you have for fixing things. In the case of a hammer, it is used to pound in a nail. So if you find a nail that is sticking out around your house, you're in luck. You have the right tool for the job.

What happens if a door won't shut because the wood is swollen or a screw has worked its way loose in a cabinet? In the case of the door, you'd probably get a plane to shave down the wood to fit the frame; in the case of the cabinet, you'd get a screwdriver and tighten the screw. But remember, the only tool available is a hammer, which means your choice of how to do the repair must fit the parameter of the hammer itself.

Rather than shaving off slices of wood to thin out the door, you're instead forced to hit the door with your hammer until you've pounded it enough to somehow force it to close. The loose screw, on the other hand, you'd treat exactly as a nail, hitting it on the head, trying to force it back into the wood from which it came. Obviously neither solution is optimal and both will result in more damage than repair. But the scenarios illustrate the point that there are two ways of looking at any repair job. You can approach the problem with what is available on hand for completing the task; that is, using Maslow's Hammer, which is not always the ideal choice.

But it doesn't take a professional carpenter to realize you can't use a hammer to complete every repair job. The same can be said for other tasks that one must perform, regardless of the setting. You need to have the right tool for the job. And what's more, you can have the nicest, best made, most expensive and time-honored hammer, but it won't be any use fixing that swollen door or that loose cabinet screw. The cheapest screwdriver around will always be better than the best hammer for tightening a screw.

Jon Corzine could have learned a lot from Abraham Maslow. It's not so much that Corzine was doing home improvement, at least not in the literal sense, but the metaphor is certainly appropriate. MF Global had a strong track record in futures brokerage and fixed income; at the same time, they were losing money hand-over-fist, and were about to get downgraded by the credit-rating agencies. Adding to the complications was the fact that senior executives had jumped ship, causing a crisis in upper-level leadership. In other words, it seemed almost identical to the situation that Corzine had inherited when he took over Goldman Sachs in 1995. That Goldman renovation project had turned out pretty well; the hope was that Corzine could put a similar fresh coat of paint on the crumbling house of MF Global in 2010. He planned to use the same hammer to solve the problem and assumed the problem was still the same nail.

Corzine's general plan was to turn MF Global into a miniature Goldman Sachs. That makes sense, given that he worked for Goldman for 23 years and it was the only securities firm he knew. In a larger sense, Corzine planned to reorganize the entire professional structure of the firm by shifting the principal business model from that of a brokerage firm to that of an investment bank over a short period of time. At the onset, he planned to reorganize the firm into four divisions: capital markets, retail services, prime services, and asset management. He would jettison the pure brokerage businesses from the firm, regardless of their profitability and shift the focus to higher-risk, higher-yielding trading, again, using Goldman as the mirror for the new image of MF Global. MF Global would move away from being predominately a futures broker and diversify into a full-fledged investment bank within five years, all the while maintaining its reputation as a major force in the futures industry. The long-term aim of this strategy was to create, in essence, a mini Goldman Sachs. That was the plan, at least.

When he pulled out his playbook from 1995, his first step was a preemptive strike of sorts against the credit-rating agencies. That meant having in-person meetings with the agencies to negotiate a deal. MF Global's financial difficulties meant that the firm was fast approaching a downgrade to a level below investment grade, which would be an outwardly visible sign that MF Global was going down, and would be the first nail in the firm's coffin, as investors and clients flee. Corzine needed to keep that from happening, so it was critical that he meet with the rating agencies in person to privately plead his case. He laid out his plans to make MF Global profitable, again in a multi-step plan.

The second stage in Corzine's rehabilitation was to slash costs. His goal was to cut the workforce by 10% to 15%, coupled with the idea of reorganizing the pay structure for front-office employees from a commission-based system to salary-and-bonus. While the existing commission structure paid employees only for money they brought in, Corzine preferred salaries because it provided him with more predictable costs, all the while incorporating the promise of a bonus. The salary-and-bonus plan also offered the firm the chance to pay a large amount of the compensation costs in stock and give traders and salespeople a vested interest in the overall performance of the firm. It was this compensation system that worked at Goldman Sachs and Corzine was betting it would work at MF Global, too.

The result of his meetings with the credit-rating agencies was that he received something akin to a stay of execution. The agencies were willing to give Corzine a year – four quarters – to turn things around. He managed to successfully leverage his reputation into a gift of time, but the gift wasn't without attachments. The agencies warned that MF Global would need to show a profit within a year after the meeting or face a downgrade; Moody's went so far as to quantify it, dictating that MF Global would need to show a minimum of $250 to $300 million in pretax annual profits by the third quarter of 2011 if the firm wanted to avoid the downgrade. That meant he had until September 30, 2011 to make it all work.

Back at the office, Corzine immediately put his plan into action. After he trimmed the fat from the company's roster, he would supplement the leaner machine with some new talent that would, hopefully, inject new levels of profit into the faltering business. He would start hiring new employees after cutting what he saw as wasted resources, and in the process refocus the front-line producers from brokerage to sales and trading. The hiring of many new employees was announced publicly.

Given the "money is no object" mentality that became so commonplace in financial institutions in the early 2000s, it should come as no surprise to learn that Corzine sometimes had to spend millions of dollars in signing bonuses in order to attract top talent to then-little-known MF Global. Much like a professional athlete demanding a multi-million-dollar signing bonus for a team to acquire him, so, too, did many new hires. And just like so many professional team owners pay enormous signing bonuses, so, too, did Jon Corzine.

One of Corzine's first hires was Brad Abelow, someone with whom Corzine was very familiar. Abelow was a partner at Goldman Sachs when Corzine was there, and he also served as New Jersey's state treasurer and Governor Corzine's chief of staff. At the newly styled MF Global, Abelow was rewarded for his service to Corzine and became the firm's new president and chief operating officer with a compensation deal worth over $2 million a year, including salary and bonuses. In total, over the two years that he worked at MF Global, Abelow would be paid a total compensation package worth in excess of $7.6 million.

Abelow was a key part of Corzine's turnaround strategy, filling the role of someone to manage the fine details of the business. And there was no doubt around the firm that Abelow was Corzine's chief lieutenant. He was the person who oversaw the cost cutting and who personally approved the hiring of every new employee. Even though he was a newly hired employee, Abelow was immediately installed as a vital cog in the machinery of MF Global.

Gregg Schonhorn was another of Corzine's first hires. He was one of the first fixed-income executives to be hired in September 2010 as part of Corzine's initiative. Schonhorn came from Jefferies, where he'd been a managing director of institutional sales. He would be assuming the role of senior vice president of fixed-income; he would be charged with serving as the co-head of the institutional sales group on the credit desk.

By the end of 2010, Corzine brought in Jon Bass to fill a position called "global head of institutional sales and fixed income." Bass cemented his status as folk hero on the trading floor when he abruptly quit his job at UBS. According to reports from people who'd witnessed the event, Bass's departure came on the heels of a conference call with the firm's investment banking division CEO Huw Jenkins. Apparently not satisfied with the explanation of why bonuses at the firm were down more than 80%, Bass told Jenkins to "sod off," the British equivalent of telling someone to screw himself. As Bass left the trading floor immediately after, he reportedly received a standing ovation from the traders who witnessed the exchange.

After UBS, Bass did a stint as head of fixed-income at the small brokerage firm BTIG. His time there did not last long, with many insiders complaining that he nearly bankrupted BTIG with his aggressive hiring practices and the guaranteed-compensation packages he offered new employees. Ultimately, the revenues generated from the fixed-income group at BTIG just could not keep up with the compensation costs, and Bass left the firm.

Bass was then hired by MF Global, who offered him a very lucrative deal. After getting a $500,000 signing bonus, Bass secured a $1,875,000 guaranteed bonus his first year. Under his direction, the plan was to build MF Global's fixed-income business to the point that they were named a primary dealer in United States government securities. He was given at MF Global, ironically, the same mandate as he'd been given at BTIG – hire aggressively. Luckily for Bass, MF Global had much deeper pockets than BTIG. He went on a rampant hiring spree, bringing on dozens of sales staff and traders, underlings that he affectionately referred to as his "animals." Well-paid animals, to be sure, but the lack of respect for those he hired was very telling.

Mortgage-backed securities (MBS) were a major source of revenues at Goldman Sachs, and became a large component of Corzine's plan. So much so that he intended to build an entire division within the firm to focus specifically on MBS trading. In order to build the right group, Corzine needed the right senior manager and was willing to pay anything to get him. A former Jeffries trader named Christopher Belhumeur, who had overseen mortgage-backed securities and derivatives there, was named head of structured mortgage trading at MF Global, reporting directly to Bass.

In much the same way that Bass had left his previous employer with a fireworks show, Belhumeur had ignited sparks on his way to MF Global. Because he stood to lose approximately $6 million in unvested Jefferies stock upon leaving, Belhumeur needed a cash payment for the money he was leaving behind at Jeffries. Corzine paid the $6 million as a signing bonus, knowing he'd make back multiple times that in the coming years.

Paul Farrell had been MF Global's head of foreign exchange since August 2009, when he was replaced by Jon Corzine's choice to be his successor, James Kemp, in May 2011. Based in the U.S., Kemp was well known in the industry as a star foreign-exchange trader. Kemp was not an expensive hire, at least by MF Global standards, and only required a $400,000 annual salary, but moving Farrell out required an $800,000 severance package.

Part of the MF Global's reengineering strategy included a major push into equities and into Asia, an area that was previously overshadowed at MF Global by the U.S. and Europe. The company planned to recruit 20 equity analysts across the world, with a specific focus on Asia and Europe. Michael Steinberg joined MF Global from Morgan Stanley, with professional experience that included heading up Asia-Pacific sales. At MF Global, he'd be the head of Asian equity sales. Bringing experience in both equities and Asian sales to the firm, Steinberg was a perfect fit to lead the firm into those two areas.

Then there was Matt Shatz, the newly anointed head of electronic equity trading and clearing at MF Global, who had been poached directly from Newedge, where he had served in the same capacity. Shatz was the last major equities trader at Newedge after most of its equity division had cleared out to go to other firms. Shatz, though, remained at Newedge, becoming the head of equities. That was, until MF Global came calling with a rumored $3 million guaranteed bonus to bring over the remaining people still at Newedge.

The hiring of high-profile people to fill high-profile jobs continued. In all, Corzine brought in approximately 1,100 new employees during his tenure at MF Global in an attempt to double the size of the firm's employee base. That number, however, stands against the estimated 1,400 who left MF Global – some willingly, some not – while Corzine was at the helm. Corzine's plan to shift focus from futures and brokerage to sales and trading was well thought out and well executed. He successfully shifted the focus of the firm, but at a cost. Recruiting those star employees weighed on the bottom line, and those who didn't contribute to Corzine's vision were let go without a great deal of ceremony.

Along with the litany of new faces that were walking the halls of MF Global came a new trading-first philosophy, which was crucial to Corzine's goal of achieving the Goldman Sachs model and generating the profits the firm so desperately needed. All the new people coming, however, weren't free from animosity. There was also a cultural change that was just as important as the new plan. There was something of a tectonic shift going on inside the walls of MF Global, as the focus of the firm's investment philosophy shifted from brokerage to trading. Despite the hopes of those in charge, the change wasn't exactly a smooth transition.

After his arrival, Corzine began walking the floors of the brokerage company, asking the brokers about their business and how it worked. He had meetings with senior executives and desk managers, trying to figure out who was worth keeping and who needed to go. In essence, he was in the process of changing a brokerage firm to an investment bank, albeit one with an emphasis on trading.

Brokers and traders are two different animals. Brokers are essentially matchmakers, bringing together a buyer and a seller, and getting paid a commission in the process. Traders, on the other hand, buy and sell securities, relying on movements in the market and successful directional bets to generate income. Not only are the jobs very different, but the cultures are very different, too. The difference between those taking risk and those who are simply filling orders for clients can be striking.

In one situation, Corzine sat down with some futures brokers at their desks. After watching them work for a while as they were taking client orders and calling the orders down to the exchange, he asked them, "Why aren't you trading?" To them, the answer was obvious. They were brokers and not traders. They had never taken market risk before, at least not unless they had an error trade and had to cover it back. Then Corzine said, "You guys are wasting some good opportunities here." He left, then later, upon speaking with the manager of the area, Corzine suggested out loud, "We need to sit some traders near these guys, so the traders can see the flows from their customers and help the traders make more money."

Over time, the cultural differences created a range of competing views and emotions across the floor. There were the legacy employees from Man Financial and Refco who were mostly brokers that were accustomed to doing business one way. Then there were the new Corzine people coming in, people who had an entirely different culture and view of the firm. It began to destabilize the core brokerage businesses and led to a schism within the firm. On one side of the divide were the old employees, looking across the rift at the new employees. With Corzine in charge, it was certainly better to be the latter.

It was made abundantly clear to everyone around the firm that risk taking was the *raison d'être* of the new Corzine era. In fact, soon after he arrived, Corzine encouraged all personnel to take more market risk in their trades, pushing the idea of profits over safety and conservatism. The new profit-making plan could potentially strain MF Global's existing resources, as Corzine planned to use what was available to support the new trading side of the business. They needed financial resources, but what limited resources MF Global had at their disposal were often already spoken for. Corzine assumed MF Global already had the infrastructure to support the strategy, including sufficient capital, support personnel, trade execution capabilities, and repo financing. Corzine knew he needed higher returns and didn't have a lot of time in which to amass them. The new profit-first mentality was the only way to get the higher returns they so desperately needed in the least amount of time.

At the core of Corzine's risk-taking plan was his plan to create a division that was charged with trading the firm's capital, a division that became known as the Principal Strategies Group (PSG). The PSG traders would commit themselves to proprietary trading, which is the term given to the practice of trading the firm's own money, as opposed to purely executing trades on behalf of customers. There would no long be the traditional emphasis on executing trades for customers. Instead, the firm would now buy and sell based on the direction of the market.

Instead of generating a commission on transactions, they would potentially make higher returns by taking a view of the market. When a firm makes the right calls, it's a higher margin business, and can function with less personnel support, capital usage, and infrastructure. There was one caveat, however: MF Global was now risking their own money with every trade, and they were not just guaranteed a fee from the customer. Taking risk meant they would not always win; sometimes they would lose. The good news was that what they won enhanced the profits of the firm. The bad news was that what they lost came out of MF Global's bottom line.

Beginning in June 2010 – just three months after Jon Corzine arrived – the Principal Strategies Group was up and running. Initially PSG was just Corzine and an order clerk, but by the end of the year, the team would grow to include four or five traders. They began to trade in a number of different asset classes and markets, trading primarily in fixed-income, equities, commodities, foreign exchange, and placing those bets through futures, options, and derivatives. They traded everything from wheat, oil, gold, foreign currencies, to U.S. Treasuries and even European sovereign debt, hoping to generate more income on the winning trades than losing ones. It was like a hedge fund within the firm and fit perfectly with Corzine; trading was his passion.

The PSG team would ultimately be composed of 10 traders: six senior traders, three juniors, and one assistant. These 10 people, according to Corzine's grand plan for MF Global, were going to account for 20% to 40% of the firm's net revenues annually. Those numbers weren't unimaginable. Goldman Sachs and Solomon Brothers had both made a great deal of money from proprietary trading, and Corzine was convinced that he could duplicate their successes.

Corzine knew hiring the right professional traders would take time, so he turned to the only other source of easily tapped talent he could think of: himself. He tapped into his own trading account and began buying and selling on behalf of MF Global. From Corzine's perspective, the trouble was that no one else in PSG had the same level of talent as he possessed. Since he saw himself as the ultimate authority – both as the CEO and as the one with the most trading knowledge – Corzine was firmly entrenched as the one calling the shots. The new obligation forced Corzine to stay up trading late at night and early in the morning, waking up at 3:30 a.m. to go to work or just check the markets. It was almost as if he were an addict, a man who literally couldn't stop. He loved trading, plain and simple. And he was good at it.

More than one MF Global employee recalled meetings in which Corzine seemed distracted, as he checked market prices and interrupted meetings to place buy and sell orders. It became such a compulsion for Corzine to trade that he oftentimes neglected other duties, choosing to spend time on the trading floor instead of focusing on the responsibilities in his office. He was completely convinced he could trade the firm into financial stability. It got to the point where Chris Flowers felt that he had to intervene, telling the CEO that he was too distracted and needed to shift his focus back to running the business.

Unlike the Goldman Sachs plan from 15 years earlier, the MF Global plan did not include an emphasis on risk management. That would become an apparent flaw in Corzine's plan that later contributed to the firm's downfall. At Goldman, the investment bankers were nervous that Corzine and his traders would take too much risk. At MF Global, with no investment banking side and no strong number two like Hank Paulson, there was no one to keep Corzine in check. In other words, there was nobody to be nervous, which meant that Corzine was allowed to run unchecked. Human nature is such that few people want to hire someone to come in and challenge their own decisions. Corzine didn't want to hire anyone who would challenge his philosophy. In fact, he didn't particularly want to hire anyone who didn't admire him for his successes. As a senior executive said of the boss, "At Goldman

Sachs, Corzine was challenged by others. At MF Global, he was worshipped."

All of that is not to say that the efforts did not show initial results. In February 2011, MF Global was named a primary dealer of government securities, and thereby became one of only 20 firms recognized by the Federal Reserve to trade directly with that esteemed financial organization. It was a great achievement for the firm and the management of the fixed-income team. It meant the firm joined an elite group of financial firms in the country. Perhaps most importantly though, it was a federal stamp of approval that meant the government had the highest level of confidence in MF Global. As a primary dealer, they would attract new customers as they served as market makers for government bonds. Corzine said in a press release, "Being designated a primary dealer by the Federal Reserve Bank of New York is consistent with our global strategy of expanding our broker-dealer activities, as we seek to serve our clients with broader execution services and greater market insight and ideas."

* * *

The stage was set for a dramatic finish. On the one hand, MF Global seemed destined to come out on top; they had a solid turnaround plan in place that proved successful at Goldman 15 years earlier. They appeared set to turn profits around and thus prove to the rating agencies they were on the right track. On the other hand, however, was the real possibility that trading risk could backfire; given the small size of the firm, a risky error could send the once-proud firm into a financial freefall. Assuming the firm was well managed and trading risks mitigated, the recipe for success seemed to be in place. Unfortunately for Corzine and company, there were unforeseen forces working against them, forces that were beyond their control.

In August 2007, the Federal Reserve had set the federal funds rate at 5.25%, which meant a large interest-rate spread for futures brokerage firms investing their customers' segregated margin funds. The higher the rate, the higher the revenues for futures firms like MF Global. As the financial crisis that wracked the country that month wore on, the Fed continued to lower the fed funds rate. At first, on September

18, the rate was cut to 4.75%. By the time Bear Stearns collapsed, the rate was down to 2.25%. Then came the collapse of Lehman Brothers, and three weeks later, the Fed cut the rate again, this time lowering it to 1.50%. By the end of 2008, the rate had been effectively cut to 0%.

While the goal of the Federal Reserve cutting rates was to reduce borrowing costs and encourage spending, the fact of the matter was that a large chunk of futures brokers' income was married to interest rates. The lower the rate went, the more MF Global's revenues fell. To put it in perspective, consider that the firm generated $1.258 billion in interest income for the quarter ending September 30, 2007. By March 2008, MF Global reported quarterly interest revenues of $632 million. In the space of six months, the firm's quarterly interest revenues had been cut in half. By the time the fed funds rate fell to zero, the firm was only taking in between $100 to $150 million a quarter in interest revenues, an amount that was equivalent to about 10% of what it was in September the year before. From the onset of the financial crisis, the entire business model for futures brokers changed considerably.

Obviously, a financial institution making $1 billion less per quarter includes other factors at work hurting its bottom line. Coupled with ultra-low interest rates was a decrease in spread on other interest-rate-sensitive businesses, including their repo and stock-loan desks. Additionally, the intensification of the global financial crisis resulted in less customer trading activity in general. That meant smaller future positions, less trading, which in turn meant smaller margin deposits. And that all added up to less revenues everywhere. Like many other firms, MF Global was caught in a bad market and a declining business model.

The financial stars seemed aligned against MF Global just as Jon Corzine's plan was to move the firm away from those businesses. He fought and clawed his way through his first year and managed to improve the firm's financial standing. When Corzine arrived, MF Global had just posted a net loss of approximately $195.4 million for the end of the fiscal year on March 31, 2010. By the end of the next fiscal year, March 31, 2011, Corzine had managed to cut that loss to $76.3 million. Within his first year, by all accounts, Corzine's strategy seemed to be working; but by all those same accounts, the firm was still losing a lot of money.

It was all about time. Corzine needed more time for his strategy to turn a profit. He'd weathered the initial storms – hiring costs had gone into the tens of millions, start-up costs of new divisions were enormous – and those costs had weighted down the initial net profits. He just needed more time. A senior manager would later say of Corzine's plan, "He was trying to change a futures broker into Goldman Sachs in 18 months. He was in too much of a rush." That said, there was a reason for Corzine's haste. He was running out of time, so to speak, and had to turn a profit by September 30, 2011.

The ratings agencies had the firm deadline of four quarters for Corzine to demonstrate that MF Global could turn that profit, and weren't interested in hearing about start-up costs or hiring bonuses cutting into the bottom line. If MF Global's rating were downgraded, it would mean a substantial hit to the firm's reputation as a whole and a subsequent loss in their client base. But it would also make it more expensive for them to do business, thus further complicating their future. In short, Corzine needed to find a way to generate another $80 million a year, or $20 million a quarter. Quickly.

Of course, it's hard to get a payday loan for $20 million, and the chances of winning a $20 million lottery every four months are equally unlikely. But hope, as they say, springs eternal, and when you're staring down the barrel of an imminent credit-rating downgrade, you hold out as much hope as you can muster. Corzine did what he had to do. He went from division to division, desk to desk, asking his employees if they had ideas to generate a quick $20 million, and then do it again three times over the course of the year.

After making the rounds on the fixed-income trading floor, Corzine noticed the repo-to-maturity (RTM) trades in the U.S. market and liked them; he thought they were a good trading strategy. What was not to like about matched risk, a little spread, no balance sheet and getting to book the income up front. The repo desk in New York said the spreads were too thin to get the kind of return he was looking for. But Corzine was desperate, so he did what many others in that situation did: he got a second opinion.

He called the London repo desk and posed the same question, "How can you generate $20 million a quarter?" Some months earlier on a trip to the MF European offices, he had noticed the seg fund investments being managed by the Treasury Department team in London. They were buying short-term securities, including Italian and Portuguese bonds and bills with fabulous yields. Fully expecting the same answer from London, he braced for the worst. As fortune would have it, London said they might just have a solution; it was risky, but still a possibility. They had wanted to increase the size of their RTM trades for a long time, but had been unable to do so. The credit limits imposed by the risk department in New York were too restrictive. If they could increase the size limits and put up some really big numbers, the returns could cover the $20 million per quarter. This was his eureka moment when it dawned on Corzine: they should be doing RTM trades in European sovereign debt.

He further developed his idea for the trade to involve more of the distressed countries in Europe. His idea was to purchase the debt of Italy, Spain, Portugal, and Ireland, then book repo-to-maturity trades with the bonds. Just like the "basis" trades early in his career, these trades were virtually risk free. Sheer volume, together with generous interest-rate spreads, would combine to generate enough revenues to put MF Global back on firm financial footing. And just as importantly, it would stave off the credit-rating downgrades.

This was the answer for buying time with the ratings agencies and building the investment bank to rival Goldman that he so desperately wanted. There was, however, one catch: Mike Roseman, the head of risk at MF Global. There were very small risk limits for the repo-to-maturity trades already in place, and Corzine needed to increase the size limits for these trades. Since it was already part of Corzine's plan to increase risk at MF Global, this was exactly what he was looking to do. What's more, it was his company. He could change Roseman's limits if he wanted to. He was Jon Corzine, the firm's CEO for God's sake. Corzine had brought out his hammer.

Unfortunately, the problem turned out to be a screw.

CHAPTER EIGHT

The European Debt Crisis

In the earliest days of colonial America there were many forms of money circulating. If a colonist wanted to buy a bale of tobacco, for example, there were different ways to pay for it. He could trade another commodity, such as some beaver pelts, or use the wide variety of coin and paper money that freely circulated.

Coins were the Spanish Peso or the Portuguese "eight-real pieces" and were typically made of silver. Paper money came in a variety of Spanish origin, some nicknamed "dog dollars," some called "lion dollars," but the best known throughout the New World was the "Spanish dollar." Collectively, the currency was often referred to as "pieces of eight," because it was worth eight Portuguese reals, and made famous by pirate films and books. The problem with having all the available coins and paper money was that there was no standard single currency, and, not only did their values differ, but they were worth more or less depending on the location.

In 1690, the individual colonies began to print their own money, with Massachusetts leading the charge. The creation of colonial currencies still had an equal number of problems. There was no central bank to back the currency, so the exchange of money between two individuals was as much an act of faith as anything else. Additionally, the weight and size of the coins varied from state to state and overproduction and debasement by some colonies led to inflation across the region.

Following the American Revolution, the nascent Continental Congress first issued a single currency, called the "continental."

Individual states continued to produce their own money, which further confused the purchase of goods, adding another layer of exchange to the existing array of choices. A person trading across state lines found that money from his home state wasn't worth as much in another state; a dollar issued in South Carolina was less likely to be accepted in Connecticut than a dollar from Massachusetts, and the federal "continentals" still weren't universally accepted by many merchants.

By the time the Constitution was signed, it was clear that the United States needed a single currency that was recognized as legal currency throughout the states. This led to the chartering of the First Bank of the United States in 1791, which was the first federally chartered bank in the new country. The new currency was officially defined by a weight of silver, which helped to stabilize its value and helped unify the mediums of exchange in the newly united states.

There was a time when a casual traveler spending time in Europe was required to carry a wide array of currencies, much like the early American colonists. Nowhere was the vast disparity in currency values more visible and many countries were geographically so close to one another but still using different currencies, all with different values and denominations. France used the franc, whereas Germany was using the deutsche mark. The Greek currency was the drachma, Italy used the lira, and purchases in Spain required shoppers to carry pesetas. Not only did someone need a large folder that doubled as a wallet to visit all of these countries, tourists needed to know the exchange rates for each currency and the value of their home currency. Businesses had many of the same issues. In order to arrange purchases and sales across Europe, companies had to transact in many different currencies in order to settle accounts across the continent, not knowing the exact value of their goods until the money was actually exchanged.

A solution to this world of multiple currencies seemed like an easy way to stabilize money exchange and the one that made the most sense was to create a single currency to be used throughout Europe. The hope was that a single currency would simplify cross-border transactions and help facilitate trade and unity that had eluded the continent for so long.

It wasn't a new idea, to be sure. The concept of a single European currency was first floated in 1929 during the League of Nations following World War I. From those early beginnings, it would still take

70 years for the governments to finally agree to a single currency, the euro, which officially came into existence on January 1, 1999.

The beginning of the European Union can be traced back to the European Coal and Steel Community, which had been around since 1951. Originally designed to bring the economies and trade between West Germany and France closer together after World War II, the association would later expand to become the European Economic Community. It continued to evolve into a free-trade zone, creating a closer political union and the federalization of Europe. Ultimately, it fostered the desire for a common currency across the region.

When East and West Germany were reunified in 1990 after the fall of the Berlin Wall, the rest of Europe, with France in particular, began to worry about German economic domination of Europe. In order to address the perceived threat of a unified Germany and maintain its central role in Europe, France pushed hard for monetary union.

But in order to get the pillar of the European economy – Germany – to participate, a grand compromise needed to be reached. Germany had always run a strict monetary policy, a legacy of memories of the rampant inflation they suffered in the 1920s. In order to convince Germany to participate in the Euro zone and relinquish control of its own monetary policy decisions, joining the Euro zone would require strict responsibilities for the new individual member countries. Interest rates and money-growth decision-making was taken away from the individual central banks. A member country could no longer lower interest rates or depreciate their currency to stimulate their economy; that ability was given to the central monetary authority, the European Central Bank, or ECB. When interest-rate policy is set, the ECB looks at overall Euro-zone averages, where Germany and France make up the largest part, giving overall European monetary policy a bias that skews towards the larger countries. On the fiscal end, Euro-zone countries were forced to limit their budget deficits and debt, which was supposed to limit the amount of money their governments could borrow and spend.

Initially, enthusiasm about the creation of the euro created expectations of a financial utopia. For most of the decade, the euro currency system worked well; the first nine years resulted in economic prosperity. In addition, during the early part of the decade, the ECB kept rates relatively low as Germany continued to absorb the former East German economy. The initial success of the euro was naively thought by many to be permanent.

Economic times were good, economies were growing, tax revenues was flowing in, so it was easy for many governments to increase domestic spending programs. The high credit ratings and stability of the currency across Europe allowed countries to easily access debt markets, thus pushing up their debt past the limits allowed under the European Union regulations. Relatively low rates led to a consumption binge and a massive housing construction boom in southern Europe and Ireland, but as long as investors assumed European sovereign bonds were unlikely to default, no one foresaw a financial cliff on the horizon.

When economies slowed down and the markets turned, the euro currency system was not as rosy as everyone was led to believe. If a country's economy weakened, those who had already hit their deficit limit found that their metaphorical hands were tied. The limitations imposed by the new system meant that, in times of economic trouble, countries were unable to stimulate their own economies. Interest rate decisions were relegated to the European Central Bank, which instituted a one-size-fits-all monetary policy. Countries' individual central banks could not cut interest rates or print money. They had no other options except to keep spending and borrowing money. After they were tethered to the euro, the government only had one way to spur the economy, which was to break the euro currency membership rules.

* * *

In engineering circles, the term "linchpin" describes a very specific component of a wheel. It is the pin that keeps a wheel from coming off an axle around which it turns. It is a vital piece to the operation of a wheel, because without it, the wheel and the axle separate. For that reason, the word linchpin has come to refer to something that holds a collection of interrelated components together.

As the old cliché tells us, a chain is only as strong as its weakest link, but a linchpin itself can be the weakest component in the construction. That said, Greece was effectively the linchpin in the European financial crisis. It didn't have the strongest economy in the

European Union – it ranked 15th out of the 27 member countries – and it didn't have a thriving export business. Tourism is its number-one industry, with millions flocking there every year to absorb the history, sun and culture of the cradle of modern civilization.

Much like the deteriorating Parthenon that suffers the ravages wrought by the elements to which it is exposed, the Greek economy was subjected to forces beyond its own control. And just like the Parthenon, the Greek economy didn't fare well when exposed to those forces. The Greeks had done away with the ever-fickle drachma, a currency that was forever declining in value for many years. Now they had the *uber*-stable euro, which meant that buyers of Greek bonds didn't have the specter of drachma depreciation hanging over their investments. It eased a lot of fears and encouraged a lot of buying of Greek debt.

Things began to go badly for the Greek economy after the financial crisis in 2008. By the time the world teetered on the brink of financial Armageddon, Greece was already spending money far more freely than their financial wherewithal could handle. The drop-off in tourism and rising unemployment meant that people and businesses began to struggle. The government fell into much of the same situation, as they borrowed more money to meet their domestic obligations. By 2009, the budget deficit was a whopping 15.4% of the country's GDP, and Greek debt that same year exceeded 127% of the country's GDP. The interest payments alone on that amount of debt were enough to cripple the already weak economy, still paying the massive amounts of interest on the debt accrued years earlier.

Everything came to a head in 2009, when in October the new Socialist government announced that the Greek budget deficits were actually double the size of their earlier estimates. Whether they wanted to finally come clean or just to stick it to the outgoing conservative government, the announcement ignited what has come to be known as the European Debt Crisis. The new Ministry of Finance cited five factors adding to the deficits: low growth; the budget deficit; government debts; the failure to comply with the established Euro-zone budget; and, quite surprising to some, unreliable data. Yes, someone finally volunteered to announce what many already knew, that Greece had been hiding their true economic condition for years.

In fact, it would later come to light that Greece had fudged their numbers in order to join the Euro-zone. Anyone paying attention knew they were overspending, and surprisingly, everyone simply turned a blind eye to them issuing more debt than allowed under Euro-zone membership. But none of that seemed to matter in 1999.

The Greek government's budget deficit was highlighted by a profit-expense report for the years 2005 to 2009. In the space of those five years, the country's output increased 40%, certainly a growth rate to be proud of, however, that increase was offset by government spending that went up by 87%. Throughout those years, the Greek government spent heavily on its professional sectors. The problem was, however, that they were mostly non-productive. A great deal of government money flowed to all areas of the country's government bureaucracy. No matter what kind of math you use, there's no way to make those numbers look good to an accountant. Once the economy slowed down and tax revenues declined, it was evident the growth of Greek spending had far exceeded Greece's ability to support it. And that was a problem.

After the government's announcement about the staggering deficit numbers, Greek debt was immediately downgraded by all the ratings agencies. In February 2010, financial markets saw a tremendous sell-off of Greek debt, which was followed by the announcement by the Greek government that they intended to implement the first round of what were called "austerity measures," which were required to qualify for a bailout from the EU. In a country whose populace had grown accustomed to reaping the benefits of their government's overspending, the idea of austerity was not welcome.

The International Monetary Fund and the European Union participated in an audit of Greece's finances, which resulted in those two institutions calling for a second round of austerity measures. That announcement led to Standard and Poor's downgrading Greece's sovereign-debt rating again, this time to junk, and the other ratings agencies soon did the same. Adding to the growing financial nightmare, tax revenues were still lower than expected, as unemployment rate increased past 12%, and, reportedly, corruption that fostered income tax evasion.

The Greek government had no other options available to it, so they again went begging, this time to the IMF and the EU, the same pair that had forced them into two rounds of austerity measures. The IMF, together with the EU, worked with officials from both France and Germany, and the collective finally agreed to the first Greek bailout in May 2010 worth €110 billion. The second bailout would eventually come almost two years later in February 2012 to the tune of another €130 billion.

* * *

As the market lost trust in Greece's ability to pay off their debts, investors became more and more worried about other countries in similar economic and political situations. Greece was definitely the hardest-hit European Union country, but there were other countries out there also hit hard by over-borrowing and the weak business environment following the crisis. Investors began to lose confidence in those economies and grew increasingly wary of holding their debts, which forced their interest rates higher and made it harder for them to issue new debt.

An acronym came to be used to collectively refer to that collection of faltering economies - PIIGS. In addition to Greece, the PIIGS included the other mostly southern European countries of Spain, Ireland, Italy, and Portugal. Many felt that Greece was a true house of straw within the European Union, and that once Greece fell, panic would spread to the rest of the countries, triggering an economic landslide. As the Greek situation deteriorated, fear of contagion would spill over to each of these countries and they would suffer a similar fate – ratings downgrades, higher yields on their debt and possibly default. If the situation spread, it would create a financial nightmare for the entire region.

It spread.

Ireland was a country with a very strong economy for many years, earning the nickname "Celtic Tiger" during the period from 1995 to 2007. When someone thinks of Ireland, many times they imagine green fields and pastures. The truth is somewhat different, however. These days, Ireland has a very limited agrarian economy, with agriculture and livestock accounting for only 5% of their Gross

Domestic Product and approximately 8% of the country's overall employment. They not only have a lucrative tourist trade, but the country heavily exports pharmaceuticals, software, and is the largest exporter of zinc in Europe.

But what propelled the Irish economy for 12 years was housing construction. As the overall economy boomed, both residential and commercial construction became a major component of Ireland's economy, and workers flocked in from all over Europe to fill construction jobs. It was, in a sense, too good to last. And it didn't.

When the housing bubble burst – set off by the financial crisis – Ireland was hit harder than most countries on the way down. It is a story that could have easily been written about the housing market crash in the United States. After the bubble burst and housing prices fell, Irish banks began finding their mortgage loans going unpaid. Missed payments led to defaults, which led to banks foreclosing on homes, homes that these banks had no way of selling in order to recoup their financial losses. As a result, Irish banks came under stress and were poised to fail. In the hopes of averting a national economic collapse, the Irish government stepped in and announced they would guarantee bank debts, later nationalizing many of the banks.

Despite the best efforts of the Irish government to stabilize its financial system, the financial crisis in Ireland deepened. On August 24, 2010 Standard and Poor's cut the country's credit rating to AA-, and when the financial situation grew even more dire, Allied Irish Bank was nationalized in September with the government injecting €3.7 billion to become the majority shareholder. By October, the government had been forced into the position of bailing out more banks and borrowing in the bond markets to finance the purchases. The government's budget deficit continued to grow, reaching the point where the deficit itself equaled 32% of the Irish gross domestic product, the largest ever government budget deficit on record.

By November, it was clear that the Irish government itself was strained and needed outside aid if a countrywide depression was going to be avoided. The European Union and the International Monetary Fund began working together on a financial bailout of the country. On November 28, 2010 Ireland needed to act fast. The country asked for and received a bailout of €85 billion from the European Financial

Stability Facility (EFSF). Ireland became the first Euro-zone country to recapitalize its banks and receive a bailout from the European Union. It was soon after that Standard and Poor's again cut Ireland's credit rating, this time lowering it to single A.

A gauge of a country's distress is shown in the interest rates they charge when they issue debt. When the rates are relatively low, it means that there is a lot of confidence in their ability to repay their debt. When the rates are high, it is a sign investors are worried the country is more likely to default. At the time of the bailout, the yield on Irish 10-year bonds shot up and was trading in the bond market at 670 basis points above German government bonds known as bunds. In other words, the interest rate on Irish bonds was 6.97% above that of German bunds. To put that in perspective, if German bunds were at 2.00%, Irish bonds would be at 8.97%.

Bonds trade at a spread above a reference country or type of security that is deemed to be risk free in that marketplace. The riskiness of bonds from smaller countries – like Ireland – are quoted at a spread above what's considered the risk-free bonds in Europe. In the United States, it's not uncommon to find corporate bonds quoted as a spread above U.S. Treasuries; in the case of European bonds, they're typically quoted as a spread above the German bunds.

Consequently, short-term Irish bonds were trading at much higher interest rates than German bunds. Irish bonds with maturities between 12 and 18 months were yielding 6.00% in December 2010, compared with 0.65% for German bunds. For an investor willing to take the risk that Ireland would not default within a year, there was 5.35% in added yield. It was a great return, to be sure. But with great reward comes great risk. And Irish bonds were the perfect example of that wisdom.

The last-ditch effort by the Irish government didn't work quite as well as they hoped. Housing prices continued to fall, banks continued to take losses, and the government's budget deficit continued to grow. Finally, on July 12, 2011 Moody's took the step of cutting Ireland's bond rating to junk, the lowest and least-creditworthy rating they bestow.

Before joining the Euro zone, Spain was surprisingly a source of cheap manufacturing products within Europe. Sometimes called a "manufacturing miracle" in the 1990s, Spain became competitive, not through innovation or invention, but from a cheap currency, the peseta. Upon joining the Euro zone, they lost all the competitive advantages of the cheap peseta, and their manufacturing base slowly disappeared as German imports took over. Luckily, Spain was blessed, in some ways, with tourism. Early in the decade, Spain became a hot spot for northern European tourists, weekenders, party-goers, and eventually vacation homeowners. That brought in tourism revenues valued at approximately €40 billion annually, and made Spanish tourism the second most lucrative tourism market in the world, accounting for 11% of the country's GDP and employing over two million Spaniards. But just like Ireland, Spain also suffered from a boom and bust in the construction and housing industries.

The Spanish economy has many weaknesses that make it less stable than other European nations. For starters, the country has few natural resources – including no energy resources – which means that all its fossil fuels must be imported. In the event of higher oil prices, the nation pays that much more for imports, directly affecting people's wallets. Outside of tourism and construction, the job market is oftentimes non-existent for those seeking work, because the entire modern Spanish economy was built on those two key industries.

Initially, the Spanish economy was stable following the onset of the financial crisis. In fact, Spanish banks were considered strong in terms of their creditworthiness for three years, and they weathered the financial storm much better than their counterparts in Ireland. However, that same widening crisis meant that fewer tourists from elsewhere in Europe had the money to spend on a vacation in Spain, or to pay for their vacation home mortgage loans, which further stagnated the country's economy. Eventually bad real-estate loans started to catch up with Spanish banks, and loans started to go sour.

When the housing bubble popped in Spain, the Spanish economy took a major hit. They ended up with vacant vacation homes and empty regional airports. The drop-off in housing demand, tourism, and then bank profits decreased tax revenues for the Spanish government, even though spending grew. As a result, Spain's government was forced to tap in to debt markets just to plug the hole. The dyke was leaking, and all the government officials could do was keep plugging the holes while they crossed their fingers that somehow the waters would recede.

The first cracks began to appear when Spain's credit rating was downgraded from AAA by Fitch Ratings in May 2010, and then again by Moody's in September of that year. It was the first time in Spain's history that they had been rated anything other than AAA. Spanish short-term debt moved to a 1.00% spread above Germany's, which was wider than before the downgrade, but not a significant setback. Fitch then further downgraded Spain again in October 2010 to AA-, at which time the country began having problems accessing the debt markets. At this point, Spanish short-term debt was quoted around 1.50% above German debt, and the funding situation continued to get worse. Then, on June 25, 2011 Spanish access to the debt markets all but collapsed and their short-term bonds were trading around 12%, which was about 11.50% more than German bunds.

For much of the twentieth century, Italy's economy, in stark contrast to many of its neighbors, was marked by economic stagnation and recession. Though Italy's economy was Europe's third largest, it was always caught in the same economic maladies as the other southern Europeans. Italy's lira constantly lost value from inflation, government overspending, an inflexible labor market, and a generally difficult business climate. But in the late 1990s, belts were tightened, services were reduced, taxes were raised, and spending was cut. The result was economic growth that put Italy well on the road to economic prosperity and allowed it to join the Euro zone.

After the financial crisis struck, Italy experienced seven consecutive quarters of economic retraction – also known as recession – as the country's economy shrank by 6.7%. By 2010, government debt was climbing again and was at 116% of the country's GDP, though Italy was still able to borrow in the debt markets at a relatively tight 40 basis-point spread above Germany. The following year it all caught up to them, though.

Citing both "Italy's weakening economic growth prospects" and the lack of the government's "ability to respond decisively to events," Standard and Poor's downgraded Italy's credit rating to single A, with the other rating agencies following close behind. Italian bond prices were sent plummeting, which caused yields to rise. Italy did not need a bailout, but investors became cautious and the interest rate on their debt remained high.

Portugal has never been thought of as a world economic power, at least not in the past 400 years. With a history of nationalized industries beginning in the 1970s that hindered the country's economic growth, they have a relatively outdated educational system, below-average productivity, an inflexible labor force, and a complicated legal system. The country has some strong primary exports, including things like wood, cork, fish, and wine – as well as a scattering of minerals, agricultural items, and other smaller industries – but more than other European Union countries, Portugal's government sector remained the largest part of their economy.

By 2005, civil service – or government employment – accounted for approximately 56% of the country's GDP, employing over 747,000 citizens of a country with a working-age population of 5.57 million. That means that one of every seven workers in the country is employed by the government, whose salaries weigh heavily on the country's budget woes.

The Portuguese economy remained relatively strong throughout the financial crisis, with less exposure to banking and housing construction than its peers. But beginning in November 2010, Portugal began feeling the effects from the debt crisis that had been wracking the rest of Europe for two years. The Portuguese unemployment rate began creeping up into the teens, and the federal budget deficit continued to climb. They began losing tax revenues as expenditures increased, further weakening the government's ability to climb out of its debt hole. The inevitable slowdown of tax revenues was increasingly not enough to support the large government sector, and they were forced to fund themselves through borrowed debt.

In December 2010, Fitch cut Portugal's debt rating to A+. Long-term Portuguese bonds began trading at 465 basis points above German 10-year bonds. The situation continued to deteriorate, and the following April the government applied to the European Union for a financial bailout. The next month, the EU gave Portugal a €78 billion bailout package, but that financial life ring didn't change the minds of the bond market or the ratings agencies. Short-term Portuguese bond yields shot up to 9.50%, trading 9.00% above Germany's equivalent bond. On July 5, 2011 Moody's further cut the rating on Portugal's bonds to junk status just when their bond yields were trading above 15%.

* * *

Meanwhile, back in the offices of MF Global, CEO Jon Corzine was on the phone with the London office. He wanted to know why the brokers were not involved with Greek sovereign debt. They were trading other European countries' sovereign bonds, and Corzine saw Greece as an exceptional opportunity that would perfectly supplement their existing business.

The answer he got was well thought out and intelligent, and one that sought to preserve the firm's financial wellbeing first and foremost. Brokers in the London office said the Greek market was too volatile, and prices were far too linked to politics. Getting involved in Greece while it was a political hot potato was potentially financial suicide. As far as that market was concerned, the London brokers felt the bid/offer spreads were far too wide and too volatile. It was a no-brainer for them. Stay away and let someone else buy and sell that market. It was financial Darwinism at work.

And while the collective wisdom of MF Global was to stay away from Greek debt, they still saw plenty of opportunity in the high yields of other European periphery debt. And Greece was the linchpin. Even though it didn't wield as big a sword in terms of the European financial markets, Greece was the epicenter of one of the greatest sovereign-debt meltdowns the region has ever seen. The country that spawned Aristotle and Homer, western-style democracy and the Olympic Games, the birthplace of modern history, was also the country that could trigger a domino effect that threaten to topple all of southern Europe.

As an investor, the yield that could be earned through buying the short-term debt of Ireland, Spain, Italy, and Portugal was very attractive. Here were single-A and double-A-rated sovereign bonds trading with abnormally high interest rates. By comparison, in December 2010, the short-term debt of Ireland was at 6.00%, Spain was paying 3.32%, Italian debt was trading at 2.25 %, and Portugal at 4.50%. These rates all compared to similar maturities in German risk-free yields of 0.70%.

For such short holding periods – assuming you didn't mind taking the default risk – they were very attractive yields. What's more, suppose you could borrow money close to the risk-free rate such as German-issued bonds for the same period of time in order to finance your purchases. Say you bought $100 million of Spanish bonds for a year with a yield of 3.32% and borrowed money at 1.00% to pay for the purchase. That's a profit of 2.32% or $2,320,000. Now let's say you could increase the size tenfold to $1 billion in bond holdings. Then there was a profit of $23,200,000. Not a bad trade, assuming you could borrow funds at such a low rate. Jon Corzine saw an opportunity. MF Global desperately needed to find a way to take advantage of these yields.

CHAPTER NINE

Repo-To-Maturity

There are few experiences in life that can compare to the feeling of driving off the lot in a brand-new car. The ride is smooth, the interior is spotless, the color is perfect. And that's all in addition to that new-car smell. You did the research and haggled with the dealer to get the best price and now you find yourself behind the wheel of your brand-new car. The whole experience is a feast for the senses, as you smile at your good fortune. The only problem, at least from a financial perspective, is that as soon as you make that first right-hand turn out of the dealership's lot, your brand-new car just depreciated by about 50%. And when you consider that you just dropped a year's worth of high-end college tuition to buy it, that hit to your wallet will echo for years to come.

In today's world, it's a necessity for most people to have a car, so there's little someone can do to avoid that depreciation. People need to have a car to go work, visit friends, go grocery shopping; so most car owners look at it as just the cost of doing business. However, there is a segment of the driving population that gets around the issue of depreciation and still enjoys the benefits of having a new car. These people choose to lease.

When someone leases a car, they are basically borrowing the automobile for a set period of time, say five years. In exchange, they pay the dealer monthly payments and a down-payment up front that serves as a margin buffer against damage or loss. The good thing is that the person leasing the car doesn't lose any money due to depreciation because at the end of the lease, the car is simply returned to the dealer.

In that regard, a lease is much the same thing as a long-term rental, albeit one that is kept for five years.

Here's where the lease catch kicks in. Assuming there are no problems with payments or damage, when the term of the lease expires and the leasee returns the car to the dealer, there's not going to get any kind of trade-in value. The car remained the property of the car dealer the whole five years. Naturally, the car dealer prefers the leasee to renew the lease or even buy it; however, if the leasee decides to return it, the dealer can lease it to someone else or sell it. In the end, the whole transaction was the lending of an "asset," the car, from the dealer to the leasee for a set period of time.

The process of car leasing is much like a financial transaction called a repurchase agreement, or "repo" for short. Today, when people hear the word repo, they typically think of some burly guy with a bunch of tattoos driving a tow truck on behalf of a finance company whose client stopped making payments on a car he bought. But in the financial world, the word has a slightly different meaning.

In the world of Wall Street wheeling and dealing, a repo is an agreement between two financial companies – usually banks – where one party sells a security (like a stock or bond) to another party, with an agreement to buy it back at a later date. That's the "repurchase" part: selling a security and agreeing to buy it back – repurchase it – in the future. The other side of a repo transaction is referred to as a "reverse-repo," or just a "reverse" for short. That's when the bank takes possession of the securities, effectively serving as the "leasee" in the car-lease transaction. Basically what you call it depends on which side of the equation you find yourself. If you're borrowing securities, you're executing a reverse-repo; if you're lending securities, you're doing a repo.

When looking at repo agreements, it's important to view them as collateralized lending. It's like a cash loan in which the borrower puts up a security as collateral to ensure that he will pay back the loan. When two entities enter into a repo transaction, the borrower receives an amount of cash and the lender receives a piece of collateral, which is valued at market prices. For that reason, a repo is also a form of secured financing. It's "secure"" because the cash being loaned is secured by the value of the securities. In other words, at its core, a repo is a cash loan that is collateralized with securities.

The financial markets have been called the oil that greases the economy and if that's the case, the repo market is the oil that greases the financial markets. The repo market enables banks and brokerage firms to borrow cash very easily on a short-term basis. If a bank buys a security and needs quick cash to hold it for a few days, they borrow the cash by loaning the securities in the repo market. Alternatively, if another bank has cash and wants to invest it with safe securities as collateral, they borrow securities and it's the reverse-repo transaction that makes it possible. Whether a bank or broker needs to borrow or lend cash or securities, the easiest and most cost-effective way is through the repo market.

Despite the fact that many people who are not familiar with the financial markets have never heard of repo, it is the largest financial market in the world. That said, it's difficult to determine its actual size, due to the fact that there is no exchange where the market trades. Whereas the stock market has the New York Stock Exchange and the futures market has the Chicago Mercantile Exchange, there is no such central exchange that governs trading in the repo market. Rather, repo trades in what is termed "over the counter" (OTC), which means trades are conducted directly between individual banks or brokerage firms. Since there is no exchange to calculate the daily volumes and trading, it is very difficult to put an exact number on the size of the market. Economists tried in 2007 to estimate the overall size and came up with numbers between $10 trillion and $12 trillion in the U.S. alone, but that was before the financial crisis. Recently, Federal Reserve economists estimated there to be at least $5 trillion in repo transactions outstanding.

Investing is, by its very nature, a sort of gamble. You're putting money down and betting that you're going to make money off that initial outlay. The market could go up, but it also could go down. That's not to suggest every investment is a long-shot gamble, since some securities are more speculative and risky than others and some investments are considered virtually risk free. The closer to no risk you can come, the less of a gamble investing becomes.

There is a specific kind of repo transaction that is as close to risk free as you're ever going to find, and that's buying a short-term bond and combining it with what's called a repo-to-maturity (RTM). Essentially, the transaction allows traders to take advantage of interest rates in two different markets: one market – the bond market – where they buy bonds with a relatively high interest rate, and the other market – the repo market – where they borrow money using the bonds as collateral.

Under a typical repo trade, the loan period is very short, usually just overnight. Party A borrows money overnight, then buys the security they put up as collateral back from Party B the next day. But with RTM, the loan lasts until the bond matures. That could be weeks, months, or even years. So whereas the normal repo loan usually gets paid back within 24 hours, a repo-to-maturity loan can take months or years to pay back.

Traditionally, RTM deals were only done with U.S. Treasury or federal agency bonds, such as those issued by Freddie Mac and Fannie Mae. These bonds are essentially backed by the U.S. government, so any transaction involving them was always considered about as close to risk free as it was possible to get.

Once bonds are purchased and they are loaned out in a repo-to-maturity transaction, the interest rates are locked in; the bond is purchased and the cash is borrowed until the bond matures, and there's no chance that the interest rate for either security can fluctuate. From an investor's perspective, it's a relatively stress-free transaction, because he knows exactly how much he's going to make, and he knows when he's going to get paid.

Returning to the car-lease analogy, an RTM is like buying a car and then leasing it to someone else for as long as it's usable. In other words, it's like sub-letting the car until that point in time just before it goes to the junkyard. For simplicity's sake, we'll call this example a lease-to-maturity. Imagine buying a car for $50,000, then leasing it to someone else who will pay you $10,000 a year for a minimum of 10 years. You're guaranteed to make $50,000 – double your initial investment – over the life of the loan. Sounds like a pretty good business, right? It's easy to understand, it's a guaranteed money-maker, it's the perfect investment. Unfortunately, it's also a next-to-impossible investment opportunity to find. But that lease-to-maturity example is the same thing as a repo-to-maturity. It's as close as possible to a completely risk-free investment product.

But people in the financial markets understand that there's truly no such thing as a completely risk-free trade. Even in the oh-so-close to risk-free world of RTM, there's always the issue of bonds losing their value. So the counterparties in a repo transaction generally require some sort of extra financial cushion before they're willing to float a large repo loan. In other words, there are margin requirements for even the largest banks that want to buy $100 million dollars worth of bonds, just like the requirements for the average investor who wants to buy 500 shares of a $3 stock.

There's another margin-related quirk that is particular to repo trades. With a repo loan, either party has the right to call for more collateral during the term of the loan if the price of the bond moves against them. In other words, if the security loses value, the lender can require more collateral to offset the added risk he's just taken on. Alternatively, if the price of the bond appreciates such that the original loan is significantly less than the new value of the collateral, the borrower can ask for additional funds to reflect that change in value. It's what is called a daily margin call. The cash lender or borrower can require that other side give additional collateral – be it cash or securities – to offset changes in the bond's value.

If the repo involves a bunch of German bonds, for example, the prices of those bonds are changing every day, and that means that additional margin could be required as a result of those price fluctuations. With short-term, highly rated debt, the price changes are usually small and the resulting margin calls insignificant, so the trader who is buying and selling AAA-rated bonds can expect some margin calls here and there, but it's nothing to be overly concerned with. So long as there are no massive changes in the bond issuer's situation, there is no reason to anticipate massive margin calls.

The thing about bonds, though, is that they are debt, which means that there's an inherent trust on the part of the bond owner that the issuer is going to make the interest payments and pay back the bond at maturity. And the lower the credit rating of the bond issuer, the higher the risk of default and, by association, the higher the level of trust involved in the transaction.

For most investors, hearing that a bond is backed by the full faith and credit of the United States is enough to instill confidence that the bond will get paid. Alternatively, just knowing that a bond is AAA-rated is yet another way to instill a similar confidence. However, a government's ability to pay back a debt can change and a rating agency can change its opinion of a bond or of an entire country. Those changes in ratings can result in a loss of confidence in a country and create dramatic declines in their bonds' prices.

And with that sudden change in opinion, a heretofore risk-free investment opportunity suddenly has the stink of potential risk arising from large price changes or ratings changes. As the potential for default changes the values of bonds, there is an increase in margin requirements. And that pairing – higher risk of default plus a higher outlay of cash in the form of margin requirements – can result in an investor losing his metaphorical shirt, if the worst-case scenario becomes reality. If the bondholder – in this case, a sovereign nation – defaults on the payment, the bond's value goes to zero. The investor loses his investment in the bonds, as well as the margin deposit. To fully understand the idea of a country's credit worthiness, it's imperative to think of the country as a consumer, just like any other consumer out there who has credit-card loans and a mortgage loan.

Just like in the case of an average person on the street, a sovereign nation like Ireland, Spain, Italy, or Portugal can face financial difficulties. Bills for goods and services have to be paid, and there's a fine line between making ends meet and spending more than is coming in. In the case of repaying debts, which is what bonds are, that fine line can mean the difference between paying debts on time or defaulting.

So while one day everything seems to be fine and the debt is getting paid on schedule, suddenly one day a country announces that they're having financial troubles. A financial crisis hit and their economy contracts, their spending becomes higher than their tax revenues, which leads to a perpetual budget deficit. As the deficit grows, their ability to repay their bonds slowly decreases, and that means the bondholders have a diminishing chance of getting paid back. Diminishing is never a good word in the financial world, unless it's being used in relation to risk. When it's referring to the chances of getting paid back the money that's invested, it's an especially bad word.

Beginning in the middle of 2010, the periphery European countries of Ireland, Spain, Italy, and Portugal were paying phenomenally high yields on their sovereign bonds. Anyone buying those bonds could invest cash at high rates and make a lot of money and, on top of it all, the repo market provided a mechanism to borrow cash to finance those purchases. Access to the largest financial market in the world, the repo market, allowed the buying of bonds of the European periphery countries and simultaneously borrowing funds at a lower interest rate to pay for it. There was a fantastic window of opportunity to do RTM trades in European sovereign debt at that particular moment in time. But no one particular bank would allow MF Global to be their repo counterparty for as long as a year with such large trade sizes, specifically trades worth billions of dollars. In order for MF Global to run up that kind of size, they needed to book the repo trades through a "central counterparty." By putting up a little margin at the main central counterparty in Europe, LCH.Clearnet, and booking their repo trades there, a firm could run up their leverage in a portfolio of European sovereign debt.

In financial markets like repo that trade OTC and have no exchanges to house and clear trades, Central Counter Parties (CCP) began to emerge about 15 years ago. Sometimes called "clearinghouses," they fulfill an important need in the marketplace to address the growing volume of trading and settlement transactions between financial institutions. Before the CCPs came into existence, purchases and sales of securities had to be cleared and settled directly between the two counterparties. The result was hundreds of financial institutions executing thousands of trades a day, generating millions of securities trades in the entire marketplace to clear each day. It was a monumental amount of work.

But with the growth of CCPs, much of that work was streamlined and simplified. For example, many of the trades involve the simple act of moving the securities from one institution to another and then to yet another all day long, so instead of one security being moved around to a hundred different institutions, the trades can be collectively settled, cleared, and netted via one central counterparty. If a bank bought and sold a bond several times in one day, they would only have to deliver or receive the net purchase amount or sales amount. Additionally, the CCP stands in the middle of the trade and assumes the counterparty risk in the transaction, so if one party to a trade defaults, it's the clearinghouse that guarantees payment to the other party.

If there are hundreds of institutions trading in a particular market, the existence of the CCP saves each institution from having separate credit lines and account documentation for each counterparty. The CCP serves the market further by comparing trades to make sure there are no mistakes and collecting all margin-related monies on the trades outstanding. In short, the CCP cuts down on settlements, mistakes, and makes the whole system more efficient, and with that efficiency it also allowed trading volumes and the sizes of transactions to increase. There are two preeminent CCPs for the bond market in the world: in Europe, it's LCH.Clearnet, and in the United States, it's Fixed Income Clearing Corp (FICC).

Based in London, LCH.Clearnet was created as a result of the merger of the UK-based London Clearing House (LCH) and the French company Clearnet in 2003. The London Clearing House was originally established in 1888 to clear commodities contracts in London and Clearnet was originally established in 1969 as Banque Centrale de Compensation SA to essentially perform the same function, namely to clear commodities contracts traded in Paris markets. The combined company is the leading European clearinghouse for commodities, repo, fixed income, swaps, and equities.

LCH.Clearnet, like all CCPs, charges margin for all the positions held and cleared by its members, so in that sense they operate in the same manner as a futures exchange. The clearinghouse establishes a system-wide margin rate for all securities, depending on the quality of the securities and the credit of the underlying country. Everyone pays the same margin amount for, say, Spanish bonds throughout Europe, based on the credit quality of the Spain and the liquidity and volatility in the Spanish bond market.

The margin rules set by LCH.Clearnet for holding and clearing repo loans are just like that of a mortgage broker arranging a down payment on a home loan. If you want to buy a house and you've got a six-figure income and a stock portfolio full of blue-chip securities, you have the opportunity to put down a smaller down payment simply because you're not as big of a default risk than if you had a minimum-wage-paying job and had a lot of credit-card debt. The logic is pretty straightforward; at least that's how it's supposed to work. The more valuable and financially stable you can present yourself as being, the lower the risk you present and the lower the down payment needed to cover that risk. If you don't have a history of paying your bills – or, alternatively, if you do have a history of specifically not paying your bills – you're a higher risk of default from the perspective of the mortgage broker, which is why LCH.Clearnet will charge higher margin rates on more volatile and lower-rated securities - the margin is a function of the LCH taking on the risk.

The CCP can increase the margin rates on its members, which they typically do when there are changes in the market. LCH.Clearnet delivers daily margin calls to all its members and that additional collateral is placed in what is known as the "default fund." In case a member defaults, a CCP will use money in the default fund to fulfill the failing member's obligations. So if the security in question loses value from interest-rate changes or a country's credit rating is downgraded and bond prices dip down to levels below where the CCP is comfortable, they raise the margin rate to compensate for the extra risk. Think of it as a sedative for nervous lenders. If the securities lose value, LCH wants to make sure they're going to get their money regardless, so they charge more margin to make sure. Once the market calms down and the sleepless nights aren't quite so commonplace, the CCP will bring the margin rates back to normal.

According to LCH.Clearnet, they officially consider the prevailing market conditions, liquidity, bond yields, credit default swaps, and market-implied ratings when determining margin requirements for sovereign-nation bonds. That gives LCH.Clearnet a lot of leverage in determining the margin rates for their members; however, the main determinant is what's called the "Risk-Free Basket," which is the weighted average of the yields of all of the AAA-rated countries within the Euro zone. Those countries include Germany, France, the Netherlands, and Luxembourg, with Germany and France making up most of the weighting in the basket.

As an example, suppose the bonds of Italy were trading at a yield of 2.00% and the Risk-Free-Basket of Germany, France, etc. had an average yield of 1.00%. The higher yield for Italy's bonds indicates the country's risk is more than "risk free" and therefore there should be more

margin assigned to Italy than a risk-free country. That, in a general
sense, is how the margin is set. That's the main principle – if a country
is riskier than risk free, then LCH is going to take more margin to clear
that country's bonds.

There comes a point when a country's yield is so much above the
Risk-Free-Basket that there is a significant risk of default. That's the
point when the country's bond yield spread reaches 450 basis points over
the Risk-Free Basket and LCH calls it "additional sovereign risk." In the
past, when a bond's yield reached a spread of 450 basis points above risk
free, LCH materially increased the margin requirements. So if the Risk-
Free-Basket yields were averaging at 1.00%, LCH.Clearnet would be
slightly more worried about a country's credit risk if the yield on their
bonds were 3.00% and much more worried at 4.00%.

But when that country's yield reached 5.50%, they worried that
it was close to "lights out." That was the case with Greece, and they
specifically announced it when Ireland was teetering on the edge. When
LCH.Clearnet raised the margin on Irish government bonds from 15%
to 30% on November 18, 2010 they cited the fact that "10-year Irish
government debt against an AAA benchmark has traded constantly
over 500 basis points" as their justification. In Europe, traders watch the
credit spreads, and 450 basis points has become a very important
number because that's when LCH margin requirements really start to
move higher.

* * *

There's a gambling strategy that people talk about around
casinos as a way for players to win back their money after they've lost
on a roulette bet. The betting strategy originated in France in the 1700s
and is called a "martingale," with a basic premise that knowledge of prior
events will help predict a future event. So the theory holds that if you
bet on black in roulette and lose, then you double the bet on black again
and are more prone to win. If the wheel comes up red a second time,
double again. Keep doubling your bet until you win and eventually you
will always get your money back. It's based on the assumption that if the
prior spin of the wheel was red, somehow there was an increased
probability of black coming up in future spins.

For example, you bet $100 on black and during the first spin of the wheel red comes up; you've lost your first bet and you're down $100. To follow the martingale theory, that means the second bet is $200 on black and let's assume there's a 50-50 chance of winning or losing, though we're not considering the possibilities of the two green number pockets. Now, assuming red just came up a second time, you've just lost the second bet, and you're now down $300 total. The next bet is, you guessed it, $400 and once again we'll assume the little ball rolled into another red number pocket, which means at this point you've lost a total of $700, with the red color coming up three times in a row. So what are the odds of red coming up again? Well, with each new spin the odds remain at 50-50, but you will notice your subsequent bets are chipping away your cash reserves. For the fourth spin on the roulette table, the bet is up to $800. If red comes up again, it will be four times in a row and if you lose again, you'll be in the hole $1,500. Looking at the prospect of dropping $1,600 on the next bet, do you keep going with the assumption that black must come up eventually? Or do you call it a day and take your losses and put it down as an unlikely event - that red could come up five times in a row?

Statistically, it is impossible for any single color to continue to hit forever, though there are many gambling stories of the same color coming up many times in a row, making and breaking top gamblers. We've all heard the stories about the gambler who got sucked into a game, losing everything to the point that he's willing to hand over his Rolex or his car keys or even the title to his house as collateral for a loan, just so he can get back to even. That said, the statistics are based on probability, so every spin still has a 50-50 chance of coming up red. The more times you spin the wheel, a martingale says there's a progressively lower chance of getting the same color every time; and although in all practicality it might take several spins of the wheel, eventually the black color will hit.

The catch with gambling – as with margin on RTM trades, for that matter – is that the gambler is limited by his available cash. In the case of European sovereign-debt RTM trades, by comparison, MF Global was limited as to how much capital the company had to put up as margin.

If MF Global wanted to own $1 billion of European debt, they were welcome to do so, as long as they met the margin requirements dictated by LCH.Clearnet. On a $1 billion debt portfolio, the LCH margin requirement was initially about 3%, or $30 million. When the Portuguese and Irish bond markets started to tank, a 15% margin rate came into existence rather quickly, just when the spreads on their bonds passed that magic 450-basis-point threshold. In the case of that $1 billion portfolio, that $30 million margin requirement became $150 million, without the profitability of the existing RTM increasing at all. Imagine the amount of money required if the margin eventually went up to an unprecedented 80%.

MF Global didn't have to imagine that number. It became part of their concrete reality when it actually happened.

However, as long as MF Global had enough funds to pay the margin calls from LCH.Clearnet, doubling up the bet on the roulette wheel, the trades would ultimately mature and be profitable. The bonds and repos were short term and would mature within a year, so everyone knew the firm would eventually get paid back in full, naturally assuming none of the countries defaulted. That meant that MF Global had to risk much of their own financial wherewithal to allow the repo-to-maturity trades to mature.

For any LCH.Clearnet member to stay in the trades, they had to be able to come up with a lot of margin money. A larger bank with huge financial resources certainly had the ability to stay in the game longer; MF Global's ability to stay would depend on the firm's limited financial resources. It would all become a waiting game; as long as MF Global had enough money to pay for the margin calls, they'd eventually get that money back when the bonds matured and they could keep spinning that roulette wheel.

But again, "probability" isn't called "certainty," and there's a reason for that. Despite all the laws of probability to the contrary, red kept coming up again and again, and MF Global kept having to put up more money and the margin requirements mounted to the point where they could no longer double down to recoup their losses. They would eventually run out of cash.

CHAPTER TEN

Managing Risk Management

Soldiers, for the most part, are an anonymous group. The vast majority of those who fight – and die – during even the most well-documented battles sadly remain statistics. For those who have seen the seemingly endless list of 58,195 names inscribed on the Vietnam Veterans Memorial Wall in Washington, D.C., it is easy to understand why so many soldiers go unnamed throughout history. That said, there are those soldiers who, for whatever reason, make a name for themselves in history's annals and are remembered by name for their actions years later. In World War II, one such soldier was a general named George Smith Patton.

Known for actions both heroic and dastardly, Patton was characterized by stern self-discipline and he expected those under his command to fall in line as to how a proper soldier should act. Military lore cites many instances of soldiers who said they would choose Patton as their leader over any other general, simply because they felt Patton's leadership would increase their chances of survival in battle. Though commonly portrayed as a rash and impulsive commander, in fact, Patton was adamantly risk-averse.

Perhaps it seems strange to think of a military general leading troops into battle while at the same time trying to avoid risk, but that's exactly what Patton did. Anytime someone goes to war there are risks involved, but Patton did everything in his power to minimize the risks his soldiers would face. In his mind, there were two types of risks: inherent and created. There was nothing he could do about the inherent risks of war; battles had to be fought, dodging bullets and shooting at the enemy was part of the requirements of a soldier. Choosing what battles to fight, where and when are calculated risks that can be determined after considering all the possible outcomes. Patton was very particular about not taking added risks and only risking when he felt the odds were in his favor; in other words, he managed the risks. To that end, General Patton famously quipped, "Take calculated risks. That is quite different from being rash."

In the summer of 2010, Mike Roseman would emerge in the spotlight again, two years after he was appointed the chief risk officer of MF Global, charged with much the same sort of thing that Patton had sought to do, namely minimizing the risk that MF Global was exposed to. It would become almost a redux of his risk management position at FIMAT, where he had focused his concern on CDO financing, only now he would be shifting his focus to European sovereign debt. Maybe fate had brought him into such a similar situation once again.

As a risk officer, Roseman had always preferred the word "no" to the word "yes" where investments he deemed risky were concerned, and he did not view his new position at MF Global as a time to change his strategy. Roseman had always been a staunch proponent of limiting the size of any trading book, credit line, or new business. A former colleague once said of Roseman, "He got nervous when he saw concentrated risk positions." In fact, Roseman had achieved his million-dollar signing bonus from MF Global by advertising his propensity to limit risk, and now it was his chance to start saying "no."

When Roseman arrived at MF Global, the firm already had some repo-to-maturity trades on the books, though the securities were mostly U.S. Treasuries and federal agencies and not considered excessively risky. Roseman was still not willing to expand the balance sheet with new U.S. Treasury or federal agency securities, so the last thing he wanted was to increase the firm's exposure to European sovereign debt through RTM trades – which he saw as an even more risky market. At the time, there was an existing limit of $500 million for these trades, but that would change.

The proprietary trading group called Principal Strategies Group (PSG) in MF Global's New York office had been effectively operating as a hedge fund inside the brokerage firm for a few months. They had already begun trading in a number of different asset classes and markets to supplement the firm's dwindling brokerage revenues, though they had not yet devoted much balance sheet or capital to any particular trade or strategy. During the end of the summer, Corzine and his PSG traders started buying some European sovereign bonds and financing them to maturity. They used their connections at Goldman Sachs and other large Wall Street firms as counterparties for the execution and financing. The first RTM trade Corzine was able to get done was $1 billion worth of bonds and he was able to book a $783,000 profit on it. The spreads were narrower than he hoped, but the risk of Ireland, Spain, Italy, or Portugal defaulting seemed remote, especially within a year. It was, hearkening back to General Patton, a calculated risk. At least that's how Corzine saw it.

They soon realized they had limited liquidity trading the European markets solely from the U.S. and managing the margin calls was not very efficient. Goldman's New York office was calling Goldman's London office to get the trades done, effectively using a middleman instead of going straight to a source in London. If they were to expand these trades, they needed better access to the European markets.

The PSG traders approached the MF Global London office to handle the trades. They knew MF Global UK had access to clear and settle European sovereign bonds directly through LCH.Clearnet. In that capacity, MF Global UK could be the intermediary for the New York office, executing and clearing the trades and pledging the margin on behalf of MF Global New York. But there was a problem. The London subsidiary was itself unable to hold the trades on its books, as they were already under increased regulatory scrutiny from the Financial Services Authority (FSA), the financial services regulator in the U.K., for regulatory violations in prior years. As a result, the FSA had increased supervision and restricted MF Global UK from developing new business lines or increasing any proprietary risk taking. For the RTM trades to be traded out of the London office, MF Global would need to transfer more of the firm's capital there and apply for regulatory approval of a new business, something that would take months to complete, at best.

But as the old saying goes, "Where there's a will, there's a way." Over the summer, PSG traders put together a strategy. The London office would provide Corzine and the PSG traders direct access into the opaque European sovereign-debt markets in order to enable them to go in and out of RTM trades at will. Corzine would speak with the traders in London, placing orders and executing trades, while the PSG traders would use an account at the London office to book and execute the trades. However, despite being executed in London, the trades would be housed in New York.

The trades would be transferred internally between New York and London, and margin money moved from New York through London to LCH.Clearnet. This arrangement seemed complicated, but it suited Corzine, as having the PSG managing the trades would mean keeping control of the positions in New York. With a workable internal structure, they were one step closer to expanding the trades.

However, there were two sticking points: Roseman and risk limits. Corzine and the PSG traders needed Roseman's approval to expand the trades, something Roseman was not inclined to do. At least he wasn't inclined to do it without a fight. The PSG traders pushed hard for the risk-limit increases throughout the summer; as they wanted to boost the size limits past $1 billion, a number that made Roseman uneasy. Roseman's hesitation was an indication, on some level, that the whole process was doomed from the start.

One thing the risk managers at MF Global learned early on was that Corzine was not a typical trader. They soon discovered that if they were thinking of a $10 million trade, Corzine was thinking $10 billion. He thought big, and he wasn't afraid of huge risk and large size. He was, in a nutshell, Mike Roseman's worst nightmare made manifest.

On one hand, it was clear to Corzine that Roseman was scared of large trade sizes. On the other hand, it was clear to Roseman that Corzine was not going to stop increasing the size of the trade. One side either had to give or there would be a perpetual stalemate. In other words, there was no outcome that would make everyone happy.

The PSG traders hounded Roseman, negotiating as hard as they could, and Roseman outlined a few hard rules that were not up for discussion. As far as Roseman was concerned, there would be no purchasing of Greek bonds, plain and simple. It was clear to anyone with a financial pulse that Greek debt was as bad an investment as there was in the market. Buying Greek bonds was the equivalent of literally flushing money down the toilet. So as a way of appeasing the risk-averse Roseman, the new group assured him they wouldn't touch Greek bonds in the RTM strategy. Besides Greece, other European debt seemed to be an untapped gold mine so it wasn't hard for everyone to agree on the rule. Additionally, Roseman wanted a limit on the maturity of the RTM trades, so that all bonds would be short term and mature before the end of 2012.

That terminal date was vital to the argument that European debt was a safe RTM bet, because it came with an insurance policy, namely the European Financial Stability Facility (EFSF). The ESFS was established on May 9, 2010 with a lump sum of cash that totaled €440 billion. Since the European Central Bank was not allowed to loan money directly to governments, a new institution was needed to support distressed countries. Functioning much like a bank for financially stressed countries within the Euro zone, the ESFS provided a financial safety net to preserve a country's solvency within the Union. The organization's function was to lend money to European nations that are unable to borrow money in the international debt markets. Insofar as it operates as a bank, however, the loans offered by the ESFS require repayment in full, with interest. It was not a charity organization.

The process for getting a loan from the EFSF followed much the same trajectory as an individual applying for a personal loan. The first step in applying to the EFSF, however, involved the applicant's losing funding in the marketplace. Once a country could no longer access the bond markets, the country entered into negotiations with both the European Commission (EC) and the International Monetary Fund (IMF). Those groups did their requisite due diligence, analyzing the finances of the applying country.

Following that analysis, and assuming EC and IMF agreed the country was capable of paying back the loan, a unanimous vote among the 17 Euro-zone states was required. After that hurdle was cleared, terms of the loan were drawn up and funds disbursed. That process could take over a month, at which point the EFSF issued bonds and other debt instruments to investors. Just like with any bond, if the country defaults on the loan, those investors – members of the European Union – risked losing their investment.

What made the EFSF different from other quasi-government banks, however, is that it had a specific shelf life; it was a temporary institution. According to its own charter, the EFSF would liquidate on a future date, with the earliest possible day being Sunday, June 30, 2013.

That June 30, 2013 date was important to the traders who wanted to jack up the risk positions on European sovereign debt. The existence of the ESFS, they argued, meant that nations who were covered by the quasi-European Union and had no risk of default. If the specific country found itself unable to make a bond payment, the ESFS would step in and make the payment for them. That logic hinged, of course, on the fact that come July 1, 2013 all bets were off in terms of whether a country was able to pay back its loan. So, to minimize the calculated risk, the traders assured Roseman that no bonds would have a maturity beyond 2012. That was, they figured, playing it extra safe.

With the backing of the ESFS, investing in European sovereign debt was as risk free as AAA-rated CDOs had been once upon a time. The only appreciable difference, at least insofar as the PSG traders were concerned, was the ability to predict the future. With the CDO market, you had no idea when the bubble was going to burst. There was no date on the calendar featuring a big "SELL" written in red block letters. But with the European bond market, you knew the best time to get out if you wanted to play it safe. So long as you exited the market before the clock struck midnight and the Cinderella-like ESFS turned into her old self, there was no default risk. It was pretty obvious to them, if you bought European sovereign bonds and funded them in the repo market, you could start printing money. It seemed as close to risk free as possible.

At the end of the day, when he sat across from Roseman, Jon Corzine brought confidence and charisma to the negotiating table. He was well connected in the financial and government worlds, and had more than a few well-known celebrities and world leaders on his speed-dial. That self-confidence meant that when he assured Roseman no periphery European bonds would default – at least as long as the EFSF was around – Roseman finally caved in. PSG would get their limit increases.

* * *

A truly risk-free investment, as history has shown, is as much nonexistent as it is sought-after. Every investment involves a degree of risk even when there appears to be none; the goal is to minimize the risk as much as possible, taking calculated risks while maximizing the return. But there's not an investor anywhere who doesn't hold out hope that the perfect investment, the one with no risk, is out there somewhere just waiting to be discovered. It's the Holy Grail of trading. High returns and low risk. Everyone's looking for it, but nobody is sure it exists. Jon Corzine and the PSG traders at MF Global were among the searchers for the elusive product, and they were pretty sure they'd found it when they paired European sovereign bonds with a repo-to-maturity.

And that was precisely the argument put forth by the PSG traders. No Greek debt. No maturities after December 31, 2012. Only debt from countries backed by the ESFS. And all trades booked with a repo-to-maturity. It was very profitable and utterly risk free. They'd found their Holy Grail, and Corzine wanted more of it.

Corzine loved the RTM trades; he saw a gold mine just waiting to be tapped, whereas Roseman still saw plenty of risk. In Roseman's defense, he wasn't just seeing risks where others either didn't or simply refused to. He was simply playing by the rules that had been previously established. As he would later state in his address to the U.S. House of Representatives Committee on Financial Services Oversight, MF Global's board of directors had adopted a statement of risk appetite before his appointment as chief risk officer. MF Global's management handed him the rulebook on his first day of work. It was his job to enforce the rules, the policies and the procedures.

"Mr. Corzine and I shared different views on the potential sovereign default risk," Roseman would later say. But despite his objections, the European sovereign-debt cap was raised to $1 billion in July. It was agreed that the default risk was nonexistent; the issue of liquidity risk – a margin call requiring more collateral – wasn't even mentioned. At the time, no one could conceive of margin calls being so large that they'd put the firm at risk. Insofar as it was even discussed, the issue of margin calls was quickly discounted.

By September, the cap had been raised and raised again, until it had doubled to $2 billion. It was about that time Roseman broached the issue of capital concerns. He began to worry about the potential for increased margin calls by LCH.Clearnet, which MF Global had relied on for funding the trades. The board chose to respond to his concerns, not by keeping the existing limit or even lowering it, but rather by authorizing a new higher limit. On September 22, 2010 John Corzine was authorized to buy up to $4 billion of European sovereign debt, funded to maturity. By the end of the month with the new limits, Corzine booked another $14 million in revenues on the trades.

Over the next few months, the PSG traders continued to repeatedly push for more increases in the sovereign-debt RTM trades. The scenario went like this: the sovereign-debt trades would be at their limit and the PSG traders would call a meeting between themselves, a repo trader, members of the risk-management department, and a senior manager. During the meeting, the PSG traders would ask for larger limits. The risk manager would state that the risks were too high already, and even if that weren't an issue, the firm did not have enough liquidity to cover their positions should the trades move against them.

The PSG traders would then look at the repo trader – who was in charge of funding the firm and managing the firm's liquidity – and ask if there was enough liquidity. The repo trader would assure everyone that there was enough liquidity. The risk department would echo their sentiment again about there not being enough liquidity to increase the size of the trades. The PSG traders would then look at management for approval, which would inevitably come. In the end, the senior manager would agree and tell the risk managers to prepare an increase request for the next board meeting.

* * *

As 2010 drew to an end, the board of directors continued to approve higher and higher limits. In November, Corzine asked to raise the cap to $5 billion. At that board meeting, Roseman was vocal about the potential risks of margin calls from LCH.Clearnet. Roseman presented various scenarios representing varying degrees of a liquidity crisis that would require MF Global to post capital that they didn't have.

The board consisted of a highly experienced and accomplished group of financial market professionals, but their resounding consensus was that Roseman's doomsday scenarios were "not plausible," as it was unlikely that such a wide range of scenarios could happen across different countries. In the end, the board approved a new limit of $4.75 billion, which appeared to be a compromise. Roseman's credibility had been diminishing over time as the board members increasingly saw him as being obstructive on most matters. When he tried to argue against larger RTM trades, the votes became as much a slap at him as a vote for more sovereign risk.

In truth, though, the $4.75 billion number was arrived at after pretty extensive analysis. Mike Roseman estimated that the firm had enough capital to meet margin calls as high as $800 million. Assuming there was a sell-off in European sovereign bonds, he estimated LCH.Clearnet could increase margin rates as high as 15% across the entire portfolio. Fifteen percent of $4.75 billion is $712,500,000, slightly less than MF Global's funding capacity. That was Roseman's hard limit. No increases beyond $4.75 billion would be approved. And everyone knew that.

Certain board members were, truth be told, seeing the same risk potential that Roseman was talking about, and they raised their concerns in regards to the European bonds at the December 2010 board meeting. The conversation became so intense that Corzine felt the need to defend himself. "I just think this is the right thing for this company to be doing," he said of the RTM trades. "If you all don't agree with this, maybe you need someone else to be running it." He'd called their bluff and he'd won.

It was, to be sure, a childish thing to say. It sounds like a kid on the playground announcing that he was leaving and taking his ball with him. But just as that technique can be incredibly effective, so, too, was Corzine's sortie at getting the board to do his bidding. This time he got another thing he wanted, too, a new chief risk officer.

Upon Corzine's taking over, there was a preliminary plan to replace Roseman by Bernie Dan, the former CEO. Corzine had initially put the idea on hold, but on January 31, 2011 Roseman was notified in writing that he was "being replaced." Roseman would stay on until April 1 of that year, and managed to pocket $1,855,740 in total compensation for his troubles in 2011. Included in that amount was a "leaving bonus" of $500,000 and a severance package of $1.3 million. Call it gratitude for service, call it hush money. No matter what you call it, it was a pretty hefty chunk of change to give a departing executive who'd just been replaced. Only time would tell, however, if Roseman's legacy of risk management would be all for naught. Despite the fact that Roseman had been sufficiently notified that he was being replaced, he'd been unaware that the search for his replacement had been going on since September.

Roseman's replacement was Michael Stockman, who apparently was not as worried about the potential risks of the sovereign-debt portfolio as Roseman was. That is to say, rather than expressing concerns about liquidity and margin requirements like his predecessor, Stockman acquiesced to Corzine's plan to acquire more sovereign debt. He was the perfect complement to Jon Corzine and his aggressive style. Stockman, from Corzine's point of view, understood the potential revenues for the sovereign-debt RTM trades.

Michael Stockman came to MF Global from UBS, the behemoth Swiss bank located in Stamford, Connecticut, just north of New York City. Years before, Stockman had worked at Goldman Sachs from 1989 to 1994, the same time Corzine was head of the firm's fixed income division. At UBS, Stockman had headed up the fixed-income risk for the United States, and eventually became chief risk officer for the Americas. UBS, being so large, had risk managers by product, by region, and by division. Coming from such a large institution with such a specific division of labor and moving into MF Global was a culture shock for Stockman and many at MF Global were surprised by the choice of Stockman. The question was posed regarding Stockman's involvement with risk management at UBS when that firm had taken a $10 billion hit on subprime mortgages in 2007, a $4 billion write-down for the first quarter of 2008 and ultimately took a total of $37 billion in losses globally related to fixed income and subprime mortgages.

Stockman's appointment as global head of risk at MF Global meant that he would be dealing with many products from all over the world, whereas his previous experience was with U.S.-based products only, a category that was further reduced to primarily fixed-income-related products. He had no global experience, nor did he have any experience in the futures markets, which was the core business of MF Global.

Perhaps most notably, he had "no idea about liquidity risk," according to people who worked with him. That was natural, given the size and liquidity of UBS. At UBS, they never had to worry about funding themselves and didn't need the funding facilities from a bank. They *were* a bank. Liquidity risk at MF Global, however, was very real, but not something people wanted to hear about. Regardless, though, it was a very tangible thing that the global head of risk would need to understand intimately. Stockman, at that point, didn't have that understanding.

During Stockman's first several months at MF Global, it was clear that he wanted to impress the people at his new firm, especially those in management. That made him temporarily a very unique risk manager in the sense that he was, at that time, a guy who was more likely to say yes than he was to say no. Stockman was in the habit of saying yes because he'd seen what happened to the guy who said no. He had been fired. Picture the situation: Jon Corzine, a legendary Wall Street trader and CEO, wants you to approve his trading positions, and the last guy who did not approve them was fired. You just got the job you always wanted, and you've been asked to approve the positions. What are you going to say?

Jon Corzine had found his yes man.

CHAPTER ELEVEN

Over-Leveraging

Necessity, it has been said, is the mother of invention, so it's no surprise that the man credited with "inventing" modern accounting wrote a book on the subject while tutoring children. Luca Pacioli, born in 1445 in what is today Tuscany, went to Venice sometime around 1464 seeking to further his education, a quest that at the time required more than a small sum of money. The need for money led Pacioli to become the private tutor for the three children of a wealthy Venetian merchant, and lacking any formal textbooks to use for mathematical instruction, Pacioli did what any resourceful teacher would do. He wrote a book.

Pacioli went on to teach at the University of Perugia and encountered the same problem again, so he wrote another book, *Tractatus mathematicus ad discipulos perusinos* ("A Treatise on Mathematics for Perusian Students"), which was a nearly 600-page tome that dealt with primarily business-related math pertinent to the merchants of the time. His next major book, however, was the one that attempted to codify the field of accounting into a single unified work. *Summa de arithmetica, geometria, proportioni et proportionalitià* ("The Collected Knowledge of Arithmetic, Geometry, Proportion and Proportionality"), printed on the famed Guttenberg press in 1494, was the first work to explain, in everyday language, the specifics of accounting, including the use of ledgers, inventory, liabilities, credits, debits, income, capital-on-hand, and expenses. In other words, in it Pacioli first began using the modern-day accounting terms for discussing balance sheets and income statements.

Summa made Pacioli something of a minor celebrity and garnered the attention and favor of many of the day's most notable thinkers. Three years after the book's publication, Pacioli was invited to go to Milan by Duke Ludovico Sforza, the man who, among other things, commissioned the painting by Leonardo da Vinci of The Last Supper, that today hangs in the refectory of the Convent Santa Maria della Grazie in Milan. It was in Milan – and through his connection with Duke Sforza – that Pacioli met da Vinci himself, who turned out to be an admirer of the mathematician's famed book. During the two years Pacioli spent living in Milan, he also taught mathematics to da Vinci.

Most accountants today don't aspire to the levels of celebrity achieved by Pacioli in the fifteenth century, nor do they typically entertain realistic notions of rubbing elbows with the likes of Leonardo da Vinci. Rather, they find themselves grounded in a very concrete world of facts and figures, where the answer is discoverable by crunching the numbers. The men and women who populate the various accounting offices around the country have it drilled into them that accounting is about rules; rules that must be followed. But what makes a good accountant – at least in some minds – is the ability to interpret those rules with a little finesse and a little ingenuity.

Today, the rules for accounting in the United States are governed by the Financial Accounting Standards Board or FASB. It was created in 1973 and became the organization responsible for setting accounting standards for public companies. When there are accounting rules to be determined, clarifications of existing rules, or just interpretations of rules, it's FASB that has the final say. In particular, a rule named FASB 140 is of particular interest, which happens to be the "true sale" accounting rule.

According to the rules of accounting, a "true sale" is defined as "a transfer of financial assets in which the transferor surrenders control over those assets is accounted for as a sale." The key word here is "control." If a party in a transaction gives control to someone else, the original party relinquishes ownership to it. But again, there's that word control. How do you determine if someone has "control" of a particular asset? While it might seem obvious in some instances – if I buy an apple at the grocery store, for example, I own it and thereby "control" that apple – things can get a little gray in the world of finance.

To clarify the specifics, FASB has set three conditions that must be met in order for an asset to be deemed controlled by another party. The rule regarding asset control states, "The transferor has surrendered control over transferred assets if and only if all of the following conditions are met:

1   The transferred assets have been isolated from the transferor – put presumptively beyond the reach of the transferor and its creditors;

2   Each transferee...has the right to pledge the assets...and no condition constrains the transferee from...its right to pledge;

3   The transferor does not maintain effective control over the transferred assets through...an agreement that both entitles and obligates to repurchase them before their maturity."

Boiling down the rules into plain language, the three conditions are as follows: The asset was transferred to someone else and the original owner has no legal right get it back. Second, the buyer has the right to re-sell the asset to someone else. Third, there is no agreement that gives the original owner the option or the right to buy back the asset. Once a transaction meets all three criteria, it's defined concretely as a "true sale."

Despite the rules established and the seemingly airtight description of what qualifies, FASB 140 is still a gray area of "true sale" accounting. Like many things in life, everything in the world of accounting is not black or white, no matter what your math teachers taught you in school. A sale must have all the characteristics of a sale in order for it to be treated as sale.

If FASB 140 were truly a standardized set of rules and everyone used one interpretation, there would not be an issue with its implementation. However, there are multiple interpretations of the rule itself, which sometimes allows companies to manipulate the numbers to their benefit. Consider the case of the repo-to-maturity trades. First, though, it's important to remember what an RTM is: it is owning a security, and then loaning it to another party until that security matures. If you've loaned it to another party until it matures, does it count as a "true sale?" On one hand, the original owner is relinquishing control of their bonds; on the other, as part of a "repurchase agreement," they would buy back the bonds in the future. However, on the day of the repurchase, the bonds mature so they really didn't exist anymore. It was definitely an accounting rule that needed interpretation.

That set of circumstances leaves interpretation of the accounting rule open, and in the case of repo-to-maturity transactions, most banks keep them as on-balance-sheet trades, where they still recognize the securities as assets, whereas some treat them as off-balance sheet. In other words, that gray area allows some banks to under-report their assets, but that's still a matter of interpretation. Luckily for MF Global, their accounting firm, PricewaterhouseCoopers, allowed the RTM trades to be removed from their balance sheet. At the end of December 31, 2010 that means there was about $5 billion in European sovereign-debt positions that did not appear on the firm's balance sheet. The firm was enjoying a very favorable accounting interpretation from their accounting firm.

The size of the balance sheet was not the only issue under consideration, since how much capital the firm was required to hold by regulators was also impacted. Whether someone bought and sold an asset is pretty important. If you bought it and have not yet sold it, then you own it and if the RTM was not a "true sale" then it's an asset. Assets have inherent risk and the values can change; a bond can even default. As a broker-dealer under FINRA and SEC rules, a company must hold capital against their assets.

Since MF Global was able to operate with the favorable "true sale" accounting view from their accountant and the "assets" were not reported on their balance sheet, they therefore did not reserve capital against the trades. That made sense given they should not reserve capital against something that did not exist, at least by accounting standards. It allowed MF Global to operate, for the time being, with substantially less capital than would have normally been required.

In terms of under-reporting or not reporting assets, the gray area of "true sales" for repo-to-maturity is only basic compared to ways other financial firms hid their assets in the past. Think of how Lehman Brothers under-reported its balance sheet in a myriad of ways, with the so-called, "Repo 105."

Repo 105 was a more complicated trick the Lehman accountants used to classify a short-term loan as a full-fledged sale. The securities "sold" were the result of a swap, with the right, but not the obligation, to repurchase them – which was again called a "sale" on the company's balance sheet. In a way, Repo 105 was more akin to Refco's "Round-Trip-Loans" fraud than the MF Global exploitation of the gray area accounting of "true sales." However, the result was the same: in all cases, a transaction was used to remove assets from the company's balance sheet, which made the company seem less leveraged than it really was. In the case of Refco, the firm was removing the assets from one subsidiary and moving them to another subsidiary. Hiding assets, in turn, reassures stockholders and the market that a firm is on more solid financial ground than it really is. The catch was that once Repo 105, Round-Trip-Loans, and the aggressive use of the "true sale" rules became part of the public record, the firms' standing in the marketplace returned them to a worse financial position that they were in prior to the "sales." In the case of Lehman Brothers, the New York attorney general called the scheme "a massive fraud," despite the opinion of a select independent auditor that the practice was in line with generally accepted accounting principles. Aggressive accounting interpretations have allowed firms like Lehman, Refco and MF Global to operate with more risk than they reported; in each case, the end result was the collapse of a major investment bank.

* * *

Over the course of the spring, Jon Corzine continued growing the PSG group. They now had huge bets on currencies, wheat, oil, and other commodities, as well as CDSs, corporate bonds, and just about every other financial instrument you can think of. If the market moved, they traded it. But the stress of managing this portfolio was leading many in senior management to openly question Corzine. They wanted him to behave like the CEO of a publically listed company, using his connections and PR to drive the overall business, as opposed to just concentrating on his trading book.

To placate the growing discord, Corzine hired a 30-something trading prodigy recommended to him by George Soros, named Munir

Javeri. When Javeri showed up to work on his first day, his hiring had not been announced internally to anyone at MF Global, so it came as a large surprise to those assembled when Javeri introduced himself to the other PSG staff as their new boss.

Javeri was hired to be global head of trading and head of PSG and, to his credit, he approached his job by behaving and operating in the ways the role required. Never mind that Corzine's over-reliance on proprietary trading was the absolute wrong strategy for the firm; Javeri was perfectly happy with the boss's emphasis on trading. The RTM trades, on the other hand, were a different matter. He saw them exactly for what they were: a plaster that was being used by MF Global to cover a multitude of deficiencies.

After only a few short months, he left the firm with the explanation that he was off to take a bigger role managing a multi-billion dollar hedge fund. Some in the firm said that Javeri saw the train wreck coming and he knew there was no way to avoid it. Others said he left because he had racked up an $8 million loss in his trading book and already knew he had blown his bonus for the year. Whatever the reason, he got out quick, while the getting was still good.

The agenda for every MF Global board meeting that convened in 2011 included an update on the sovereign-debt portfolio. That update, as the year progressed, showed larger and larger positions in European debt and an increasing tendency to extend the trades and maturities, as those bonds promised bigger profits. That was, in effect, a necessary evil from the perspective of the decision makers, because MF Global's other businesses were still mostly unprofitable. The firm – especially Stockman – was under intense pressure to ratchet up the risk threshold to get the RTM profits higher. And the pressure wasn't just implied. Stockman would later say that he was overtly "warned he would face 'tremendous pressure' to support higher risk limits." The justification was that MF Global, as a result of losses elsewhere in all core product areas, risked losing its investment grade rating without showing more revenues.

The RTM trades were becoming like an ATM machine for Corzine. Anytime the firm needed additional revenues, all they needed to do was make a quick trip to the RTM machine. Get the risk-management team to increase the position limits, book more trades, book more profits. Who could resist? On the surface, it seemed like it was just too easy. And truth be told, it was.

One of the temptations of the RTM trades was that they allowed for immediate profits, no waiting for the bonds to mature because MF Global and Corzine took the easy road when they booked their RTM profits, they booked them all up front.

In RTM trades, the profit is the difference between the yield they received by owning the bonds versus the interest cost paid in the repo transaction. It's accounting at its most basic: income on one side, expense on the other. Most firms account for their profits by calculating the net interest they received on the bonds each day for the life of the trade, so if the trade was for one year, most firms booked a little bit of profit each day for 365 days.

MF Global, however, was doing things a little differently. Instead of accruing the profits daily, they booked them all up front, taking the full year's worth of interest accrual all at once. In trader jargon, that's called "moving your P/L forward." Typically, better traders tend to avoid that practice and instead move their P/L out further, being that it's better to have long, steady returns than large, quick profits as a professional trader. No doubt Jon Corzine knew that he was making what amounted to a rookie mistake, but he needed immediate revenues in order meet quarterly revenue targets. To illustrate the point, just by moving the profit forward, MF Global was able to show $25 million in revenues from the RTM trades for the fourth quarter of 2010 and another $47 million for the first quarter of 2011.

Regardless of how you book the profits – and remember, RTM profits were a relatively sure bet – conceptually it goes back to whether or not RTMs qualify as true sales under the rules of accounting. If you interpret the rules to state that RTMs are a type of true sale, it makes sense to book them on the day the trade was done. The securities were bought and sold, and the profits should be realized, especially if you're in a position needing to show positive cash flow in a hurry. Once again, most banks subscribe to the opposite point of view, and let profits on those trades accrue daily over the life of the bonds. That way, the profits are realized as the actual interest is booked, not all up front.

The incentive to move profits forward went back to the hope that over time, the RTM income would be replaced by brokerage revenues from elsewhere. It was the classic "buy now, pay later" equation that plagues so many credit-card users around the world. Spend the money now in hopes that you'll somehow get a financial windfall down the road. The problem arises, however, when the bills start coming in, but the longed-for turnaround for MF Global had yet to materialize.

MF Global needed positive cash flow, and if showing that meant they had to do some aggressive accounting, so be it. The mandate from Corzine was to generate $20 million a quarter in income as soon as possible, and the most practical method for doing that was to grow the sovereign-debt business. As another way of forwarding that agenda, the board approved what was euphemistically referred to as a "temporary increase" in March 2011 in the authorized amount of the sovereign-debt portfolio.

The agreement stated that MF Global could purchase up to $5.8 billion in sovereign debt, but that number was supposed to fall back to $5 billion in September 2011. For six months, the increase didn't bother the chief risk officer at all. In fact, in April he would report "good news" to the MF Global board. At that time, he announced that Jon Corzine was aware of the limits imposed by the firm and that Corzine agreed with the strategy as a whole. It was astonishing that someone would have to report that the CEO finally recognized the risk limits; it was equally astonishing that the recognition would be termed "good news" by the firm's chief risk officer.

Then, on June 6, 2011 the MF Global board once again convened and once again voted to increase the limit on sovereign debt. This time, the approved limit went up to a blistering $9.75 billion, a decision made based largely on the input of Jon Corzine, who lauded the strategy as an amazingly profitable venture. In addition to the increase, the board also approved the addition of Belgium as an approved country in which to do the RTM trades.

The new limits led to more RTM trades, and the firm immediately booked a $38 million profit. However, the margin requirements had the potential to put the firm in a precarious position in terms of liquid capital. But the collective wisdom felt it was a manageable number. At the time of the board meeting, the firm was pledging $170 million in margin at LCH.Clearnet, which was an amount that they all agreed was within reasonable limits.

It would be the final increase authorized by the board. But not surprisingly, neither the board of directors nor the risk limits was able to stop Corzine from growing his positions. To do so would just take a little more creative accounting.

By the end of June, the firm was up to $11.5 billion in European sovereign debt, but still appeared to the outside world – and the inside world, for that matter – to be within their risk department limits of $9.75 billion. In other words, within weeks, MF Global had managed to actually increase their holdings in sovereign foreign debt without breaking their internal risk limits or increasing their margin requirements.

This seemingly paradoxical situation was achieved through yet another financial sleight-of-hand. They were able to report a smaller position for their internal risk management in their sovereign-debt holdings if they hedged themselves through the use of the opposite trade in very similar securities.

While it might sound complicated – and, truth be told, the explanation is somewhat convoluted – it's actually a simple transaction that once again goes back to what's allowed under the rules of accounting. The transaction is, in essence, a reverse repo-to-maturity. Specifically, it was the double-entry accounting system that allowed MF Global to downplay the extent to which they were invested in sovereign debt. They could use short sales of the bonds of other countries with similar maturity dates to offset their existing long positions.

For example, by short-selling the bonds of a country like France and then borrowing the bonds back to maturity – that's the reverse repo-to-maturity part of the entry – they could net some of their positions down and not show them on the balance sheet. If they owned Italian bonds and then short-sold French bonds, being long Italy and short France would appear as a different kind of trade than just being long the Italian bonds. So when it came time to report the trades in their internal system, the French short positions would offset the Italian long positions, and the total assets were decreased. Thank you, Luca Pacioli.

MF Global, however, received another benefit from the reverse repo-to-maturity trades, namely a hedge against declines in their other positions. In the event the entire European bond market declined, the

French short-bond position would increase in value while the value of the other trades decreased. The added bonus there is that the positive margin from the French short positions would offset some of the margin requirements they faced otherwise. It was another hedge, a fail-safe that would protect the firm in the unlikely event of a global economic collapse. That's how it was supposed to work, anyway.

MF Global was into the repo-to-maturity trade up to their eyeballs with sovereign-debt bonds as the traders increased the size of their holdings to $11.5 billion. With the positions that large, the firm was beginning to feel the strain on the balance sheet, specifically through the massive margin requirements associated with such a huge position. But through the magic of reverse repo-to-maturity trades, they were able to offset the size of their assets and reduce their margin requirements at LCH.Clearnet. All told, the reverse-RTM trades managed to knock nearly $5 billion off the MF Global balance sheet and substantially reduce margin requirements. In short, they were able to make everything appear smaller.

Despite the financial smoke-and-mirrors campaign, it took until July before Stockman became nervous about the firm's dedication to the sovereign-debt market. He was so concerned about it, in fact, that he went directly to CEO Jon Corzine and announced, "I am not currently supportive of buying more sovereigns." His fears were grounded in the fact that he had been notified of new margin requirements by LCH.Clearnet, and he had the unpleasant task of notifying the board about the increase. Suddenly Stockman became very aware of liquidity risk, something about which he had to learn the hard way.

The margin requirements to that point had never been much larger than $100 million. But with the European financial crisis looming on the horizon, the bonds of periphery countries – specifically Ireland and Portugal – began to sell en masse, and that meant that the margin requirements associated with those countries' sovereign debt were growing. By the end of June, MF Global was posting an astounding $550 million in margin to LCH.Clearnet. That amount was an increase of over $450 million in just a matter of weeks. What's more, that staggering figure took into account the margin offset from the French bond reverse-RTM hedge. At this point, the RTM trades were becoming a severe drain on the firm's liquidity, and it appeared no one could do anything about it.

The downfall of the RTMs would come when MF Global's accounting firm and FINRA began to question the regulatory capital requirements of the RTM portfolio. The calling into question of the accounting practices was the equivalent of a single low-pressure front building off the American coast. The decision was about to be handed down that MF Global's "sale" in the repo-to-maturity transactions really didn't qualify as "true," at least insofar as the accountants were concerned. When that happened, $11.5 billion in European sovereign bonds would magically reappear on the balance sheet.

It was the first component of a perfect storm, one with amazingly destructive powers. Unfortunately from the perspective of MF Global, however, nobody at the firm knew it at the time. But it was coming, and Corzine was like a foolhardy sailor, heading straight for the teeth of it. And he was taking his entire crew with him.

CHAPTER TWELVE

Downfall

In the world of politics, people often joke that reality is what people think it is. Oftentimes it isn't so much what a politician does while in office that matters as what people interpret that action to be. There is a name for people who make their livelihoods by creating the perception from the actual reality. They are colloquially referred to as "spin doctors." Lee Atwater, a well-known political strategist (a title which may, in a way, be read as "spin doctor"), once famously said, "Perception is reality."

When dealing with financial matters – especially in the world of an investment bank – perception is the lifeblood of a firm. As the Bear Stearns collapse illustrated, if the perception is that a firm doesn't have enough liquidity to continue operating, it doesn't matter what the reality is. If there is public sentiment that a firm can't continue operations, sooner or later it will collapse.

Of course, oftentimes the perception is based in reality, at least in part. But like so many things, what is deemed perception and what is deemed reality depends on one's own interpretation. Such was the case with MF Global as the calendar pages turned to 2011.

After 18 months with Corzine at the helm of the firm, MF Global's profits weren't increasing, but the headcount was. Corzine had cut the company's work force to about 2,600 from 3,200 employees overall. He had trimmed the old workforce down, then proceeded to build up the firm with new employees. Many of these new hires were traders coming out of big investment banks, traders who didn't understand a brokerage company or how risk is managed in a brokerage organization; instead, they understood big-bank risk culture – take big risks and make big bonuses. And the new hires cost a lot more than the employees let go. Many of the old employees received large severance packages, while the new staff members were enticed with sign-on bonuses and big stock awards. Those severance packages and signing bonuses, paired with guaranteed compensation, were a mounting expense to the firm.

On top of that, there was entirely new management. These new leaders had difficulty managing both the new Goldman-esque employees and the legacy Man Financial, GNI, and Refco employees. There was a clash of cultures and divisions at all levels of the organization. You were either part of the Corzine team or you were *persona non grata*. At Goldman Sachs, there had been checks and balances for Corzine, and that system served to keep the firm under control. At MF Global, however, there were no such controls, as Corzine hired ex-Goldman cronies and surrounded himself with yes-men.

Representative Randy Neugebauer, who would be instrumental in the later investigation of MF Global's collapse, said of Corzine that his actions demonstrated that he "was autocratically running this organization." There was no one to challenge his authority, and he was free to run the business his way. Management and board meetings became sycophantic hero-worshipping sessions. It's not that any of these people were somehow bad or unintelligent. It's just that they were compromised by their love of Corzine. By agreeing with and supporting his every move, they were doing exactly what they'd been hired to do.

The company, like many banks in the industry, initiated a deferred bonus plan to be paid in MF Global stock that had a three-year vesting period, meaning some of the stock could not be sold until three years had passed. Corzine's bonus plan meant that employees would take up to 60% of their annual bonus in stock with much of the rest deferred, so in some cases as little as 10% was paid in cash. As one manager put it, "For a $100,000 bonus, I walk away with $10,000 in cash? After taxes, that amounts to almost nothing." It wasn't what the status-quo traders had become accustomed to in the years of huge bonuses paid in the world of high finance.

As such, the bonus plan was not met with open arms by many of the employees, a majority of whom had been with MF Global through years of MF being on the acquisition trail. Being that many legacy traders and salespeople had little faith in Corzine, the institution, and especially the company's stock, they were visibly disappointed in the new compensation plan. They were used to commission-based compensation, based on sales and brokerage, and not taking stock as compensation. Now, not only were they receiving a majority of their bonus in stock, but they had to wait up to three years to receive it. Many of the employees – especially those in sales and trading jobs – saw this is a cut in pay, and some were preparing to leave the company as a result of it.

And then there was Peter McCarthy, the former head of fixed income at MF Global. McCarthy had been the head of fixed income at Refco, and arrived at Man Financial through the Refco purchase. McCarthy had developed the firm's repo and clearing business and had grown it into fantastic profitability. His knowledge of financing and the firm's liquidity were an important part of the undercapitalized firm. But as Jon Bass and the new Corzine hires arrived, it became clear that his services were no longer considered of value to the firm. McCarthy asked Jon Corzine if he'd be willing to negotiate a severance package so that McCarthy could be on his way to greener pastures.

In September 2011 McCarthy was given a lump-sum cash payment of $60,000 from MF Global in exchange for his stock holdings. At the time, Corzine saw that as a major coup; he felt that the stock was grossly undervalued at the time and by getting McCarthy to accept a buyout, the firm would come out ahead. The final severance payment of $3 million was made to McCarthy in the middle of October.

Aside from adopting a strategy that was akin to using lottery tickets to fund one's personal retirement, Corzine's plan at resurrecting MF Global had other shortcomings. For starters, he didn't hire sufficient support staff, specifically in the fields of record-keeping and back-office personnel. That was a problem that would come back to bite the firm when things started to go wrong.

Additionally, given the level of risk he was encouraging his traders to take with the firm's money, Corzine failed to give the risk department adequate time to keep up with the company's growth. The department's policies and technology lagged severely as the trading desks continued to take increasingly risky positions in a wide variety of asset classes. Unlike the Goldman Sachs turnaround plan that had included heavy emphasis on risk management, the subject of managing risk was largely ignored at MF Global. In fact, as Mike Roseman could testify, if anyone stood in the way of increased risk, Jon Corzine showed them the door.

A 2011 internal audit noted the lack of a comprehensive risk-mitigation policy, citing the fact that "risk policies had not been updated to reflect the current operating environment." The audit also noted "the absence of reliable liquidity reporting tools," pointing out that the firm was relying on an assistant treasurer's personal expertise to mitigate risk. It is important to remember that finding came after the much-publicized Dooley debacle. Clearly either Corzine hadn't learned from the firm's disastrous history, or he thought he knew better. Or, perhaps he still thought he had the right tool to fix the problem.

* * *

MF Global became a Primary Dealer on February 2, 2011. That designation gave the firm the ability to purchase government securities directly from the United States Treasury at auction, securities that they could in turn resell to customers. The new designation was both good and bad. Along with the recognition came more responsibilities. As part of the Primary Dealer application's approval, the firm was ordered by CFTC to overhaul its internal controls. That overhaul was never really completed.

In June 2011, an internal audit report identified gaps in the firm's management of liquidity, capital, and systems for monitoring its funding. Too many processes were manual: operations, accounting, and compliance. Additionally, it was reported that the front office relied on spreadsheets for functions that should have been automated. There were requests to the IT department to automate many things that were never delivered, so the systems and tools to enable real-time monitoring of liquidity were never implemented. Instead, they continued to use an "ad hoc" system, developed by the front office called the Liquidity Dashboard.

Despite the fact that they were relying on outdated systems, the firm functioned perfectly for years. MF Global had a long, proud heritage as one the world's leading global futures brokers. In truth, the systems and support were not as much the problem. They were sufficient for the work that needed to be done. One real problem facing the firm was a failure to have in place a group of employees dedicated to supporting the work of those bringing in the revenues. While management added many sales and trading staff, the firm remained short-staffed in operations and support. The entire management and support structure was weak and fragmented, and the organizational chart couldn't clearly identify reporting lines of internal communication.

By the summer, MF Global still needed more earnings to avoid the looming ratings downgrade, but could no longer increase the size of the RTM portfolio anymore. In fact, Corzine was forced by the board to reduce the RTM positions. By the end of September, the trades were down to a number settling in at $6.3 billion, a significant decrease in volume from their $11.5 billion peak in June. That avenue was closed, so there was certainly no way to squeeze more profits from more RTM trades.

Throughout the summer and fall, margin calls were still growing, even though the size of the positions was contracting. The European debt situation had deteriorated, which meant that LCH.Clearnet was requiring more margin on some country's bonds in the portfolio. Even though the positions were cut, the existing ones were still eating up more and more capital. And there was nowhere for that capital to come from. At least, not in any sort of traditional manner of speaking.

At the end of June 2011, the LCH.Clearnet margin requirement had been up to $550 million. By the end of September, even with the size of the RTM positions cut by almost half, the margin at LCH was still as high as $417 million. The two anchors that were weighing most heavily on the firm's sovereign-debt portfolio were Portugal and Ireland. The margin rate had moved up to 65% for Portugal and up to 75% for Ireland in June. Both of those LCH margin rates would peak in July, when the clearinghouse required 80% margin for both countries. To put it in perspective, for every $100 in European sovereign bonds, LCH required $80 to be put up as margin. In short, the LCH margin requirements were becoming a severe drain on the firm's liquidity.

Edith O'Brien, the assistant treasurer based in Chicago, was not completely naïve to the fact that there was a financial sleight-of-hand going on at MF Global. Referring to their liquidity situation as a "shell game," she recounted in an email that she was "rendered speechless" upon being told by CFO Henri Steenkamp that MF Global had plenty of operating capital. "I wanted to say, 'Really, why is it I need to spend hours every day shuffling cash and loans from entity to entity?'" The financial wheels were beginning to come off at MF Global.

There was still a major problem in MF Global's core business, futures brokerage. That division was still mostly unprofitable. The economy was weak and short-term rates remained near 0.0%, so the firm was struggling to make minimal revenues from investing their clients' margin cash. Business divisions that had always been profitable, like foreign exchange and fixed income, were struggling with volatile markets and declining volumes. MF Global's revenues were further blighted by unprofitable quarters in the equities and retail brokerage divisions, both of which continued to bleed the company's resources.

All of these factors came to a head in the middle of 2011. The firm was plagued by funding problems, new hires who were not performing, unprofitable businesses, lax internal controls, long-time employees leaving, and zero-percent interest rates. All it would take was one more event to accelerate the decline that was already in motion. For MF Global, that single event came in the form of an obscure accounting rule change.

The rule in question was FASB 140. The issue was one of interpretation, and it all boiled down to whether MF Global actually sold assets or not. It seems like common sense, on the surface. Either you sold something or you didn't. But in the world of RTM trades, it's all about how you interpret the transaction. The question came down to whether or not the MF Global RTM trades qualified as "true sales." The bonds were sold to LCH.Clearnet under a repo agreement. The assets were then out of the reach of creditors in the case of bankruptcy or default. However, there was a little problem, one that was particular to the policies of LCH.Clearnet, that threw the proverbial wrench into the works.

As it turned out, the RTM trades MF Global was executing weren't exactly sold to maturity. LCH.Clearnet's policy is that they will not accept bonds financed to the full maturity date. Instead, the closest they will clear and settle bonds is two days before maturity. That means that what were previously termed RTM trades really weren't RTM. Instead, they were what could be called "RTM-minus-two." What that means is that any creditors who would be in line to take over control of the bonds would have access to those assets during the last two days before maturity.

LCH.Clearnet does not let counterparties book a true repo-to-maturity, blaming it on their internal systems constraints. It is also quite possible that LCH did not want to assume the default risk over the last two days before a bond matured. Regardless of why, however, it meant that the default risk was assumed by MF Global during those last two days of each trade. Because the bonds were returned two days before, the RTM trades were clearly not a "true sale," per the accounting definition of that term. As has been discussed, there were questions as to whether an RTM is a true sale to begin with, but with a two-day period shy of maturity, it made the trades even more questionable. Or, alternatively, it made the issue crystal clear. The RTMs weren't true sales.

* * *

Right around the time when MF Global's RTM trades were at their peak, FASB, PriceWaterhouseCoopers, and the SEC were looking into the firm's accounting practices. On March 16, the SEC sent a letter to MF Global asking them to justify how it accounted for their RTMs for the year ended March 31, 2010, the year prior. MF Global responded that they treated RTMs as sales, but that was just the beginning. A few weeks later, FASB revised the interpretations of the rule, as did MF Global's accounting firm, PriceWaterhouseCoopers. According to an MF Global staff member, PWC "helped MF Global take the RTMs off balance sheet, then three months later changed their minds and told us to put them back on the balance sheet."

PWC advised MF Global that if any mark-to-market losses on the RTM trades were greater than $10 million, the firm should make a provision in the company accounts. In other words, the accountants were telling MF Global that they needed to show for losses on their balance sheet since the RTM trades were now assets. As one MF Global staffer put it, "PWC screwed MF when they changed their opinion."

Even after the March financial statement reflected the RTM trades, few people outside the company really took the time to delve into it. CFO Henri Steenkamp discussed the RTM on investor calls, but no one seemed to care. The risks of the European sovereign-debt trades were still not on anyone's radar.

It wasn't until June when the RTMs were finally referenced in MF Global's annual report, appearing on pages 77 and 78: "The Company also enters into certain resale and repurchase transactions that mature on the same day as the underlying collateral . . . the Company de-recognizes the related assets and liabilities from the consolidated balance sheets, recognizes a gain or loss of the sale/purchase of the collateral assets." Over $11 billion European sovereign-debt repo-to-maturities trades had gone from nothing to something, seemingly overnight. The disclosure was not overt, but it set other things in motion. Once the RTMs were an asset on their books, it made sense for the firm to reserve capital against them.

The Financial Industry Regulatory Authority (FINRA) submitted questions to MF Global and asked how much of their $11 billion RTM portfolio qualified as "riskless." After some review, MF Global responded that only $500 million of the total could be considered completely riskless. That meant that there was a large discrepancy between the riskless portion and the risk portion. The regulators viewed those risky components as assets and informed MF Global that they'd be required to take capital charge over the summer. Once FINRA concluded that some capital needed to be set aside, they initially dictated that number to be $150 million. MF Global personnel did not agree with their findings, and the negotiations began.

The problem with the capital charge was that RTM trades weren't specifically addressed in FINRA rules. Evidently, there was something of a gap in the rules. Again, it was a matter of interpretation. FINRA viewed the RTM trades as being closest to "long positions in sovereign debt," which meant they should be treated as "nonconvertible debt" in FINRA rule language. In that way of viewing them, the trades would have a large capital charge.

MF Global, perhaps not surprisingly, had a different opinion. They had been treating the European sovereign-debt RTM trades in the same fashion as they did the RTMs on U.S. Treasury and federal agency bonds, which do not have a charge. That seemed like quite a stretch since MF Global had pushed the boundaries of the original RTM trade from "risk-free" bonds into periphery European sovereign debt.

FINRA refused to let the issue pass and decided there definitely was a risk, and because of that, there was a capital charge that was required. The only problem was that they were not sure what to call it, so they asked MF Global to call it a "potential default risk charge," and MF Global could suggest some scenarios of how to calculate it. The MF Global accounting department assembled five possible scenarios, based on different assumptions. The capital required, according their findings, ranged from $7.6 million to $98.2 million.

By August, MF Global's accountants and the FINRA regulators were still haggling over the size of the charge. On August 11, FINRA decided the "potential default risk charge" should be $55.8 million. That meant that the MF Global broker-dealer needed to set aside an additional $60 million in capital, effective July 31. That number was acceptable to MF Global and would be manageable for the firm, being it was well within their expected range. At that point, employees at MF Global assumed the issue was mostly resolved.

Even before the final ruling on the capital charge came down, MF Global knew they needed to raise more capital. The margin calls from LCH.Clearnet continued to increase, and the RTM trades were consuming cash, time, and now regulatory capital. The firm needed more capital, and it was decided that a bond offering was the best alternative. The firm issued $325 million in debt, but there was a problem. Investors were worried that Jon Corzine would not stay at the firm. There were rumors Timothy Geithner, the U.S. Treasury secretary, would resign, and if the Treasury secretary job were open, Jon Corzine was the perfect candidate to fill it. He'd served as a senator and governor of New Jersey, and was a loyal Democrat. He was also an accomplished Wall Street executive. And what's more, Corzine really wanted the job.

    In order to sell the debt, MF Global had to write in a provision to pay the bondholders an extra 1% interest if Corzine left MF Global for a government job. But that was another problem for another day. The bonds were issued, investors' worries were soothed, and MF Global got some much-needed money. With another $325 million in capital, it seemed like the firm was well capitalized again.

    A week later, on August 24, the final word came in from FINRA on the capital charges. MF Global was completely shocked. They received notification that they were required to take a $257 million charge. It was almost four times as much as had been initially expected. Naturally, this set off multiple calls to FINRA and the SEC. Whereas a $60 million charge could be absorbed by the existing capital base of the broker-dealer, now they needed to increase the broker-dealer's capital by as much as $183 million. With the new charge, the broker-dealer, as of July 31, had a net capital deficiency of $150.6 million. Being under-capitalized is bad for regulatory standing, not to mention that it creates bad press and bad feelings from customers.

    At a minimum, MF Global needed to put more capital in their broker-dealer to satisfy the regulatory net capital minimum threshold. To make things worse, they had to file a public "hindsight notice" of the capital deficiency in July. They would have to make public their financial statements with the details of the capital set-aside related to the RTM portfolio. This meant that a lot of attention would be drawn to the RTM trades, the capital deficiency, and the restatement.

    With all of the problems still facing the firm, management needed to look at alternatives. A number of those options included selling off all or pieces of the firm. One suggestion was selling the retail futures broker, Lind-Waldock; another was to sell the institutional futures brokerage business to a competitor. In Corzine's grand scheme, the futures business barely played a role, so he deemed a retail futures brokerage operation as negligible. If MF Global was to go down that road, why not sell the entire futures brokerage division? Futures margin investment income was low and the business was only marginally profitable. On top of that, the expectation of higher short-term interest rates had been quashed by the Fed's policy announcement statement in August, announcing the economic situation would "warrant exceptionally low levels for the federal funds rate at least through mid-2013."

Other ideas included getting a capital injection or becoming a joint venture with an institution with a large capital and balance sheet, specifically with The Bank of New York Mellon. BNYM had struggled for years to expand beyond its custody and clearing business. From their perspective, here was the opportunity to enter investment banking, fixed-income sales and trading, and the futures business, all in one shot. They'd also acquire the talents of Jon Corzine and his management team. But such a union would take weeks, even months to complete. BNYM did not move fast like Jon Corzine and his traders in the market; they moved more like a custody-and-clearing bank, slow and steady. There just wasn't enough time for that to work.

The final question, then, was whether to merge with another futures broker. In April, Corzine reached out to Newedge about a possible merger or the purchase of MF Global's futures business. Newedge was a prime candidate because it had a similar business model. Both firms began as futures brokers and expanded into other business lines. The problem was that Nicholas Breteau, the CEO of Newedge, was not part of the New York investment scene. In fact, he was rarely in New York. Breteau owed his rise from internal auditor to CEO to inter-company politics and staying close to the Newedge power base in London and Paris and had few relationships with financial executives in New York.

Corzine and Breteau had dinner at Manhattan's Fresco By Scotto restaurant on 52nd Street. Sitting at a small table for two in the back of the restaurant, the two discussed possible combinations. Corzine told stories about the markets and about being CEO of Goldman and governor of New Jersey, the whole time staring at his Blackberry as he spoke. Breteau realized that the Newedge/MF Global combination would not work. Newedge had its own problems, and just like MF Global, Newedge was for sale. Newedge had two French bank parent companies, Calyon and Société Générale, which were divesting assets to shore up capital for the upcoming BASEL III capital rules.

Even if Newedge hadn't been for sale, there were too many similarities and overlaps between the two businesses. Newedge was suffering from the same impairment as MF Global: the collapse of interest rates that had eliminated their interest revenues on customer deposits. What's more, Newedge was bloated with support staff and a large amount of personnel in Europe who were mostly immune from layoffs. Newedge management was already unsuccessfully wrestling to reduce costs. Their only hope was to make the company appear profitable in the short term by fixing it up for a quick sale. There was no way Newedge could purchase MF Global. Newedge was desperate itself._

Interactive Brokers was the firm that had bid against Man Financial for the Refco business. If they wanted it back then, perhaps they were still interested. The firm was started and mostly owned by Thomas Peterffy, a Hungarian-born billionaire. Peterffy always showed up for distressed sales of futures brokers, because he could extract significant value out of the acquisitions. Peterffy ran a very efficient business. He shunned traders and salespeople, preferring to keep as much of the business automated and computerized. His vision was to combine the MF Global clients with Interactive Broker's systems. "I wanted to put together all their messy broker business under Interactive's technology," he said. Corzine met secretly with Peterffy, but nothing came of the discussions.

Growing increasingly desperate, Corzine wanted another meeting with Breteau, and began calling him again but could not get through. Breteau would not return his calls, so Corzine looked for other senior Newedge executives to speak with. As he began calling other Newedge personnel to arrange another meeting with Breteau, he had problems getting through with them. As his personal secretary went through the rolodex, some people never picked up the call because Corzine used a phone line with no caller ID; he didn't want anyone to know it was he or MF Global calling. After making initial contact with a senior executive at Newedge, Corzine was even more secretive. He told the Newedge executive that he did not send emails, claiming he learned to avoid written trails from his time as governor of New Jersey. "If there's something to discuss, let's meet at my club and we can talk about it."

His contact at Newedge tried to put Corzine in contact with the elusive CEO, but Breteau would not bite. Breteau later claimed that he saw MF Global's books and would not touch the firm. And what was worse, Breteau's French sensibilities saw Corzine's behavior at the dinner the two had shared in New York as extremely insulting. Breteau was put off by the stories, and especially by the attention Corzine had paid to his Blackberry instead of his dining companion. It had been, in Breteau's mind, a *faux pas extraordinaire*, and the whole evening had turned him off entirely from doing business with Corzine.

As the FSA in London became worried about MF Global's exposure to European debt and the growing margin calls, they required the MF Global London subsidiary to have a contingency plan. At the same time, the risk department worried that the London office could face up to $900 million more in margin calls on the RTM trades. The firm needed to know where they would get the funds under a disaster scenario. The board of directors liked the idea of an emergency plan, and requested that management prepare such a plan in case they were downgraded to junk status. The report was 23-pages long and described the firm's access to liquidity. The main strategy was to draw down the $1.2 billion revolving credit facility, sell assets to raise cash, and hire an investment banking firm to arrange a sale. The report went so far as to suggest that they use customer seg funds, which was certainly controversial. However, the plan concluded the firm would survive.

By October, the year-end deadline to meet the profitability targets was approaching. The rating agencies, specifically Moody's, wanted to see the firm post $200 million in pre-tax profits in order to maintain their investment grade rating. The FSA was still not satisfied with the liquidity plan, and announced that they were "uncomfortable" with MF Global's liquidity position. There was fear around the company that disaster was at hand. That fear became much more real with the news of the pending earnings report. MF Global was expected to report its quarterly results on October 27. A year prior, in the previous year's third quarter, the firm had posted net income of $13.3 million on revenues of $314.5 million. At that time, those earnings had been considered low, but at least the firm was in the black.

That was not the case this year. MF Global was about to report their worst quarterly profits ever. Most of the loss was generated by the auditor's requirement to take a $119 million accounting charge that was a write-off of tax credits that had accumulated after years of losses. The outside accountants even concluded that MF Global would not be profitable anytime soon. With an operating loss in the business and the tax write-off, it brought the quarterly loss up to $191.6 million. There was little doubt that the firm's credit ratings would be downgraded to junk.

Losing a notch in a credit rating might not seem like such a tremendous change. After all, there's really just one level between a triple-B and a double-B rating. But when a firm is downgraded to "junk" status – especially an investment bank – it's a huge problem. First, there are clients who can only trade with investment-grade counterparties. Once the rating threshold breaks below BBB-, the company is no longer investment grade, which limits the potential client base. Even for those clients who can trade with non-investment-grade counterparties, the label of junk is oftentimes enough of a turn-off to send them elsewhere to do business. Additionally, the central counterparties, like LCH.Clearnet, would increase their margin requirements if MF Global dropped below investment grade. Basically, all the problems that MF Global was already facing would be exacerbated by the downgrade. Being downgraded to junk status was not something to be taken lightly.

All the strategic alternatives that had been under consideration over the past few months were now being considered again with renewed intensity. Ideas were tossed around like paper airplanes: dump the RTM portfolio, speak with BNYM again, find a buyer, sell a division. Perhaps they could transfer the RTM portfolio to the MF Global London office or to one of the unregulated subsidiaries, or even to a third party. That would ease their liquidity crunch, at least from a regulatory perspective.

By engaging in any of these possible solutions, it would be an admission that Corzine's plan had not worked. Corzine said of the ideas that were bandied about, "We don't want to do those types of things." He knew that the rating agencies would be a major problem, so he hired J.P. Morgan for advice on how to handle them. He figured he'd personally explain the situation to the agencies and to investors. Tell them why everything would be all right. Basically, he pulled out the 1994 Goldman Sachs plan once again. It had worked before, so why not use it again for a third time?

Adding to the crisis the firm was facing was the fact that there was still no long-term plan to make the company profitable. So even if they managed to chew themselves free from this trap, they still had a minefield to navigate. He needed more time to figure out a viable solution. But time – like available capital – was a resource Jon Corzine was rapidly running out of.

On October 17, 2011 the *Wall Street Journal* published an article with the headline "MF Global Told to Boost Capital." While an obscure headline that a casual reader might have skimmed over while sipping a cup of coffee, the content served as the spark that would become a bonfire. That article finally brought all the problems to light.

When almost two months had passed since the initial news was out, someone had finally taken notice. The capital situation, which was mostly ignored before, was not to be ignored any longer. In a sense, the article seemed to come out of nowhere. In another sense, it was long overdue. The article got much attention and would serve as the spark that would ignite a fire. It would be, to reference another financial author, a bonfire fueled by vanity.

One week later, on Monday, October 24, Moody's downgraded MF Global by one notch, to Baa3. Luckily, that designation still qualified as "investment grade", but just by a hair. Standard and Poor's followed two days later on October 26, and put MF Global on "Credit watch with negative implications." S&P warned investors that it might downgrade MF Global from BBB-, the firm's lowest investment grade rating. On Thursday, October 27, both Moody's and Fitch downgrade MF Global to junk, a rating of Ba2.

All the dominos had fallen. The first domino fell when the RTM trades were declared assets with risk, which led to the capital charge. The capital charge showed that MF Global was undercapitalized, and the *Wall Street Journal* article sparked the downgrades. Those downgrades led to the liquidity crisis. Now, customers were fleeing and counterparties were grabbing cash and margin. MF Global was in a full-blown crisis. The crisis would culminate one week later in bankruptcy, when the perception of risk and lack of liquidity became reality.

CHAPTER THIRTEEN

Bankruptcy Week

"Turning and turning in the widening gyre,
The falcon cannot hear the falconer;
Things fall apart; the center cannot hold;
Mere anarchy is loosed up on the world."
                    -William Yeats
                        "The Second Coming"

Written in 1919, William Butler Yeats' poem "The Second Coming" describes a world that sits on the precipice of coming to a final end. Yeats was writing immediately after World War I, "the war to end all wars." Wounded men returning home told stories of trench warfare, chemical attacks, and commanders blindly leading their troops to their deaths. An estimated 17 million human beings lost their lives during the war years, including seven million civilians. The time immediately following the armistice was, to be certain, one of fear of what the future of humankind would hold. Yeats captured that sentiment in his poem, describing an imminent apocalypse that would result in a second coming, but in Yeats' vision, it wasn't any sort of philanthropic messiah that would return the world to peace and happiness, but rather a "rough beast." In short, Yeats saw no hope for humankind's salvation. The world and its inhabitants were doomed, destroyed by their own ferocity.

The precursor to this utter obliteration is the image of a falcon flying in ever-widening circles. As the falcon flies further and further away from the falconer who is, at least in theory, the controlling force in the falcon's life, the bird can no longer hear his commands. That metaphor, representing the world's inhabitants as a whole, leads to a situation where "things fall apart" and "anarchy is loosed up on the world."

And while Yeats was speaking in metaphor about the post-war world in which he lived, "The Second Coming" is an accurate reflection of what was happening in the MF Global offices in the last days of October 2011. Just as Yeats described a world void of any hope, so, too, was the future of MF Global.

Things began to unravel for Corzine and his firm on Monday, October 24. MF Global had just posted a staggering $191 million quarterly loss, which had resulted in the decision by Moody's to downgrade the company's credit rating to one notch above junk. To make matters worse, State Street Bank – one of many financial lifelines that MF Global was struggling to hold on to – had just cut all their credit lines, including all their financing lines. Following on the heels of that revelation, Corzine instructed the repo traders not to discuss the cut credit lines. The repo desk didn't listen, feeling there was an obligation for senior people in the company to know, and an email went out to all business heads about the situation.

Corzine was irritated by the taboo communication, and asked the sender, "Why did you do that? You're just going to worry everyone." The situation was, in his mind, still a speed bump, a small storm that the firm could weather without any undue hardship. But Corzine knew, too, the power of perception, and his fear was that if customers and counterparties sensed trouble, they would begin pulling their money out. If that escalated, it would create a financial landslide the firm would not be able to withstand.

That evening, Corzine took matters into his own hands, seeking to calm nerves that were upset by the news from the rating agency. He sent an email to all MF Global employees, explaining the situation. But in the same email, he reassured them that there was nothing to worry about. "While I am disappointed by this action," he wrote, "it bears no implications for our clients or our strategic direction at MF Global." It was classic Corzine, always the politician.

It would seem obvious to any impartial observer that when an investment bank declares a massive loss, has its credit rating cut, and loses credit lines, those things will bear heavily on the clients and the firm's strategic direction. And perhaps Corzine sensed that his words might ring a little hollow with some, so he added a further reassurance, just to buttress the feelings of safety: "Many of our peers are experiencing similar changes to their counterparty credit ratings." In other words, there's safety in numbers. No need to worry, nothing to see here, move along.

From where Jon Corzine sat that Monday night, things might have seemed manageable. The collection of bad news was an unfortunate development and it would definitely cause a short-term hit to MF Global's financial health. But he'd been through rough patches before, and he'd always come out on top. At its essence, this was just a setback on the road to greater financial success. MF Global would get through this. At least that was Corzine's view of things. The next day, though, the falcon flew a little further away, and things began to fall apart.

Regardless of what his calm façade suggested, Corzine was clearly operating from a defensive perspective. He needed to reassure everyone inside and outside that there was nothing substantially wrong with the firm's finances. On Tuesday morning, October 25, he created a PowerPoint deck that he emailed to MF Global's clients and counterparties. In the 10-page presentation, he outlined the firm's RTM trades, explaining the size of the positions – $6.3 billion – and the strategy behind the investments. He also detailed the firm's exposure to each country whose sovereign debt MF Global was holding.

At the time of the presentation, MF Global's sovereign-debt holdings were primarily in Italian bonds, which accounted for 51% of the portfolio. Spain was next, with 18%, followed by Portugal at 16%, Belgium at 9%, and Ireland at 6%. But that wasn't the real point of the PowerPoint deck. This was supposed to be calm anxious nerves, and those numbers really didn't do much in that regard.

The main thrust of the presentation was that MF Global's short-term European sovereign-debt portfolio was a gold mine, and there was no need for investors or customers to panic. Peppered throughout the pages were buzzwords investors love: words like "diversifying revenue" and "limited risk," and in the event that things turned bad, investors would be protected by "solid risk management." There was even mention of the fact that the European Financial Stability Facility had "pledged backing of these countries to June 30, 2013." Of course, given the volatile nature of Europe's economy, it seemed only fair to point out to investors that "risk of loss would be due to default of the issuer of the underlying securities." But fear not, investors, Corzine was quick to point out the fact that there was $1.3 billion in French short positions that were a hedge. So really, there was nothing to worry about.

Obviously Corzine hoped that the deck would assuage any fears and return life at MF Global to a semblance of financial normalcy. His hopes were quickly dashed, however.

Throughout the day on Tuesday, more counterparties began to decline to do business with MF Global, leaving the company with securities they were unable to fund through repo transactions. Hard-to-finance securities are usually also hard to sell, so the company was in the unfortunate position of holding debt obligations that they couldn't finance or resell. The remaining counterparties that were still trading with MF Global started requiring increased amounts of margin deposits to continue to do business.

In a more perfect world, those margin requirements wouldn't have been such a huge burden. With extensive credit lines from which to draw funds, MF Global could have easily come up with the requisite money to cover the margin calls. But following on the heels of State Street Bank's cutting off all MF Global business, the London office of HSBC did the same thing. They ceased doing business with MF Global altogether, which mainly consisted of the company's stock-funding credit lines.

With fewer lines of credit available to use in their quest for financing, management decided to partly draw down the $1.2 billion revolving credit facility (RCF) they had established through a conglomerate of four banks: JP Morgan, Bank of America, Wells Fargo, and BNP Paribas.

A revolving credit facility – colloquially referred to as a "revolver" – is essentially a credit card for businesses. It is a fund from which a business may draw money as needed – usually for daily operating purposes – up to whatever pre-established limit has been set by the lenders. In exchange for the use of the "revolver," the borrowing company usually pays a commitment fee – the same thing as an annual fee a credit-card holder pays – and interest on any outstanding loan. In the case of MF Global, dipping into the RCF wasn't a case of needing a little extra spending money to make payroll, it was the last option available to borrow cash before the liquidity squeeze impacted the rest of their business.

One of the major obstacles they faced, however, was that Bank of America, Wells Fargo, and BNP all had limited counterparty credit lines to MF Global. So as they drew on available credit in the revolver, those same counterparties began to return securities that they were funding elsewhere. So as the firm's liquidity grew as a result of drawing on the revolver, their liquidity contracted as those banks cut back funding in other areas. It was self-defeating – just when MF Global needed more credit, especially in light of the fact that the revolver actually cost MF Global in annual payments – they lost liquidity through other funding sources.

As a further way of supplementing the RCF funds – and also as a way of cauterizing the bleeding wound that was MF Global's financial situation – management ordered the repo desk to reduce the balance sheet through the liquidation of the "REIT trades." On paper, it seemed like a logical idea. Return all the mortgage-backed securities (MBS) they were financing for REIT customers – which accounted for approximately $6 billion in positions – to reduce the balance sheet and risk, but the new managers did not really understand liquidity and liquidity risk.

What the powers-that-be who ordered the closing of the trades didn't realize – or at least didn't take into account – was the fact the repo desk was generating that 3% margin on financing the MBS. Those trades generated between $150 and $180 million in cash liquidity for MF Global, money that the firm used to finance their operations. So by closing down the REIT customers, management effectively put a larger burden on MF Global's already precarious liquidity situation. The falcon was circling further and further away from the falconer.

By Wednesday, October 26, what had begun as a relative trickle of clients leaving the firm had morphed into a deluge. MF Global clients were calling all over Wall Street, searching for a safe haven for their accounts. It was clear to them that the firm was not stable, and customers were looking for new homes for their business. Throughout the day, salespeople at other banks fielded calls from worried MF Global refugee clients, all of whom seemed to be asking the same question: Can you get me out of MF Global and into your bank by close-of-business Friday? Salespeople who wavered in their assurance – after all, transferring assets from one bank to another typically takes a little longer than two days – lost out on the client. The desperation was palpable.

There is, at least in recent history, a tradition of Wall Street investment banks going from solvent to bankrupt in a rapid spiral. Bear Stearns took five days; the rumors started on Monday, and by Friday they were basically insolvent. The company spent the weekend looking for a buyer, and by the next Monday, they were a historical footnote. Lehman Brothers followed much the same trajectory several months after Bear's demise. And now it was Wednesday, and all that history was weighing heavily on MF Global's client base. Would the firm survive the week? Could they limp through the weekend? What about the days after that? Would they find a buyer? The general consensus was that after Friday, it would be too late.

Many of the customers who chose to stay at MF Global began closing their trading positions, leaving only cash in their accounts. The prevailing wisdom dictated that if MF Global went bankrupt, cash was the safest thing to have in their accounts. If the firm entered bankruptcy, there was no guess to whether customer trading positions might be frozen, and no trader liked a position they can't sell. Many MF Global salespeople worked frantically trying to unwind clients' trades and they were desperate to keep those clients solvent. As many of the salespeople knew from Refco just years before, once your firm is bankrupt, your clients are all you have left. By keeping them happy and helping them as much as possible, including closing their accounts, the MF Global salespeople were hoping to keep the clients who they'd worked so hard to woo in the first place. Assuming MF Global did slip into bankruptcy and the salespeople went on to other firms, their collective hope was that their clients would follow.

The activity was so frantic on Wednesday that the employees – not to mention the computer systems – were having extreme difficulties in keeping up with the volume of activity. The sheer number of transactions was unprecedented in the history of the firm. By the end of the week, a total of $105 billion in cash moved in and out of the firm and over $100 billion in securities, approximately $1.1 billion of customer funds, representing thousands of customer accounts, would be withdrawn from MF Global's coffers. That was partly margin money that, prior to its withdrawal, had been generating positive funds for the firm, capital they'd been using to help fund their business. The rapidly draining customer cash reserves put yet another strain on MF Global's finances.

The panic that had set in was forcing the MF Global employees to unwind the entire MF Global business, trading positions, client accounts and all their various components in a matter of three days. That's a tall order to complete in a month; three days is next to impossible. To describe the scene at MF Global headquarters as chaotic does not quite do it justice. Money wires were being sent in and out constantly throughout the day, as salespeople were holding multiple conversations on multiple phones simultaneously. Whenever a phone was hung up, it immediately started ringing again. The overwhelming majority of those calls were from clients instructing salespeople to close their accounts.

Between the lost funding from State Street, HSBC, Bank of America, Wells Fargo and BNP, the liquidation of the REIT financing positions and the loss of client funds, MF Global was losing vast amounts of money in the form of financing and margin funds. That was money they relied on in order to fund their own business. Now that the source of that funding had disappeared, the firm was on life support. They needed to do something drastic, and do it soon.

It was then that the "Break The Glass" idea of siphoning off from the seg funds was floated. Of the approximately $7 billion the firm maintained in their seg funds, approximately $300 million was MF Global's own money. That money was meant as a cushion, a sort of rainy-day fund to be used in case of dire need. In daily operations, it wasn't uncommon for the company to dip into that money, usually taking out $50 million here and there as needed.

If more than that $300 million was needed, it could be temporarily used, but the money had always been replaced at the end of the day, and up until then, the sacrosanct customer seg funds had never been missing when the time had come to tally the numbers. It was, in the minds of MF Global personnel, acceptable to dip into the firm's own money and the client funds, so long as the customer funds remained untouched. That is to say, so long as the money was always repaid by the end of the day, everything was as it should be in the minds of the executives. It was, for lack of a better term, a policy of "what they don't know won't hurt them." And after all, it was only used in cases that qualified as dire need.

And given the nature of the current situation, "dire need" seemed to be an appropriate description. By the end of Wednesday, the firm had withdrawn the full amount of their own money from the seg funds. And while the customer funds had been shuffled around, moving funds in and out of the seg accounts at JP Morgan, the client funds had, up until then, always found their way back to where they belonged by the close of business.

By Wednesday evening, that $300 million wasn't even enough to cover the new margin call from LCH.Clearnet, an amount that currently stood at $601 million, and all the other cash liquidity going straight down the drain. The firm needed more cash immediately if they hoped to be in business tomorrow.

At 5:53 p.m. an employee from the MF Global treasury department named R. Jason Chenoweth, who worked in the Chicago office, asked a co-worker named Joseph Cranston to rush a late-day transfer. Chenoweth was requesting that $165 million be transferred from a JP Morgan "house account" that belonged to MF Global to another JP Morgan account "seg account" that held customer funds. The transfer was, Chenoweth explained, to cover the day's clearance settlements. The account the funds were supposed to be drawn from, it needs to be made clear, was an account maintained by MF Global Finance, a subsidiary. In other words, the original intent as it was stated was a completely normal, legal transaction.

A minute later, Cranston came back and approved the transfer. Such a request was, again, a relatively mundane one, even though it was only seven minutes before the money wire closed at 6:00 p.m. Perhaps it was because of the late hour, or maybe it was because of the insanity of the day, we'll never know for sure, but for whatever reason, the account "CHASEFIN" was written in the internal money wire code as opposed to the correct code, "MF Global Finance USA." The error resulted in funds coming out of the customer seg account instead of an MF Global house account. The first dip into the honey pot of customer money had just occurred.

Upon realizing the error, the pair immediately sent instructions to have the money wire reversed. But by the time they caught the mistake, the Federal Reserve money wire system had closed for business that day. Their concern about the improper transfer suggests they were not engaged in any sort of premeditated nefarious behavior. However, such a mix-up is not a minor oversight, and one that people of their experience level wouldn't make in the normal course of business. In other words, it could be a nice cover story to say the transfer was made at the end of the day and, despite your best efforts, you didn't catch the mistake until after the wire had closed. You're only human, after all. And it was a great way to ensure that the MF Global "house account" was balanced at JP Morgan at the close of the business day.

If we give the pair the benefit of the doubt and accept the error as an honest mistake that they tried to correct, one thing is crystal clear: the coding mistake is testament to the fact that the last days of MF Global were uncontrolled bedlam. Or, as Yeats might have said, anarchy was being unleashed upon the world.

Regardless of their intentions, the fact of the matter was that at the end of the day on Wednesday, the heretofore sacred cow that was the customer seg funds ended up $300 million below what it should have been. It had not been repaid as it should have been.

Alarmed by the massive drawdown on the revolver, those people at JP Morgan who provided the vast majority of the loan – a substantial $930.6 million – were concerned about the financial wellbeing of the firm. The JP Morgan clearing and settlement group contacted MF Global, offering to "help with deliveries and settlements." MF Global was at first hesitant to accept the offer, but the JP Morgan clearing group literally pleaded and they finally relented. On Wednesday evening, a team from JP Morgan took over a conference room in the MF Global offices, essentially barricading themselves inside and refusing entry to anyone from MF Global. From that point on, JP Morgan's people would be handling much of the firm's settlements, including securities and money transfers.

Wednesday night was the first of many sleepless ones for Edith O'Brien, the 46-year-old assistant treasurer at MF Global's Chicago office. O'Brien was listed on the firm's organizational chart as being part of the "liquidity management" team, which included "cash management" and "meeting regulatory requirements." She oversaw 48 separate bank accounts and was charged with moving funds between the accounts, as well as keeping track of both the firm's and the customers' money. Due to their lack of automated functions and support staff, the firm relied heavily on O'Brien for liquidity management. Beginning Wednesday night, O'Brien stopped leaving the office altogether, choosing instead to nap periodically on a bench.

She wasn't the only one who had taken up residence inside the MF Global office. CEO Jon Corzine, too, was now sleeping at his office in New York. He sensed the impending disaster that was to befall MF Global, but he wasn't going down without a fight. Employees would later say that Corzine fought for the firm with everything he had, doing anything in his power and calling in any favor he could in order to save the company from bankruptcy.

* * *

On Thursday, October 27, the morning news was once again not good for MF Global. Their credit rating had been cut to junk by both Moody's and Fitch, a move which triggered JP Morgan, as their clearing bank, to place the firm on "debit alert." That new status meant that all money and securities transfers in and out of MF Global were slowed considerably, and they're access to intra-day credit was terminated.

Intra-day credit is basically an extremely short-term loan. Typically an intra-day credit loan is for a few hours at most, and it is used to facilitate the delivery of securities. When JP Morgan took away MF Global's ability to borrow those funds, it meant that all funds required for the clearing of securities had to be in the MF Global account, a balance that was by now sliding to new depths. It was yet another set of handcuffs placed on the financial arms of the dying company.

Tellingly, JP Morgan also restricted MF Global's ability to access their own accounts online. Clearly the clearing bank had concerns, and they were watching every move MF Global made in regard to their money. Meanwhile, margin requirements continued to increase for MF Global's trades, with the LCH.Clearnet margin topping $665 million, an increase of more than $60 million over the past day's amount.

On that Thursday, when the previous night's erroneous transfer had been discovered, initially MF Global tried to reverse the faulty $165 million transfer – an action called "back value" – from the day before, but the money was already gone and they had no access to their JP Morgan accounts. Ordinarily, the clearing bank would have let the reversal go through and approved it; but again, they were closely monitoring MF Global's activities, and they refused to allow the reversal to go through. They, MF Global, had no choice but to drain their remaining credit on the "revolver" to cover the cash shortfall, now thought to be about $165 million.

At that point, two regulators from the CME Group made an unannounced visit to the Chicago offices of MF Global, saying that there were some "immaterial discrepancies" in money transfers. They requested documentation on the seg funds, and began poring over them. Soon after, they emailed three MF Global officials – including the firm's general counsel – notifying them that "effective immediately, any equity withdrawals from MF Global's brokerage unit much be approved in writing by the CME Group." In other words, MF Global was now in the position of having to ask written permission in order to access their own money.

* * *

The Financial Services Authority (FSA) is the securities and banking regulatory agency based in the United Kingdom. Wielding something close to judicial power, the agency operates independently of the government, despite the fact that its board members are all appointed by the governmental treasury, and functions most like the SEC in the United States. The Financial Services and Markets Act of 2000 bestowed on the FSA four major tasks: maintaining confidence in the market; protecting the stability of the United Kingdom's financial system; protecting consumers; and working to curtail financially related crimes.

One tool in the FSA's arsenal that the organization uses to carry out its collective mandate is the requirement of a "liquidity buffer" to be held by all banks operating under its jurisdiction. The amount of the buffer varies from bank to bank, and is determined for each bank by the FSA. In addition to the amount, the FSA also regulates the types of securities that can be used as part of the liquidity buffer, securities that are labeled "near cash." Appropriate securities include central-bank deposits and government-issued securities. The thought behind the requirement is that such a buffer will ensure that a bank has the needed funds to survive a financial catastrophe like the one MF Global found itself in the middle of.

The MF Global office in London had approximately $600 million in working capital, plus a $500 million buffer – as required by the FSA – that they kept at the Bank of New York Mellon (BNYM) in London. Given the current situation, the London office felt it wise to access their liquidity buffer, which again was there for just such an emergency. They planned to withdraw all their securities – the buffer consisted exclusively of government-issued securities – and either sell or loan them in the repo market to raise much-needed cash.

Personnel from the London office contacted BYNM in the morning, explaining their need to raise capital and requesting that BNYM release the "liquidity buffer" securities. MF Global personnel were told that they would have to speak directly with the specific bank manager who handled such requests and were transferred to that manager's direct line. Whoever answered the phone there replied that the man in question was "away from his desk," and they'd need to call back. About an hour later, on the second attempt, the manager was reportedly "in a meeting," and the third call resulted in the manager's being "out to lunch." On the fourth try to reach the manager, the answer was blunt: "He'll call you back."

He never did. And MF Global was never able to gain access to their liquidity buffer. Without access to their own funds, they would need more cash from their New York office ASAP to send into LCH.Clearnet for the next margin call.

While the London office was struggling in vain to get at their liquidity buffer, Citibank, just like JP Morgan in New York, had sent a representative from its London office to "advise" on the clearing of securities directly into the MF Global London offices. For the most part, settlements flowed well throughout the course of that Thursday. But at the end of the day, there were many small trades and a single large trade that were not settling. It was a large Spanish stock transaction that represented a buy from ICAP and a sell to Macquarie, both considered reasonably high quality counterparties. The deal was worth over a few hundred million euros, and there was no apparent reason as to why the trade was being held up.

Initially the Citibank representatives explained that they were waiting to see MF Global's credit line usage for the day; they needed approval from the New York office before they'd settle the trade. The only thing the Citi representatives would tell them was that the Citi computer system would not process the trade, so it was out of their hands.

The actual explanation for why the trade wasn't settling was because Citibank had reduced MF Global's credit line to zero while they made a global assessment of their risk exposure to MF Global, and there wasn't any credit available to clear the trades. In reality, there was no risk to Citi associated with the trade, as it was a matched buy and sell, meaning the transaction had been prearranged with both the buyer and the seller. All that needed to happen was the settlement, and everybody would get what they wanted.

As the MF Global employees grew weary of what they perceived as a bureaucratic game being played out by Citibank, they literally took matters into their own hands. They stood in front of the door of the office occupied by the Citibank employee from the outside blocking the door from opening and refused to let him leave until the trade had settled. A few minutes later, the trade miraculously cleared.

Back in New York, the situation was much the same as it had been in London; both JP Morgan and the Depository Trust Company (DTC) were not settling MF Global trades. Like JP Morgan a day earlier, DTC had placed a credit restriction on MF Global's clearing account for corporate bonds, stocks and for U.S. Treasuries through their subsidiary, Fixed Income Clearing Corp (FICC). The credit restriction included the requirement for MF Global to send more margin money to DTC and FICC refused to return over $100 million in margin money owed to MF Global. It was as if all the clearing accounts had been frozen and no money was moving either way. In the hopes of speeding things up, MF Global transferred some cash from its BONY "house account" to JP Morgan and DTC. The expectation was the money would be returned to MF Global at the end of the day after all the trades had settled. JP Morgan declined to return the cash and it left MF Global's cash, at least what seemed to be their cash, in even shorter supply.

With no access to their "liquidity buffer," the JP Morgan clearing group in London also seemed to be dragging its collective feet in terms of settling MF Global wire transfers and requested more margin. Whereas JP Morgan had previously settled wire transfers by taking into account the balances of other currencies in the account, they now refused MF Global credit for these funds. It was obvious that JP Morgan had its own agenda and had grave concerns about the activities at MF Global. No doubt they were using whatever means to accumulate as much of a margin buffer and leveraging that by refusing to clear MF Global's trades otherwise. Their concerns, as it turns out, were well grounded.

By day's end, the deficiency in the customer seg fund accounts had climbed to $413 million.

* * *

For many office workers in America, Friday is a day to look forward to. The simultaneous end of the workweek and the beginning of the weekend, the day has been regaled throughout popular culture, from song titles to restaurant names. But for the employees of MF Global, Friday, October 28, was not a day to look forward to. Rather, it was the day of final reckoning.

JP Morgan had taken complete control of securities settlements, and lack of intra-day credit prevented many securities from being released and delivered to clients. The delays resulted in calls from angry clients complaining that MF Global was failing to deliver securities. Margin calls were coming in from all corners, and the firm was struggling to keep track of all of them. So common were margin calls by Friday that they barely registered with many of the traders when even the Federal Reserve actually issued two of its own margin calls against MF Global-held mortgage-backed securities.

Early on Friday morning, Jon Corzine received word that the London office had overdrawn its account at JP Morgan, and needed an immediate infusion of $175 million. As long as the account was under-margined, JP Morgan refused to clear any European securities or participate in any MF Global auction liquidation. Business was at a standstill until the overdraft was cleared up. Upon learning of this, Corzine took it upon himself to personally phone Edith O'Brien in Chicago. He told her to "resolve the issues," though it's unclear what he expected her to actually do.

There is an old saying about not being able to get blood from a stone, and it was a perfect cliché to describe MF Global's situation. The New York office literally had no available cash to send to London. The revolver was maxed out, and there was no capital available in the firm's accounts.

O'Brien then sent an email to Vinay Mahajan, the MF global treasurer. "I need $175 million sent immediately," she wrote. Mahajan responded, "Edith, if you don't hear from London in the next five minutes, please provide them funds today to cover this overdraft position." He didn't suggest how O'Brien should make the money materialize or offer ideas as to where she might find it. He only said that JP Morgan was "HOLDING UP VITAL BUSINESS IN THE U.S. AS A RESULT" of the overdrawn account. His use of all capitals reflected the frenzied chaos that was engulfing the firm.

Emails were flying across the network – and across the Atlantic – at a furious pace. The head of the treasury department in the London office sent an email to New York asking for $175 million immediately. He followed that up with another email that said, "Edith just said she is paying us $175 until our repo settles."

At about 9:30, O'Brien sent instructions to have $175 million sent from the MF Global New York account to London; almost simultaneously, she instructed JP Morgan to move $200 million out of customer seg funds and make it available for MF Global's use. In an act that can only be called that of a woman trying to cover her own ass because she knows she's doing something questionable, O'Brien forwarded the email she'd been copied on from the London office announcing that she would be sending funds to several members of MF Global management. The only addition she made to the email was to add the phrase "Per JC's direct instructions" as an introduction to Jon Corzine's call she'd received earlier that morning.

The transfers did not go unnoticed by the JP Morgan personnel who were still in residence at the MF Global office. They decided to research the transaction, and noted that it originated right after a $200 million transfer from a customer account. There was a notation that the money was to be repaid after the London office settled a repo transaction, but sirens were going off for the JP Morgan employees. In other words, $200 million had been transferred from a customer account to the firm's account, and then $175 million went to London. In that order.

Soon after that, Corzine got word that money had been possibly withdrawn from customer seg accounts. He called Edith O'Brien in Chicago, demanding an explanation. He wanted assurances that she hadn't wired customer funds to London. It was, according to Corzine, the first he'd heard of any customer seg funds being withdrawn for operational costs.

According to Corzine, O'Brien reassured him, telling him the money that had been wired to London had been wired from a house account. It was a lie of omission at best, assuming that the conversation went the way Corzine said it did. While technically the money that was wired to London had originated from an MF Global house account, the money in that account had originated from a customer seg account.

Corzine would later use this conversation – without any kind of corroborating evidence to support his claims – as evidence he had no idea what happened with the customer seg funds. He would say that the back office "explicitly" said that that the transfer was legal. He would go on to deny that he ever approved the movement of seg funds to the house account, reiterating the fact that Edith O'Brien "explicitly confirmed to [him] that the funds were properly transferred."

Later in the day, Jon Corzine got an anxious phone call from Barry Zubrow, the chief risk officer at JP Morgan. Zubrow was concerned about the transfer that had been approved earlier in the morning. Specifically, he was worried that customer funds had been used inappropriately. Zubrow was certain that MF Global was using customer seg funds to cover their money problems abroad. Corzine assured him that that was not the case, but Zubrow wanted written confirmation of that fact, so he told Corzine he'd send a letter saying "no customer funds had been used," and that O'Brien, as the one who'd authorized the transfer in the first place, should sign and return it.

The letter, when it arrived, asked for written assurance the $175 million that had been transferred from MF Global's Chicago office to the London office had come from MF Global's own account and not any customer account. It seemed pretty cut and dried. If she'd done it the way she'd said she did it, then there was nothing to worry about. But O'Brien refused to sign the letter.

Both Laurie Ferber and Dennis Klejna, the MF Global general counsel and deputy general counsel, respectively, worked on a revision of the letter, which they then sent to O'Brien again for her signature. She replied to both via email, stating that she was too busy to focus on the letter. To Klejna, she said that she was "swamped dealing with customer wires," and to Ferber that she had "numerous moving parts under critical deadlines." Both attorneys got the same message, though. She wouldn't sign it.

A third draft of the letter would make its way from the JP Morgan office to the MF Global office, this one seemingly more benign than the first two. O'Brien still refused to sign. To her mind, it wasn't appropriate for her to be signing the letter, as she wasn't a company officer. She felt that it was better to have a member of management sign it, but Corzine was insistent that it should be O'Brien's signature at the bottom of the page. The subtext of the situation was that MF Global management didn't want to take responsibility for the transfer. Instead, they were looking – and hoped they'd found – a "fall guy" in the person of Edith O'Brien, who individually could take the fall for the entire company.

* * *

Throughout the day on that fateful Friday, the employees of MF Global operations were struggling to reconcile the previous day's securities settlements. For those who have never tried to reconcile settlement bank balances before, rest assured that, even for a small bank, it's a profoundly complicated operation. Factor in to that difficulty the fact that MF Global was a behemoth, international firm – a firm that

lacked sufficient technology to do the reconciliation electronically –
and the process becomes exponentially more difficult.

The CME regulators that were in Chicago asked to view the
documents relating to the seg funds, which they examined for some
time. They concluded that everything looked fine to them, and they left
for the weekend. However, through the reconciliation process, it was
discovered that there was a noticeable discrepancy in the seg funds. As
the day wore on, the deficit mysteriously grew.

It was a staggering sum of money that had disappeared. In fact,
because it was such a huge number, the operations group worked under
the assumption that it had to be some kind of accounting error that was
causing the discrepancy. Employees said that it was "simply too large to
be accurate." It is still unclear today whether or not anyone in the
operations group in Chicago reported the discrepancy to anyone,
though CFO Christine Serwinksi would later say in a tacit
acknowledgement that she knew, though she was "under the belief that
there must have been an accounting error, because such a large deficit
was simply inconceivable."

Because they were looking for a billion dollars that appeared to
be missing, the operations group concluded that a $540 million BONY
money wire must have been booked incorrectly. Specifically, it must
have been booked backward as a debit instead of a credit. And that was
close enough to the amount they were looking for to make them believe
they'd found the problem. Everyone heaved a sigh of relief. The $540
million adjustment was reversed in the books, and the books were in
balance.

Corzine was told by the operations group that, as a result of "an
erroneous $540 million manual adjustment," the balance had appeared
to negative. However, upon examination, they'd discovered the
problem and corrected it, which had resulted in the firm actually having
an excess of liquidity in the amount of approximately $150 million. So
instead of an exorbitantly negative balance, they were happy to report
that the firm had a financial cushion.

But the problems didn't end there. At 4:27 that afternoon, it
became clear that there were missing funds that couldn't be explained
by a reversed transaction. The customer seg fund accounts were short
$952 million, and nobody could come up with any explanation as to

where the money had gone. Matt Hughey, an employee in the controller's office in New York, sent an email to the firm's assistant controller, in which he asked if his instructions were to "give [the regulators] the preliminary [report] showing the $(952) seg deficit?"

The Chicago office stuck to their story about an accounting error – that was the only plausible story that could explain the missing funds – and that was the answer that was given to the regulators, as well as senior management in New York.

As the sun set on Friday – an apt metaphor for MF Global's future – after much computation and vague explanations, the seg accounts would ultimately show a final deficiency of $891 million. Compounding that deficit was that the margin call for LCH.Clearnet would creep up to $973 million by the open of business on the next Monday.

The falcon, it seemed, had flown too far from the falconer to hear that the Second Coming was imminent.

CHAPTER FOURTEEN

Interactive Brokers

Deus ex machina is a classic dramatic plot twist that involves the resolution of a given situation through intervention by the gods. It is an unexplainable act with no basis in human experience that serves to solve plot problems that are otherwise seemingly irresolvable. It is, to use a sports metaphor, a Hail Mary pass with no time left on the clock. When ideas fail the writer who's trying to wrap up the twisted plot he's created, he calls in the gods to clean up the mess he's wrought to this point. It's brilliant, because nobody can argue it. After all, it's the will of the gods. So it must be truthful.

In real life, there are plenty of times when things happen that humans can't explain, and often these incidents need a resolution that cannot be fixed by human means. By Thursday, October 26, it was clear that MF Global was not going to survive, without some sort of *deus ex machina*. The board of directors was notified by regulators that "in the absence of a solution acceptable to them, they will exercise their powers on Monday to seize the assets of the company's regulated businesses." In layman's terms, that meant that MF Global was about to be foreclosed upon if they didn't come up with a solution to their existing financial nightmare. They needed a Hail Mary.

The search was immediately begun to locate a buyer for the dying business. It was a last-ditch effort and the hopes were truly slim. Just to make a bad situation worse, they had until Monday to find a buyer. It was *deus ex machina* time. For MF Global, the receiver they threw their Hail Mary to was a firm called Evercore Partners, an investment advisory firm with a history of advising major corporations in uncomfortable financial dealings. At about the same time, MF Global got a call from CME Group and despite CME's declaration that they had what was described as a "very motivated buyer," nothing ever came of the potential acquisition.

The team at Evercore got to work looking for the buyer for MF Global, and by Saturday, they had identified Interactive Brokers as the most likely candidate to take over the struggling investment firm. There were other potential buyers who'd been identified, to be sure. Heavyweights like JP Morgan Chase (who acquired the defunct Bear Stearns in 2008 in what many called the investment bank sale of the century), Goldman Sachs, The Bank of New York Mellon, and Jeffries were on the list, but Interactive Brokers was the favorite, especially since they were the only ones to actually make an offer. They had tried, at one point, to buy Refco, and had actually had discussions with MF Global to purchase the firm several months earlier. Their willingness to act quickly made them the most likely candidate, and MF Global pursued that angle.

Interactive Brokers, is a highly rated online brokerage firm that is considered one of the best in the business. Headquartered in Greenwich, Connecticut, the firm specializes in futures brokerage and stock-based market-making. Interactive, given the niche they fill, is not a personnel-heavy business. Their virtual existence means they operate the vast majority of their operations via the Internet, and financial efficiency is one of their selling points.

Self-made billionaire Thomas Peterffy is the brains behind Interactive Brokers, having built the firm from scratch beginning in 1993. Born in Budapest, Hungary, in 1944, Peterffy emigrated to the United States in 1965. He arrived in New York City speaking no English, but determined to make a name for himself and to realize the oft-mythicized American Dream. He began his professional career in New York as a computer programmer, but soon realized he had a knack for trading options. He bought his own seat on the American Stock Exchange in 1977, and started making his own fortune. He founded Interactive Brokers in 1993 and 20 years later, found himself worth an estimated $5.4 billion. American Dream realized.

Peterffy is also known for secrecy. Though the main office is a large office building based in Greenwich, the executive offices are tucked away nearby. The executive office address is not listed on the website or in the financial statements. It's located in a small Greenwich office park, away from the main roads and virtually in the woods. There's no "Interactive Brokers" sign on the building, on the door or in the elevator to indicate the financial heavyweights who work inside.

Another marked difference between Interactive Brokers and the firm they'd targeted for acquisition lay in the amount of revenues each firm generated from interest margin spread. Whereas MF Global relied heavily on the revenues generated from investing client margin, Peterffy was much more conservative in his approach. Interactive Brokers didn't charge clients a mark-up on interest rates on their margin balances, so the firm didn't make the eye-popping numbers for much of their history. But as the race between the tortoise and the hare taught us, slow and steady wins the race. When interest rates dropped to near zero, Interactive Brokers felt no major impact on the profitability of their business, leaving them in strong financial shape while other futures firms were struggling.

With the announcement that Interactive Brokers was in play as a potential buyer, MF Global went on the offensive. On Saturday, October 29, a "war room" was set up at the headquarters, and executives from both firms were in contact throughout the day. As a part of their requisite due diligence, Interactive Brokers reviewed MF's books, those same books that indicated a discrepancy with the seg funds.

When they were initially asked about the missing seg funds, MF Global personnel claimed the funds were all present, just not all accounted for. They blamed an accounting error – an oversight, even – and suggested that securities and cash had simply been recorded incorrectly. The sort of thing that happens all the time, and easily explained. In other words, it was nothing to worry about.

And in truth, such an accounting error was not completely unbelievable. A review of the accounting practices employed by MF Global earlier that year showed they were relying on an antiquated system for determining the correct account balances. The system they used did not specifically look at the customer seg funds held at their clearing bank, JP Morgan, which meant they could honestly say they had no idea how much was in the accounts. It was equivalent to an argument in a marriage between a husband and wife, with one spouse telling the other how much is in their bank account, with no one really sure how much is there. Call it an honest oversight, call it willful negligence. Either way, their ignorance was, albeit on a small scale, a viable defense.

The team from Interactive Brokers did not rely on MF Global's accounting system, and instead went straight to the source. They examined and re-examined several days' worth of seg funds reports provided by JP Morgan. Their feeling was that if the money was where it was supposed to be, those statements would say so. In other words, the statements from JP Morgan were the financial gospel that told the absolute truth, the gospel according to John Pierpont Morgan. Unfortunately for MF Global, that gospel didn't quite jive with what they were claiming. The JP Morgan accounts showed deficits in the seg funds accounts for three full days. There was definitely client money missing.

At that point, things got harder for MF Global to explain. Go back to the discussion between husband and wife about the bank balance. The husband reviews the bank statement and discovers money missing – let's say several hundred dollars, for our purposes here – and he wants to know exactly where it went. His wife, at this point, has a couple of options. She can fall on her sword, admit that she bought a gorgeous pair of Christian Louboutin shoes, and offer the excuse that she bought them so she could look pretty. Alternatively, she can continue to back-pedal and say that there's another explanation. Both have their own set of pitfalls, especially the latter. In the end, as the old saying goes, the truth always comes out.

In the case of MF Global, they opted not to heed the inevitability of the truth's emergence and instead clung to the increasingly unlikely tale of funds misplacement. Given the limited amount of time they had, perhaps their excuse could be forgiven, though clearly they should have gone with the truth. Interactive Brokers informed MF Global personnel that the seg funds were "not exactly" all at JP Morgan, and it prompted a conference call for a more detailed explanation.

During that call, MF Global's treasurer Edith O'Brien gave her version of what happened. "I was told to send the wire," she explained. "I sent the wire. But the money never came back." She went on to say that she'd done the same thing the next day, sending money wires as instructed, but the money never came back. The long and the short of the conference call was that MF Global had sent out funds to settle securities, but those funds never came back. For their part, the MF Global folks on the call agreed, saying that the funds did seem to be missing. But they left it at that, leaving out any suggestion of culpability on their part. If the funds hadn't come back, it wasn't their fault. Attempting to resolve that little hiccup would take up the better part of the entire weekend for Interactive Brokers.

Upstairs, MF Global executives, Evercore Partners, and Interactive Brokers leaders finally reached a deal, at least on paper. As a precursor to the acquisition, MF Global would declare Chapter 11 bankruptcy, and then transfer control of client accounts to Interactive Brokers. In exchange, Interactive Brokers would pay $1 billion to MF Global for effectively all of their assets. Given the situation, it seemed like fair deal for both sides, but it had a few strings attached.

The founder of Interactive Brokers would be financing the deal with $800 million from his own personal account, but he couldn't get the full amount to MF Global on Monday, he could only get $750 million, followed by another payment of $50 million on Tuesday. Peterffy asked them, "Is that okay?" The remainder would be paid when the deal closed. It was an agreement that a firm in a less precarious situation would have questioned, but MF Global was not in the position to question any suitor at this point. Not surprisingly, the financially destitute firm agreed without hesitation.

While they were waiting for the deal to finalize, MF Global would oversee the reduction of proprietary positions held by its subsidiaries, and the deal would require the approval of a variety of regulatory agencies. Assuming all the conditions were met, the deal would go forward. MF Global would become part of Interactive Brokers, and everyone would be at least content, if not happy. At least they thought.

The question always comes up in a situation like this about what the buyer hopes to gain from the acquisition. Especially in the financial sector – where both sides are convinced they're getting the better end of the deal – one has to question the motives of a buyer who accepts a sketchy explanation for missing client funds to buy a firm that will be bankrupt. And all for the low, low price of a billion dollars.

Interactive Brokers, for their part, saw a diamond in the rough. Peterffy felt that MF Global had a large amount of profitable customer accounts; they just needed to be squashed into the mold he created to realize their potential. It was, on one level, a micro version of a leveraged buyout. Peterffy would assume control of the firm, cut the number of personnel that he saw as a drain on profits, and make the new lean and mean MF Global a part of Interactive Brokers. Peterffy said that MF Global employed "3,000 people to do the work that maybe 1,000 could do." Cut out the fat and largess, and, at least in Peterffy's mind, MF Global's business would be on the road to financial success.

But a funny thing happened on the way to Nirvana, and that was a sticky little academic subject called math. Interactive Brokers personnel had been scouring the books, searching desperately for the misplaced funds that would explain the discrepancy in the seg funds. In the afternoon on Sunday, October 30, the accounting and operations staff realized there was no explanation that anyone could find; $952 million was missing, plain and simple. It hadn't been misallocated, it hadn't been deposited in a different account. The MF Global seg funds were short nearly a billion dollars, though the search for the money continued anyway.

At 6:00 p.m., Edith O'Brien announced what seemed like a solution to the missing funds question. It was sort of a *deus ex machina* within a *deus ex machine*: "There has been an item(s) identified that may offset the seg debit. The figure appears to be @ 900 million. Matt and I shared this with both the CME and CFTC…Jason is proving this out," she wrote in an email. The "Matt" she references in the email is Matthey Hughey, the firm's regulatory capital controller. The person referred to as "Jason" is Jason Chenoweth, the one involved in the seg fund movements earlier in the week.

It took a half an hour after that for the treasury team to accept the truth, and it wasn't a pleasant discovery. There was, in fact, no offsetting item. They determined with a high degree of certainty that nothing offset the apparent imbalance; the actual amount the seg funds were missing totaled $952,047,822. Additionally, the $540 million adjustment from a few days earlier on October 28 was, in fact, wrong.

That meant that the deficit on Thursday, October 27 had really been $339,821,088.

Whether or not she knew the extent of the firm's financial misdeeds is another matter; she was cognizant that things were not as they should be. O'Brien's culpability would come into question in later weeks, when friends of hers would come forward in later days to defend her, saying she'd been set up to be a corporate patsy by her bosses at MF Global.

Still, despite even those "discoveries," there was no smoking gun to explain the missing seg funds; by 11:00 p.m., that information had no yet trickled upstairs, and all systems still seemed a go. The deal was going to go through, and people had finally begun to shuffle their tired ways out of the office where they'd been holed up for the weekend. The division chief of the Securities and Exchange Commission was emailed with the details of the deal, and everyone fully expected the deal would go through.

At approximately 11:30 p.m., the phone rang in the MF Global CFO's office, and Henri Steenkamp was informed by his counterpart at Interactive Brokers that the missing seg funds still had not been accounted for. Further, it was determined there was no error in accounting, no overlooked bank account, no oversight in classifying a deposit. The money was missing, it had been transferred out of the firm, no two ways about it.

Following that phone call, Steenkamp took a few moments to think to himself about what to do. One can imagine a Japanese Kamikaze pilot who's just been told he's about to take off on a suicide mission. The pilot would toast his homeland with a final glass of sake, strap dynamite to his body, and board his plane. As he taxied his plane down the runway and climbed into the sky, he'd take a last farewell glance over his shoulder at the county he loved, then turn his attention to blowing himself up in the hopes of inflicting damage on an enemy naval ship. Once he'd taken off, there was no going back. Steenkamp needed to rally his inner Kamikaze before doing what he had to do.

At midnight, Steenkamp finally worked up his resolve enough to go into the boardroom to address everyone still there. He gave them the unfortunate news that Interactive Brokers had searched high and low for the missing seg funds, but their efforts had proved futile. While offering them the carrot that the search would continue, he tempered that optimism by telling them there was no rational explanation for where the money had gone. It was, as the Interactive Broker CFO had told him, just plain gone.

At some time after 1:00 a.m. on Monday, two things were crystal clear to both teams. One, the missing seg funds were gone, and nobody from MF Global could offer an explanation that made any sense as to where the money had gone. It had, for all intents and purposes, evaporated into thin air. There was no way for either side to resolve the missing money.

The other obvious thing was that the deal was not going through. Upon learning of the finality of the missing money saga, Peterffy pulled the plug on the acquisition. The money was gone and MF Global could neither dispute that fact nor explain what had happened to it. Peterffy would later comment, "There is a big difference in having a substantial amount of time and putting accounts onto our technology in an organized manner versus taking in a bunch of accounts where you have no idea of how much money these accounts made or lost since last Friday." One investment banker had suggested that Peterffy buy MF Global for a dollar, more or less a token sale. Peterffy declined the offer, as even a token sale was more risk than he was willing to assume.

The deus had spoken. There would be no eleventh-hour stay to keep MF Global alive. It was over.

* * *

Halloween, in its original incarnation, was a celebration held the night before the Christian feast of All Hallows, thus the original name ascribed to the holiday, "All Hallows Eve." Despite its Christian etymology, there is a school of thought that traces the roots of the holiday to more pagan traditions. In ancient Celtic traditions, the day was thought to be when the natural and supernatural worlds were closely linked, and festival participants would invoke the powers of various gods to help them ward off the evil spirits. For the Christians, All Hallows – or All Saints Day, in the more modern vernacular – was a time for praying to the saints, as well as for the souls of those who had died recently.

Today, children relish the holiday as a night when rules about candy seem to go out the window. Costumed trick-or-treaters make the rounds of local houses, bags in hand, hoping to unearth the mother lode of candy by night's end. It's a time of fun – albeit paired with a little bit of fright – for everyone involved.

Suffice it to say, though, that Halloween 2011 was not one for the memory book for MF Global. This particular Monday morning was worse than most at MF Global, because at 10:30 a.m., they officially filed for Chapter 11 bankruptcy protection. It was, without a doubt, the only protection that they had left. There were no other buyers on the horizon, and the specter of missing seg funds was looming large. It would be a matter of time before the firm was called to account for itself.

As soon as the news was public, the last remaining financial crutches of MF Global were knocked out from under them, one at a time. First came the announcement from the Federal Reserve that MF Global's status as a primary dealer had been revoked. That meant that MF Global would no longer be allowed to serve as a counterparty in financial transactions with the Fed, which was an immediate indication all that the federal government had lost faith in the firm's financial solvency. That action was quickly followed by Fixed Income Clearing Corporation's ending MF Global's membership, an action that tied MF Global's hands in terms of settling transactions. And if securities couldn't settle, they couldn't make the money in their business.

As the day wore on, the news only got worse. At 3:07 p.m., the declaration came down from CME that all futures trading for MF Global and its clients would be restricted to liquidation sales only, meaning that there could be trading by anyone. If you had a position, you could liquidate it for cash. That was your only option, no pun intended. At 6:30 p.m., CME sent down another order, this one directed specifically at MF Global itself. The firm was ordered to liquidate the entirety of its own futures holdings, regardless of loss. There would be no more futures business conducted by the futures brokerage firm of MF Global.

The salt in the wound at the end of the day was the ugly pimple that was the firm's seg funds. At close of business – if you can call it that – on Monday, October 31, the MF Global seg funds showed a deficit of approximately $891 million. It seemed increasingly likely that All Hallows 2011 would include a short prayer for the soul of the dearly departed MF Global.

CHAPTER FIFTEEN

Liquidation

The first recorded instance of the term "fire sale" is thought to come from an advertisement posted by Maraton Upton, a resident of Fitchburg, Massachusetts, who had suffered through a massive fire at his home in December 1856. Following the destruction, Upton no doubt needed money for recovery, so he took out an advertisement that read in part, "Extraordinary fire sale; customers are invited to call and examine goods which are still warm."

These days fire sale is a term used in many facets of American life. Regardless of the setting, however, the meaning is almost always the same: something is for sale, condition notwithstanding, for significantly less than it would cost new. For that matter, not only is it less than a discounted price, the term implies the items are being sold at a drastically reduced price.

As the sun rose on Monday, October 31, MF Global was, for all intents and purposes, defunct. The firm had access to no more cash reserves on which to draw, legal or otherwise. It was, to quote a cliché, all over but the crying. There was no trading the firm's positions or executing sales for customers on Monday; despite being Halloween, there would be neither tricks nor treats for the employees of MF Global. Rather, there would be legal formalities, while the firm sought the somewhat paradoxical relief of bankruptcy.

The initial bankruptcy paperwork had been filed the day before, and the action represented the fourth-largest financial bankruptcy filing in the history of the United States. While Jon Corzine originally hoped a buyer would materialize – what is affectionately known as a "white knight" in the financial world – the revelation that the firm couldn't explain hundreds of millions of dollars of missing customer funds put an end to any thought of that salvation. The only option left was for MF Global to declare bankruptcy and hope for the best.

Declaring bankruptcy is not quite as simple as a two-word description might imply. For starters, there are several different classifications of bankruptcy an entity may declare, the most common being Chapter 11. Chapter 11 is a tool used for reorganization, which is a nice way of saying that it's used by people and businesses who are over their heads with debt and need relief in order to continue with their everyday lives or to continue operating their lives or business. A committee determines a specific plan and places requirements on the entity declaring bankruptcy. Assuming the bankrupt entity keeps to the plan and meets the obligations set forth by the committee, they are granted a blank financial state, albeit one that comes with a marred credit record.

Chapter 11 is substantially different from Chapter 7, which is a bankruptcy proceeding that is specific to businesses. In the event a business finds itself without the ability to continue operations and pay its debts, it may petition for Chapter 7 protection. If that petition is granted, the business ceases any and all operations, and declares itself as no longer in operation. Control of the company is transferred to a trustee appointed by the court, and that trustee oversees the sale of all company assets. The money generated by the sale is used to pay off as many of the outstanding debts as possible.

A key difference between the two types of bankruptcy is that Chapter 11 allows the company to continue operations, whereas Chapter 7 does not. However, Chapter 7 has the advantage – from a business's perspective – of allowing a company to unwind itself and to continue looking for a buyer.

But for a brokerage firm like MF Global to qualify for Chapter 11 bankruptcy, the brokerage component had to be separated from the larger MF Global Holdings, the parent company of all the subsidiaries. The separation of the broker-dealer from the holding company filing was set up prior to Monday morning's court appearance, but during the court proceeding the two became surprisingly reattached.

Kenneth Ziman was the attorney representing MF Global Holdings, and he entered the courtroom on that Monday morning intent on securing Chapter 11 protection for both MF Global Holdings and the broker-dealer, MF Global. There was no attorney specifically representing the broker-dealer, so the job fell on the holding company's attorney. He'd spent the night before preparing his case, which was built on a shaky foundation. The major issue, of course, was the missing money. No doubt he was relieved to know that he'd be presenting his case to Judge Martin Glenn, a former colleague of Ziman's with whom he worked at another law firm several years prior.

Per the bankruptcy code, "The court shall order the appointment of a trustee…for cause, including fraud, dishonesty, incompetence, or gross mismanagement of the affairs of the debtor by current management," so everyone was expecting a Chapter 7 filing for the broker-dealer. Since missing customer funds were expected to be determined to have been the result of fraudulent activity engaged in by MF Global personnel, the attorney's petition for Chapter 11 would be denied. At least that was the expectation.

In court that morning, the presiding judge asked Ziman about the missing money. Ziman replied, "All funds are accounted for, and I'm talking about the broker-dealer." In other words, Ziman was denying in open court that there was any money missing from MF Global, customer money or otherwise.

Or was he?

It's interesting that the attorney didn't openly declare, "No money is missing," or "There are no missing funds." He said that "all funds are accounted for." By saying that all money was "accounted for," there is a chance that Ziman was operating in a legal gray area. Accounting for money simply means that you know where it is. It is not a definitive declaration that all money is exactly where it should be. It's just a statement that you know where it is.

Regardless of what he actually meant, the mood in the courtroom was one of patent disbelief. Spectators in the courtroom – a group that included regulators from both the SEC and the CFTC – looked at each other in shock, as if they wanted to make sure they'd all heard the attorney correctly. Additionally, and more importantly, the legal interpretation by the judge seemed to be that Ziman was saying the more affirmative, "No funds are missing." Whether Ziman misspoke in court – or if he was simply wrong – didn't matter. The Chapter 11 application was approved by the judge.

The approval meant that MF Global – both the brokerage firm and the larger holding company – had officially collapsed. It also meant that every asset the company still owned would be liquidated, and that every employee on the payrolls would lose their jobs. There would be no sale of the business and all customer accounts would be temporarily frozen. From there, trustees and liquidators would take control of the proceedings, selling off everything associated with the dead firm.

All things considered, the whole process of placing MF Global into Chapter 11 protection was rushed, and there were many problems with it. For starters, Chapter 11 is commonly used to reorganize a business and provides substantial advantages to creditors because the business can continue operations without a trustee. Chapter 7, on the other hand, is used for the liquidation of and sales of broker-dealers, as was the case with Refco a few years earlier. So the decision to place the firm under Chapter 11 didn't make a lot of sense on the surface.

Another issue arose when the Securities Investor Protection Corporation (SIPC) sought to get the liquidation rights to MF Global's brokerage business, despite the fact that the broker-dealer maintained approximately 38,000 futures customers and only 318 securities customers. One percent of the firm's customers qualified as securities clients, but that seemed to be sufficient to give liquidation powers to an organization that dealt with securities firms.

From the perspective of creditors like JP Morgan, DTC, and Bank of New York Mellon, the Chapter 11 outcome was the most favorable option, because it meant they would have more influence over the liquidation of the firm. But most significantly, the decision to place MF Global under Chapter 11 protection is that with two different entities, it meant two different trustees –each with different goals and agendas – would be overseeing halves of the same whole. And that doesn't take into account MF Global's UK operation that would be assigned its own dedicated trustee in London. All total, there would be three different trustees, each pursuing their own goals and agendas.

James Giddens was named the trustee of the broker-dealer component, MF Global. Giddens served as a special liquidations trustee for Lehman Brothers when that investment bank had collapsed. His job was to get money for U.S. customers and unwind the firm, a job that was complicated by many subsidiaries and accounts. It would take teams of lawyers over a year to get anywhere near finishing the job.

Louis Freeh was appointed as trustee for the holding company MF Global Holdings. Freeh was the former director of the Federal Bureau of Investigation, today probably better known as the man who spearheaded the investigation against former Penn State University assistant coach Jerry Sandusky, who was recently convicted on several charges. His task as trustee would be to recover money on behalf of the firm's creditors, while preserving whatever assets he could.

In London, the firm KPMG was appointed trustee. In the United Kingdom, an accounting firm is traditionally appointed to handle the unwinding of a London bank, but this job wouldn't be an easy one for KPMG; MF Global in London had over 3,300 claims from customers who wanted their money back.

Typically the process of liquidation doesn't take place – at least not in the legal sense – until after a company has gone into bankruptcy protection after the initial legal hearing. Once the process begins, the bankrupt firm starts selling the assets they still control. In the case of MF Global, that meant securities that they still managed, including the vast portfolio of foreign debt, corporate bonds and RTM trades.

* * *

In truth, the liquidation of MF Global's securities had begun a week earlier, on Monday, October 24 in a last-ditch attempt to save the firm from collapse. The liquidation began very slowly with the reluctance of Jon Corzine, who was still holding out hope that he'd be able to sell the firm before the unthinkable became reality. Whatever happened with MF Global, whatever it was to become, Corzine's business legacy would be forever linked to that finality. He would either go down in history as the man who managed to save MF Global by selling it in the nick of time, or as the man who oversaw the colossal collapse of yet another Wall Street investment bank.

On that Monday, MF Global had approximately $20 billion in assets that they needed to begin selling. Over $9 billion of that was made up of sovereign-debt RTM trades, with the remainder coming from positions they were holding in federal agency bonds, U.S. Treasuries, and other securities that included mortgage- and asset-backed securities, and miscellaneous corporate debt. And of those securities, some were being held in the firm's customer seg funds, an amount that approached $2 billion, split between commercial paper and corporate bonds. While no one was advocating a distressed sell-off just yet, there was a sense that something was imminent.

Early Tuesday morning, Corzine began quietly selling off some of the firm's European debt positions, despite his continued defense of the trades. But that wasn't the only suggestion that something was amiss. Corzine contacted Gary Cohn, president of Goldman Sachs, whom he worked with during his Goldman days, and asked for assistance in getting bids for the securities that MF Global was holding. All told, over the course of the day, Corzine managed to unload approximately $1.5 billion in the foreign-bond RTM positions. But as the firm's liquidity situation worsened by the end of the day on Tuesday, it was apparent that nothing short of divine intervention was going to save MF Global. The time had come to break the glass.

The firm's emergency plan outlined the conditions that defined the worst-case scenario. According to the Break-the-Glass plan, if two of the three conditions were met – or, even worse, if all three were met – it was time to "Activate [the] Contingency Funding Plan." And at around 7:00 Tuesday night, Corzine went with his chief operating officer Bradley Abelow to a meeting with J. C. Flowers, who happened to have an office in the same building. It was time to activate the plan.

Crisis management was the topic of discussion. The situation was dire, at best. Because clients were fleeing the firm and taking their money with them and credit lines were closing, MF Global needed to reduce the size of their trading positions, which meant they had to sell assets – fast. Assuming they could get fair prices for those assets, they expected they would get back much of the margin they'd used to fund their various positions, which would then ease the liquidity problems and might just keep them afloat a little longer. But that was a short-term solution at best. Problems of the magnitude like those facing MF Global didn't just go away. They needed to bail out while they still could. So the end result of the meeting was that the best course of action for MF Global would be to quickly sell assets en masse.

That was not necessarily the message that Corzine wanted to hear, however. It meant that he'd have to become someone he was unaccustomed to being, namely a trader forced to take losses in a trade he still believed in. He needed to sell, regardless of profit or loss, and unload his positions quickly. It went against every fiber of his being as a professional trader.

Every instinct in his psyche told Corzine that if he were just able to wait out the current storm, his trades would become profitable. It was just a matter of time. But time was a luxury not afforded to those men who oversaw companies on the verge of collapse. He would have to sell his positions, regardless of the losses those sales might incur, and regardless of what his brain was telling him. There were no other options available. This was, in every sense of the term, a fire sale.

On Wednesday morning, David Schamis, a managing director at J. C. Flowers and MF Global board member, moved in to an impromptu office inside an MF Global conference room to assist with the liquidation and help retain the services of an investment bank to pursue a sale of the firm while selling was still a realistic option.

Survival is perhaps the strongest instinct in any animal. Stories abound of wild animals willing to sacrifice their legs by chewing through their own flesh and bone to escape the clutches of a trap. Ted Tally posed the question in *Terra Nova*, his play about the race between Robert Scott of England and Roald Amundsen of Norway to be the first person to reach the South Pole: "Think of the fox, with his leg caught in a steel trap. He'll gnaw through his own flesh for the chance to save his life... *Become* the fox – feel the metal grinding into bone, smell your own hot blood running – and then ask yourself which it is you really love most: the leg or the trap?" At that very moment, Jon Corzine found himself in a similar position. He needed to decide whether he loved his trades more than the firm's survival.

Initially, it seems that Corzine favored survival, as he began to liquidate positions, albeit somewhat slowly and without the typical trader's aggression. He sold off some holdings in corporate bonds, but soon stopped. He just couldn't shake the trader mentality of avoiding losses, no matter what the cost. Maybe he decided he loved the trap more than the leg.

Corzine got on the phone with Gary Cohn, trying to negotiate mutually agreeable prices and to minimize the losses on his positions. The pair haggled, but could not agree on prices that Corzine could live with. He continued to drag his feet in liquidating the positions.

The MF Global senior management collectively decided that Corzine needed to abandon his principles in favor of doing what was best for the firm. He was attempting to "trade out" of the positions, one employee said, and he needed to "dump them, not trade them."

Corzine replied, with his trader mentality clearly taking center stage, "We need to keep something with some yield around here." He either didn't understand the peril the firm was facing or he was simply refusing to acknowledge it. Either way, it was decided that the RTM portfolio needed to be liquidated immediately. It was time to institute Project Plaza.

Though code-named operations seem more suited to military outfits and highly classified missions, MF Global had its own coded projects, and Project Plaza was one. It was the name ascribed to a confidential analysis done in conjunction with BlackRock about the sale of the RTM portfolio. BlackRock is a well-known New York-based money manager that also specializes in "risk management and business-process challenges." If anybody fit the bill for that description, it was MF Global at this exact moment in time.

The findings of Project Plaza determined that it would take five days in total to fully liquidate the sovereign-debt RTM portfolio, and that the liquidation would incur a net loss of approximately $280 million. It was a tough pill to swallow, to be sure. This was the can't-miss portfolio, the one that was guaranteed to turn a profit. Again, as Corzine say it, it was just a matter of time, a matter of waiting for the bonds to mature when they would mature and the firm would get back all the margin money at LCH.Clearnet. Fifty percent of the portfolio would be maturing at year's end, which was only two months away. But again, time was an enemy of MF Global. They just didn't have any.

What made the RTM trade liquidation process even more complex – and which necessitated the five-day window – was the fact that it wasn't simply a matter of selling off the positions. Selling the bonds was the easier part, albeit with large bid/asked spreads, but they had to unwind the repo portion of the trade. In essence, they were going to be executing reverse repo-to-maturity transactions, which meant borrowing back the securities they'd sold. That would require paying a financial premium for specific securities used as the collateral. Additionally, the bonds had to match the maturity dates of the original RTM transactions. All of those factors made unwinding the repo positions complex and incredibly time consuming.

On the chopping block Thursday morning in Chicago were the securities in the customer seg funds, specifically the commercial paper and corporate bond holding. In two large chunks, MF Global unloaded nearly $2 billion worth of commercial paper, taking losses on the sales. In the first and larger sale of the two, the firm sent $1.35 billion worth of commercial holdings to Goldman for $1.33 billion, incurring a loss of $15 million. But that was the tip of the iceberg in terms of losses, as the second round of sales, $418 million in the corporate bonds, went for a mere $384 million, costing MF Global $34 million. No doubt the folks at Goldman were reveling in their own good fortune while their counterparts at MF Global lamented the opposite.

The fire sale continued into Friday, when $4.5 billion worth of federal agency bonds went up for auction. From a trader's perspective, the nice thing about the federal agency bonds is that they're very liquid securities that are easily sold. In what can only be called a potential light on a cloudy day, JP Morgan agreed to settle the sale on the same day, whereas it would have ordinarily taken a full day, meaning MF Global would have access to the funds immediately instead of Monday.

Some time on Friday, Jon Bass, the global head of institutional sales for MF Global, reportedly made some phone calls in order to take the liquidation into his own hands. Bass had worked at UBS many years prior, and he still had some connections with the traders. He told his friends there that MF Global had very large sovereign-debt positions to sell, and wondered whether or not UBS might have any interest in bidding on them. Bass asked them to take a look at the entire portfolio, they agreed to look, but declined to give any bid.

Various MF Global personnel believe that UBS – who themselves had positions in European sovereign debt – took full advantage of the insider information they now had and the traders took the opportunity to short-sell some of the bonds in the MF Global portfolio, specially the Italian bonds.

It's a common occurrence that when the market knows of a distressed seller, many traders will short-sell bonds that are about to go to auction or be liquidated. The theory is that, knowing a distressed seller was about to auction off its entire debt portfolio, they can push down prices further, which results in a lower price for the auctioned bonds, and an opportunity for them to buy back the bonds at a lower price. But here's the catch: it's important to know which bonds are about to be sold, which gives opportunistic traders an even better opportunity to short-sell and then buy back those bonds in the auction and pocket the profits.

And while it's easy to discard this accusation as mere conspiracy theory, consider the fact that at the time, prices for the overall Italian sovereign-bond market was up over the course of the last few days of MF Global's life – that is, except the specific Italian bonds that MF Global was about to auction.

It wasn't just UBS secretly acquiring information about the positions. Management at MF Global asked their colleagues at Jeffries to look at the sovereign-debt portfolio, and they too declined to bid, though it wouldn't be discovered until several weeks later that Jefferies had no serious interest in actually acquiring the portfolio, as they were already heavily invested in the sovereign-debt RTM trades themselves. Once again, it was just another firm simply trying to get a sneak-peek of what MF Global had on its books, to see what was going to get sold in the fire sale within a few days.

In many eastern religions, the idea of karma is a major tenet. Briefly, karma is the idea that a single deed or action is part of a greater whole, which is referred to as the cycle of action. So a single act by a single person has ramifications beyond the immediate. The term has been colloquialized in several contexts, ranging from the Beatles song about "instant karma" to the more blunt "karma is a bitch." In short, the idea is that what comes around, goes around. And for Jon Corzine, it was coming around.

During the Russian debt crisis in 1998, Jon Corzine and his traders had pocketed a lot of money shorting securities that were part of Long-Term Capital Management's positions after seeing their books under the guise of investing in the dying hedge fund. Now, it seemed, he was on the receiving end of exactly the same treatment. Maybe it was the rule of the financial jungle, where firms both live and died by the sword; a world where no mercy is shown the weak at the expense of the strong. Before, Corzine had been in the position of the strong, as he sent traders to sift through the positions of another collapsing firm; now he was on the other side of the collapse. Regardless of whether or not those firms used underhanded tactics to profit off of MF Global's misery, at least insofar as karma is concerned, what went around finally had come around, and Corzine was feeling the results of karma.

In another last-ditch attempt at liquidating the entire portfolio, Corzine turned to Carl Icahn, a Wall Street mogul who was either a financial genius or a heartless corporate raider, depending on your interpretation of his tactics. No matter what you thought of his business plan, the fact remained that he was a wildly successful investor, with a lot of money. Corzine offered to sell the entire portfolio to Icahn at what amounted to a $187 million loss; Icahn declined to pursue the offer, however, and the deal fell through.

By the end of Friday, MF Global had managed to sell off billions of assets, including some portions of the RTM portfolio. Those sales had freed up some money for the firm, but liquidity was drying up faster than the sales eased up on the drain. The only option left was to auction off the remaining positions.

The auction was arranged for Saturday, October 29. All remaining MF Global positions would be on the block, and the participating investment banks scheduled to take part in the auction included JP Morgan, Goldman Sachs, and Bank of America. In the end, though, none of the firms opted to participate in the auction, given the set of extraordinary circumstances. For starters, the auction was on a Saturday and markets were closed; additionally, there was a tremendous amount of uncertainty swirling around the financial world, with MF Global teetering on the brink of collapse. Interestingly, JP Morgan had used their pre-arranged participation in the auction as their own sort of leverage to milk more margin out of MF Global for clearing their trades. In short, the potential calamity that could arise if MF Global failed, for the winning bidder would have no way of unloading the positions before the markets opened on Monday. MF Global was left holding their positions for another day.

It's no surprise that JP Morgan failed to appear at the auction on Saturday and they were not interested in buying any more of MF Global's trading positions. As MF Global's clearing bank, JP Morgan was already worried they'd get stuck with the securities in the clearing account if the firm failed. JP Morgan staffers were holding their own auction and assembled on Sunday at their office to begin preparations for liquidating the MF Global "box positions," those positions in the JP Morgan clearing account that MF Global had been unable to fund since earlier that week. The total value of the securities was approximately $600 million and traders were busy pricing the securities with plans to liquidate them in their entirety on Monday, in anticipation of MF Global's announcing bankruptcy. In addition to the box securities, the traders also planned to liquidate all the MF Global-held mortgage-backed securities and other collateralized securities currently in the account.

JP Morgan traders lit up the phone lines, calling their trading brethren at other firms, trying to entice them to show up at their offices on a Sunday to participate in the auction. A smattering of traders showed up, including some from Morgan Stanley. In the end, Morgan Stanley's traders declined to bid, citing the fact that it wasn't entirely clear who owned the securities in question. Since MF Global had not yet declared bankruptcy, how could JP Morgan sell securities that officially were not theirs, at least not for several more hours? Regardless, JP Morgan would liquidate the securities in their entirety the next day before the world learned that MF Global was no longer in business.

* * *

After the bankruptcy was declared, there was much less of a rush to sell the remaining positions. Over the next few weeks in November, LCH.Clearnet would complete its liquidation of MF Global's securities, most notably, the sovereign-debt RTM positions that were turned over to KPMG in London for liquidation.

The RTM positions were reportedly offered to a select number of major investors, including JP Morgan, George Soros, and an unnamed hedge fund. What would have been deemed a tactical error in a traditional sale, a major mistake added to the massive losses suffered on the sales. LCH.Clearnet ran the sale, but they separated the bonds during the auction. In other words, LCH.Clearnet offered investors the opportunity to buy Italian bonds in one auction; then offered others the chance to sell the French bonds in a separate auction.

From a trader's and liquidator's standpoint, this is a major error by effectively giving up the "bid/asked spread." In a spread trade, where MF Global was "long Italy" and "short France," the two securities are simultaneously traded, one bought and one sold. The idea is to create a net position, based on the difference between the bid price and the offer price. By not liquidating both the long positions and the short positions together, the liquidation of the RTM trades just added to the growing losses in the liquidation.

In the end, all the sovereign-debt securities were sold at deep discounts. So much so, in fact, that the MF Global personnel were shocked at how low the prices had been. Those securities with A-ratings had sold at 10% below the current market prices, whereas the lower-rated BBB securities were sold in bulk at a price that was $250 million below what the market said they should be. On November 29, LCH.Clearnet announced that they had completed the liquidation of all the MF Global European securities, a gross amount of $14.7 billion. As a result of the sale, they were happy to report that they were not forced to draw on their default fund. In other words, netting the sales against the margin they were holding, neither LCH.Clearnet nor its members lost any money as a result of the MF Global collapse.

One of the investors who benefitted the most from the fire sale was George Soros, the 81-year old hedge-fund investor that managed approximately $26 billion. Soros' name became synonymous with investing success in 1992, when he famously bet against the British pound. Soros had shorted the pound, and on the day that came to be known as Black Wednesday in Britain, the currency was withdrawn from the European Exchange Rate Mechanism, the value of the pound subsequently plummeted. His gamble paid off to the tune of over $1 billion, and is still today considered to be one of the single most successful trades in the history of investing. It earned Soros the moniker "The Man Who Broke The Bank of England."

While not necessarily on the same level as his bet against Britain's currency, Soros' purchases of MF Global securities were wildly lucrative. In total he purchased approximately $2 billion worth of the $4.8 billion RTM securities that were offered for sale. For Italian bonds, he paid approximately $0.89 on the dollar, compared to the market price of $0.94. Within a month, it was reported that those bonds were back up to a price of $0.96, making Soros a $140 million profit in the space of a month.

There is, of course, no way of knowing the full extent of the losses directly due to the rushed fire sale and certainly under better circumstances a liquidation could have been handled better. Looking at the numbers, we can surmise the approximate damage done to MF Global's bottom line. For starters, the firm took a $7.3 million loss on the sale of $600 million worth of RTM positions before Bankruptcy Week. The sale of commercial paper to Goldman Sachs for $1.33 billion had resulted in a loss of $15 million. Soros had paid $2 billion for a portion of the RTM portfolio, costing MF Global another $120 million, with the remainder of the RTM positions selling at a 10% discount, which adds another $280 million to the loss ledger. Moving on, we come to the $418 million worth of corporate securities the firm held, which were sold for $384 million, a loss of $34 million. An additional $600 million worth of relatively illiquid securities were on the books, which we can conservatively guess were sold at a 10% discount, meaning they lost the firm another $60 million.

Assuming a negligible loss or even a slight profit realized on the sale of the remaining assets in the firm's holdings – which included several billion dollars in federal agency, U.S. Treasuries and other positions – the total cost of unwinding the trading positions topped out at over $500 million.

The collapse and liquidation collectively cost over half a billion dollars as a result of the MF Global fire sale, money that could possibly have been used to prop up the dying firm or, at the very least, used to offset money that had mysteriously gone missing.

As long as we're speculating, it's interesting to note what happened to the markets following the liquidation of MF Global's holdings, if only to imagine what might have been. Soon after the bankruptcy, the European sovereign-debt markets recovered. Irish and

Portuguese margin requirements – which had reached levels as high as 80% at LCH.Clearnet – fell dramatically to approximately 15%. Of the Italian bonds in the MF Global portfolio, 91% of them matured in December 2011, just two months after the bankruptcy; their value at maturity was approximately $3 billion. The remaining European debt positions matured in 2012.

As for the RTM trades that Corzine had worked so hard to push through, all of them would have matured and MF Global would have gotten all of their margin money back since none of the bonds defaulted, all would have paid out in full. Naturally, that was assuming MF Global had enough money to stay at the roulette table while the margin calls were accumulating against them. But the panic that gripped the investing world – paired with MF Global's decision to over-leverage itself – led to the firm's ultimate demise.

Jon Corzine has been criticized, and rightfully so, for his management skills. He was perhaps not best suited to be in the CEO's office. It can be argued that his success was that of a fixed-income trader. He can be accused of being too focused on trading rather than running a business. But he cannot be criticized for his devotion to the RTM trades. He was right about the portfolio. It was a good trade that made the firm a lot of money, and it would have made the firm more if he had the luxury of time, and money, to allow them to mature. But he wasn't making wine. He was making money, and money doesn't wait for anyone in the fast-paced world of Wall Street. And the people who populate that world aren't any different from any other consumer. When they smell a good deal, they jump on it. Especially when they hear about fire-sale prices.

CHAPTER SIXTEEN

The Money Noose

It's a scene most of us have only seen in old black-and-white photographs and old movies. A line of people – perhaps better described as an unorganized mob – crowd around the front of a bank, all them of the clamoring for their money. They want to withdraw the deposits from their bank accounts and want to do it immediately. It's what is known as a "run on the bank," and perhaps the best known "bank runs" took place in the early 1930s, when panicked people feared that many banks had become insolvent and they worried they would lose the last precious funds they had. These bank runs arose as a result of the fact that banks are inherently illiquid. The assets they hold are long term, like mortgage loans, and the deposits they take in are short term. The mortgage loans cannot be recalled or sold upon demand in the same way the deposits can be. Since banks only keep a fraction of their deposits in the form of cash in the bank vault itself, they have a limited ability to pay off their deposits. When that aforementioned mob shows up at the front door and wants their money, the bank just doesn't have enough to give out.

Most people living today have not experienced a "run on the bank," and that's mostly attributed to new banking regulations in 1933 and the establishment of the FDIC to insure people's deposits at the banks. In a crisis, individuals no longer need to line up outside a bank and wait for it to open to take their money out; that problem was mostly solved. But institutions can still experience much of the same thing – MF Global had the sorry experience of suffering from a modern-day version of the "bank run."

Suppose you have the typical checking account, savings account and mortgage loan and they are all at the same bank. Chances are that you use the money in your checking to pay everyday expenses and bills and your mortgage is a loan just like any other mortgage loan, but in this case it happens to be held by the very same bank. Let's give you a little benefit of the doubt and say you're a conservative financial mind, so you've got a pretty high balance in your savings account. Maybe you've saved enough to last for a year if you lost your job. Now, let's also assume you're secure in your profession, and you're not too worried about that unthinkable event coming to pass.

But then, out of the blue, the unthinkable happens. The economy tanks, the housing market crashes, and economic recession grips the country, much like it did beginning in 2008. You lose your job. It's a setback, to be sure, but again, you've got that savings account to support you. There's enough money in there to carry you through the "rainy day" or days, or months.

But the bank doesn't necessarily believe you'll be quite as responsible with your savings account as you believe you are. After all, with no income, people have been known to do crazy things with their money. The bank is concerned about their outstanding mortgage loan and they are very worried that you won't make good on the payments going forward.

Given their concern, the bank begins to look at the situation more closely. From their perspective, they traditionally have only one option. They stand by you and wait to see if you actually miss a mortgage loan payment; as long as you don't violate the terms of the loan agreement by missing a payment, there's no other action they can take.

But suppose there's another option available for the bank – and one that is potentially more prudent for them in terms of minimizing risk – which is to freeze the funds in your checking and savings accounts to be held as margin against your mortgage loan. It's their way of hedging themselves against the potential losses associated with the foreclosure process. While a foreclosure is a terrifying proposition for a homeowner, it's also a nightmare for the bank. They'll spend up to 18 months going through eviction proceedings, and they'll have the time and effort associated with selling the house. Given the fact that the real estate market has crashed, they're not optimistic about being able to sell the house for the amount still outstanding on the loan, which means they expect to lose money on the transaction.

You call the bank and tell them what they're doing isn't fair, because you're a responsible person who pays his bills, and you've got enough in your savings account to get you through until you find another job. They should have nothing to worry about. But amazingly enough, that doesn't do much to convince them. They proceed with taking control of your accounts.

You are now in an impossible situation. The money you had set aside for just such an emergency has been taken away from you. In a sense, the bank is now using it for the exact same purpose as you: they are making sure they'll have the funds to cover the mortgage loan in case you can't make the payments anymore. But without access to your funds, you can't pay the bills and when you still can't find a job, you can't make your mortgage loan payment. You find yourself in default, and your home is foreclosed on by the bank.

You had the money to pay the bank, but they took that money away from you to protect themselves in case you couldn't pay it back, and then when you couldn't pay it back, they took your home. Had they not seized your assets in the first place, you would have been able to pay them, you would have kept your home, and the bank wouldn't have had to endure the issues associated with foreclosure. Nobody wins in the end. You've just experienced a run on yourself by a bank.

As much of a nightmare scenario as this creates – and as truly unimaginable it is to think of this happening – the exact same thing happened to MF Global. As of the end of September, the firm had approximately $1.5 billion in capital and an unutilized Revolving Credit Facility of $1.2 billion. Then suddenly, customer accounts were withdrawn and the LCH.Clearnet margin requirements shot up to nearly $1 billion. And when paired with the other collective margin requirements of their clearing banks, MF Global suffered total margin requirements of over $2 billion. After they'd drawn down their revolver to the point it was gone, they were left with no way to function. The combination of withdrawn customer accounts, the frozen "liquidity buffer," and margin calls left them with about a billion-dollar deficit.

But what really caused this situation to come to be in the first place? Obviously the economic climate at the time was a major influencing factor, but again, the firm started with nearly $1.5 billion in capital. After the firm was downgraded, however, fears began to emerge that MF Global was soon to be out of business. Nearly $1.5 billion can only go so far in the world of high finance, so both customers and counterparties began to prepare for the worst. Ironically enough, it was their preparation that caused MF Global's liquidity crisis. It was, in a sense, a self-fulfilling prophecy, much like the one theoretically created by your bank when they took control of your bank accounts.

* * *

Central counterparties like LCH.Clearnet and Fixed Income Clearing Corporation wield a great deal of power and influence in the financial markets by controlling access and margin in the markets. Many firms won't trade with another unless that firm is a member of the club, so to speak. In order for a bank to trade fixed income in the United States or in Europe, for example, membership to the central counterparties is required. Losing access is akin to being out of business, so faced with losing access to a CCP membership, a firm will do whatever it takes to stay.

Clearing banks like JP Morgan, Citibank, and Bank of New York Mellon control the extension of credit and margin for settling and clearing securities, and that gives them power over a financial firm that is basically unlimited. By having the power to extend or contract credit through margin requirements, they literally control a firm's cash flow – as was the case with MF Global – that can directly affect that firm's ability to pay debts, move money, or deliver securities. In other words, a clearing bank's decision on whether or not to clear trades directly controls a firm's ability to be in business.

Think of what happened to the MF Global's London office. They desperately needed their "liquid buffer" reserve fund from the Bank of New York Mellon; they had $500 million in securities deposited and needed an infusion from their "rainy-day fund." The bank held up the transfer and that meant that MF Global had trouble meeting their final margin requirements for the RTM trades. That $500 million in funds, which were supposed to be there for just such an event, could have helped stave off bankruptcy.

And BNYM wasn't the only bank shackling the hands of MF Global. JP Morgan did their part too, by the simple act of scaling back MF Global's intra-day credit. By requiring that securities transfers had to be cleared on a pre-funded basis, MF Global needed to provide more actual cash in the bank before anything would settle. Without credit, the entire settlement process was slowed down considerably, increased counterparty's doubts they'd get their money out and added to the operational confusion.

Perhaps the strongest nail in MF Global's coffin came in the form of the "debit alert" issued on October 27. That action required pre-approval by JP Morgan for any transfer of funds, just like the restrictions on securities settlement, and there was again no credit extended on money transfers. In other words, MF Global couldn't transfer money to a client if they didn't have the exact amount in their account already, which also destroyed MF Global's ability to move funds in between their own accounts and to and from customer accounts. All totaled, it was estimated JP Morgan collected $430 million additional margin while MF Global was sliding into bankruptcy. The simple act of removing credit extension to clear trades added to the squeeze on MF Global's liquidity situation. Instead of receiving support from their clearing bank for their liquidity situation, the bank's actions made everything much worse.

Depository Trust Company was another firm that followed the herd in restricting MF Global's cash flow. In terms of clearing securities, at first DTC reduced MF Global's "debit cap" from $334 million to $100 million, so MF Global was required to send in $200 million more in margin deposits in order to cover the difference in order to settle trades. One day later, DTC eliminated all credit extension, thus requiring yet another deposit – this time $100 million – in order to settle trades. It was yet another restriction on MF Global's credit and cash flow, slowing down their securities settlements and transfers, just when they needed more help.

Fixed Income Clearing Corporation (FICC) – which clears federal agency and U.S. Treasury bonds – kept a substantial portion of the margin MF Global had on deposit after their repo book was largely wound down. As MF Global closed out positions held there, they expected that they'd receive their margin deposits back, but FICC held on to those funds. The traders at MF Global expected to have $108 million returned to them of the $170 million they had on deposit, but FICC would not release the funds.

A case can easily be made that central counterparties and clearing banks have too much influence in the financial markets. The fact that they can literally cut off a company's access to the market or settle securities through margin requirements illustrates this point. If a CCP or clearing bank wants to restrict trading in a particular market or by a particular customer, all they really need to do is raise the margin requirements to the point that nobody can afford to stay in.

It is, of course, a decision left up to individual banks as to how they will process transactions for their clients. On one hand, it can be argued that no bank is required to extend credit to their customers, so that it was a business decision that these banks made in regard to MF Global's transactions. However, on the other hand, even that argument offers no excuse for their decision to not return excess margin to MF Global while the firm was obviously foundering.

That said, the individual actions by each bank and CCP – with the exception of the failure to return margin deposits after positions were closed – are easily defended. Each firm was doing what they believed correct to minimize their own exposure to the dying MF Global. In other words, they took actions that were potentially more prudent for them in terms of minimizing risk. For those banks, that meant freezing the funds in MF Global's accounts. Individually it made sense because they were doing what seemed best at the time. However, collectively they drew the last bits of liquidity away from MF Global, the only money the firm had left to keep it alive.

Because there is little competition in the central counterparty market, banks and financial firms are at the mercy of those few organizations that control margin and leverage in the market. It is ironic that an economic system that is based purely on supply and demand is held captive by what effectively amounts to a mini-monopoly.

And central counterparties operate free of regulations, despite the amount of control they have in the markets. They generally operate under the assumption of "self regulation." That lack of oversight makes the equivalent of price gouging in particular markets not only possible, but a very distinct reality.

There are positive aspects to the central counterparty system. Most importantly, the existence of these institutions ensures that other firms won't be doing direct business with defaulting counterparties. That situation would invoke more panic in the marketplace, which could inevitably lead to contagion as countless other firms suffer losses as a result of their exposure to a dying firm and possibly meet the same unfortunate fate as MF Global. And given recent legislation, including the Dodd-Frank Act, it appears that not only are central counterparties here to stay, but also that they are the wave of the future, and we can expect to see a proliferation of them going forward.

Interestingly, past bankruptcy cases demonstrate that central counterparties are, in fact, good for the overall market. Consider the case of Lehman Brothers. On September 15, 2008 the venerable Wall Street investment bank filed for bankruptcy. The liquidation of the firm's assets fell primarily to the Depository Trust & Clearing Company, the parent company of Fixed Income Clearing Corporation. It would be the largest closeout in the firm's history.

By the end of October that year, FICC announced that they had successfully liquidated over $500 billion in mortgage-backed securities and another $190 billion in U.S. Treasury securities. They did it all without drawing on their default funds, meaning that none of their other members experienced losses resulting from the liquidation of Lehman's assets. LCH.Clearnet was the firm tasked with liquidating Lehman's holdings in London, and they met the same results in terms of incurring no losses to their default fund. Those successes were due in large part to the existence of the central counterparty system.

Just as in all things financial, however, there is a price to be paid for the consistency and reliability afforded financial institutions by central counterparties. In the event of any loss in a bank's liquidity – or even in the event of rumors of a loss – the central counterparties tend to take drastic action, as was evidenced in the case of MF Global. Those drastic actions usually take the form of jacked-up margin requirements, which come at the same time the suffering firm needs extra liquidity in order to stay in business.

Which brings us to the unsavory topic of those firms who end up defaulting. Those same central counterparties and clearing banks, as has been illustrated, can actually hasten the collapse of a firm when it finds itself in a dire financial situation. Their unilateral ability to raise margin rates at the slightest provocation – a downgrade, a rapid decline in the stock price, a large quarterly loss, what have you – can be a death knell for firms.

* * *

Much like the old-time photographs and movies of bank runs, most of us have only seen similar images of the macabre hangman's noose. Just the sight alone – even in a grainy photograph – is enough to cause a sense of fear in the average viewer. It is a symbol of suffering and death.

The hangman's noose of the past worked in one of two ways to kill its victim. In the version of a sanctioned execution, a noose was rigged from a platform with a trapdoor underneath the condemned criminal. At the precise moment, the trapdoor springs, leaving the victim to fall through, and the drop is what breaks the condemned's neck. Death is typically quick and painless in this form of killing.

However, there is another form of hanging, the one that is generally associated with a noose. In the other method, the victim hangs from the rope where there is no trapdoor and no sudden death. Instead, the person slowly suffocates, as his airway is constricted and his body is starved of life-giving oxygen. It is, to say the least, a slow and painful death, often taking 10 minutes or longer of extreme suffering before life is finally snuffed out.

Despite the noose's morbid connotations, it is an apt metaphor for the death of MF Global when the firm experienced the prototypical run on the bank. Throughout the last week of October 2011, as MF Global's financial situation grew worse, the noose tightened in the form of higher margin requirements and tighter restrictions on accessing their own cash. The firm found itself caught in what can only be called a money noose. MF Global had its neck in the noose and no matter what they did to try to escape, the money noose tightened. In an attempt to escape, they relied on the temporary use of customer seg funds to get them through. Raiding the clients' funds could not save the dying firm; it just postponed the inevitable. The firm was condemned the minute the mob of financial firms instituted a run on the bank. At that point, all liquidity dried up and the money noose would not loosen. It was an institutional run on a bank, just like people lining up in the past to take their money out, but a modern-day bank-run is orchestrated by institutions. In this particular story, central counterparties and clearing banks served as the hangman, cinching the knot around the firm's neck and pulling it tight, literally choking the life out of MF Global.

CHAPTER SEVENTEEN

Finding the Money

For new parents, the experience of a child being born is second to none in terms of the excitement. All of the months of anticipation, preparation and worry are rewarded by the arrival of the new addition to the family. Family and friends gather and wish the new parents well, often bringing gifts for the baby and parents – some of those gifts more practical than others. The truth about those baby gifts is that the more practical the gift, the more it is appreciated by the parents. Children outgrow clothes and toys, and in all honesty, how many stuffed animals can fit on one bed? The reality with kids – just like with getting married or buying a first home – is that the expenses of raising a child are just beginning.

As a parent, you're responsible for the well being of your child, and for many parents, that includes the child's education. With the necessity of advanced education in today's professional world, college is all but a requirement for graduates hoping to break into higher-paying jobs. And for many parents, the obligation to pay for that college education falls to them; and to pay for that future college expense, parents often set up a savings account for their child's education.

Four years of college is, to be certain, a prohibitively expensive prospect. Because of the skyrocketing costs, many parents have taken to starting college funds for their children almost as soon as the child is born. Luckily these days, one option available to parents planning for their kids' education is the 529 Plan, which is offered in most states today.

Named after Section 529 of the IRS tax code that set up the plan, a 529 Plan is an investment account that allows parents to contribute money annually to a child's education. In turn, the growth of the balance from any investment income is tax-free. It is basically the same thing as a 401(k), but deposits into the account have the specific goal to pay for the child's education.

Sometimes people can get into a little trouble with their 529 Plan. Let's say one year you overspent a little on Christmas shopping. Your kids wanted gifts that were a little more than you expected to spend, and maybe your spouse deserved an extra-special gift this year. Just to top it off, your Christmas bonus at work was less than you were hoping for. In the end, you spent more than you intended, plus you didn't get quite the financial boost you were expecting. But it's on a credit card, so you'll pay it off when you can.

But then the dog had to have emergency surgery and a water pipe burst during the same week and suddenly you're not just a little short. You're in need of some immediate cash to cover your current bills. Be it a good thing or not, the 529 Plan holder has access to the funds in the account and can make withdrawals for whatever reason, with a small penalty.

So you dip into the 529 Plan funds. It's not a big deal; it's legal, although morally a little questionable. It's your child's education money, but they won't know, they're too young and soon enough you'll pay back the money. You take the cash to make the payment on your credit-card bill, and nobody gets hurt.

The next month rolls around, and there are other expenses that need to be attended to. Life keeps on happening, and often that means spending money you weren't counting on spending. So in the end, that withdrawal from the 529 Plan doesn't get paid back. It gets put on a back burner until it's forgotten altogether. It is the all-too-often scenario of buy now, pay later. Only in this case, you never pay. Nobody is any the wiser, until it comes time to pay the college tuition. With any luck, you didn't have to draw on the account any more than that one time, and the money you took out won't be missed. But what happens in the event it is missed?

That is, in essence, what happened with the MF Global seg funds. The firm dipped into the accounts like they'd done in the past, promising themselves that they'd pay them back. And truth be told, if they had access to money elsewhere and had paid the seg accounts back, nobody would have had any idea the funds were gone in the first place. But there are legal penalties, including jail time, that govern the withdrawal of customer seg funds by investment firms, whereas the penalties for borrowing from your child's 529 Plan amount to only a 10% early-withdrawal surcharge.

For starters, a seg account is technically a customer's private property. It contains the client's own funds that are supposed to be available only to that customer. The accounts are required to be segregated – thus the name – from the firm's own funds, and are kept in a completely separate bank account by an independent third party. The funds are only supposed to be invested and transferred with that client's consent.

The segregation of customer accounts follows a long history in the industry of protecting customer assets and is an important a matter of safety. Not in the sense that an investment firm like MF Global would necessarily use the funds, but rather they are segregated as a fail-safe against a firm going bankrupt. If the company does go under, those funds are supposed to be safely and quickly ensconced to another, theoretically stable, bank. Consider an air traveler who is flying on a plane. Suppose while he's in flight, the airline declares bankruptcy. His luggage can't be taken and sold off in order to help the airline pay its creditors; it still belongs to the traveler even though the airline is technically holding it for him. It's the same with seg funds. If a firm declares bankruptcy, the seg funds don't belong to them, so they can't be used to pay off creditors. Rather, the customer property must be returned to the original owner.

In the end, someone at MF Global committed a crime when they dipped into the customer seg funds. It doesn't matter that they planned to pay it back. As soon as the money was taken out of those accounts – regardless of reason or justification – it was a criminal act.

There are plenty of people who could rationalize that breaking the rules was an attempt to save many jobs or even to save the company itself. And while those are certainly lofty goals worthy of praise, when their achievement – or the attempted achievement – comes as a result of illegal activity, the fact of the matter is that a crime was committed and anyone who broke the rules deserves to pay the consequences associated with the crime.

The history of Wall Street is filled with men and women who did illegal things under the guise of noble causes. Theft of company funds, altering of company records, lying to officials. All of these things and plenty of others are examples of acts committed by well-respected businesspeople who said they were either doing nothing wrong or were only doing something wrong to achieve something better for the firm or their investors. Regardless of your opinion of what these people did, they knowingly committed crimes.

In the case of MF Global personnel, they operated under the assumption that they wouldn't get caught because nobody would know what they did. Much like that parent who dips into his kid's college fund, the folks at MF Global figured that they'd be able to pay the money back before anybody knew the funds were gone, so in the end, nobody would get hurt. But just like that parent, when it came time to pay the account back, there were other expenses that needed to be paid first. The seg funds were suddenly secondary in importance while the firm was falling into bankruptcy, at which point there was no chance of paying the money back. But their absence became of the utmost importance after the bankruptcy. And who was to blame for the missing funds became a question of equal importance.

Questions swirled around the lack of internal controls MF Global had in place, especially in the final days before the bankruptcy. Employees were being pulled in multiple directions simultaneously, trying to keep the business going, so it's entirely possible the funds were withdrawn as the result of an honest mistake by a well-meaning staffer. Alternatively, there is always the chance an unscrupulous executive took it upon himself to withdraw the funds in direct violation of the law, knowing full well what he was doing.

The main argument refuting the second idea is that there isn't an obvious paper trail pointing to a specific individual as the one who'd authorized the withdrawals. There would have been an approval – sent via email or recorded conversation – for the sending of the money wires. And any such email would have been in the records obtained by the bankruptcy trustees, but no such email ever surfaced.

* * *

The days immediately following MF Global's bankruptcy were filled with finger-pointing and denial of culpability in regard to the missing funds. The firm was bankrupt, under the control of James Giddens. A trustee is not someone you want to see walking the halls of your company; Giddens was named a liquidation trustee, and was operating in the same capacity for the defunct Lehman Brothers. MF Global's existence was over. Giddens and his team began an in-depth investigation of MF Global's practices and accounts.

Despite the trustee's best forensic efforts, however, many questions remain unanswered. Specifically, who knew what and when did they know it? Giddens concluded that the $175 million wire transfer from Chicago to London had, in fact, originally been customer seg funds. That much was clear. But what the employees who handled the transaction knew was still up for speculation.

On the one hand, Edith O'Brien's refusal to sign the letter from JP Morgan that would have acknowledged her involvement in the transfer suggests that she knew something wasn't right. But on the other hand, had she known that the funds had come from seg accounts, she – or anyone else, for that matter, especially Jon Corzine – could have very easily reversed the transaction in a matter of minutes. But nobody did anything. MF Global desperately needed the cash, and that need superseded any desire to know the origin of it.

More telling is the action O'Brien and others took after it had become clear on Sunday night that money was siphoned out of customer accounts. Upon confirming the facts, O'Brien immediately worked to transfer all of MF Global's "box collateral" into the customer accounts to offset the money that had been taken out.

"Box collateral" is the term given to those securities held – in this case at the clearing account at JP Morgan – as either margin collateral or simply as a trade waiting to be funded. In the case of MF Global, they were the unfunded securities that nobody really wanted. But that said, they had a monetary value, and by moving them into the MF Global seg accounts, O'Brien was exercising the only option available to her in terms of returning money back to those accounts. While it might have been seen as being too little too late – or even just an empty gesture of replacing cash with junk securities – it was something, and it's an important something to consider.

The overt suggestion offered by this action is that O'Brien knew that taking money from seg funds was ethically wrong, not to mention illegal. It also suggests, however, that she was honestly naïve as to the fact that during the preceding days, money in those customer accounts had been used. If she had been aware of the source of the money, it makes sense that she would have replaced it with the box collateral immediately – on Friday – as opposed to waiting until after the weekend.

There is, of course, the possibility that it was merely willful ignorance, that she didn't know where the money had come from because that knowledge could somehow make her complicit in a crime. O'Brien's actions following the announcement come very close to proving her innocence; however, just like in so many other parts of this story, there is room for interpretation.

As for Jon Corzine, he was fired from his position without a severance package on November 4. He denied knowledge of the seg funds being used for operational expenses, saying forcefully, "I did not instruct anyone to lend customer funds to anyone." But the questions still linger: what did he know when?

The only real tangible evidence to suggest that Corzine knew of the nature of the transfer comes from the email forwarded by Edith O'Brien, the one in which she inserted the phrase "Per JC's direct instructions." The email came on the heels of a phone conversation, which provides no paper trail. So we are left with O'Brien's words to try to divine the truth.

According to a statement he made public, Corzine claimed that he was unaware "that customer funds had been used" to cover the overdraft at the London office. He would later plead ignorance before a Congressional subcommittee investigating the missing money, saying, "Since I had no personal knowledge of the issue, I asked senior people in the back office and the legal department to become directly involved." In other words, Corzine wasn't denying giving the order. Rather, he was denying knowing about what was going on.

In this day and age, with technology and communication as readily and easily accessible as it is – especially at the highest levels of one of the largest corporations – it is extremely hard to fathom a CEO in Corzine's position not knowing the severe liquidity squeeze the firm was facing, and it's equally hard to believe that he didn't have at least an inkling as to where that money had miraculously materialized from.

In the end, there was no question about whether money was missing from the seg funds. It had been documented that money wasn't where it was supposed to be, though the final destination of that money was up for debate. Remember the statement made by MF Global's attorney, Kenneth Ziman, who said, "All funds are accounted for, and I'm talking about the broker-dealer." The suggestion there is that the firm knew where the funds were, meaning they could be returned to the customers.

Notwithstanding, however, there was still that nebulous question as to how much of the money was actually "accounted for," despite not being where it was supposed to be, namely in the customer seg fund accounts. Soon after the bankruptcy declaration, the liquidators overseeing the unwinding of MF Global announced that the seg funds were missing a combined total of $891 million. While that's enough money to raise more than a few eyebrows, the news got worse. On November 21, just three weeks later, the total was raised by the trustees, who were now somewhat confident that the firm was missing in excess of $1.2 billion in customer seg funds. The number would finally settle at $1.6 billion in seg funds that weren't where they were supposed to be.

How is it that people who work with money – people brought in specifically to figure out how much money there is – could not account for over $700 million over the course of several weeks? The jokes are easy, to be sure, especially given the MF Global attorney's assertion that the money was "accounted for," but they couldn't exactly tell where it all was. There is an answer to the question that pulls the curtain back on the complexity of the regulatory rules that financial firms – not just MF Global – operate. And that illumination helps to show, too, how easy it is to manipulate numbers and work within the gray area of regulation.

The simple answer to the wildly disparity in numbers goes back to the Alternative Method. The Alternative Method was that obscure futures accounting rule specific to the U.S. Commodity Futures Trading Commission that allowed MF Global and other commodity futures trading firms to distinguish between traditional seg accounts and what were labeled as foreign secured accounts, which were specifically for customers trading on foreign exchanges.

So in other words, you could be an MF Global client and have your money in two different seg accounts: one for domestic trading and the other for foreign trading. The domestic account was legally untouchable by the futures broker – it was customer property. But money deposited for the foreign account didn't necessarily go straight into a segregated account. That money could be mixed in with the broker's own funds and it was entirely legal for MF Global to use it how they wanted. And that was thanks to a little magic from the Alternative Method.

Because of the fact that foreign futures margin and domestic futures margin are both customer-owned monies, they were all due to be paid to MF Global's clients once the firm had declared bankruptcy. And when the money in the missing customer seg funds accounts were added up, that number did, in fact, total $891 million. It wasn't until the Alternative Method money was counted – and found to be short over $700 million – that the number was finalized. Those dollars destined for foreign exchanges – money that MF Global was very much within their legal rights to use as they wanted – comprised the extra missing money, a fact that took a few weeks to discover because of the complexity of the unwinding process.

* * *

So if it's "accounted for," then where's the money? That is – pardon the pun –the million-dollar question. One possibility for the missing funds was that they had been paid out in margin calls with different clearing counterparties. JP Morgan, Bank of New York Mellon, CME Group, and other institutions had a lot of MF Global margin money on deposit when they declared bankruptcy. Could that be the source of the missing seg funds? If so, it's entirely possible that Ziman knew about it at the time of the original bankruptcy hearing, and that his declaration in court had not been a premeditated attempt to mislead the judge, but rather the actual truth of the situation.

On December 16, 2011 Jill Sommers, a commissioner for the U.S. Commodity Futures Trading Commission who was serving as a point person for the MF Global bankruptcy, told the Reuters news agency that "all MF Global funds have been accounted for." Her major concern at that point, according to an interview she did with the *Wall Street Journal*, was determining whether or not each transaction involving the customer seg funds had been "legitimate." Richard Heiss, a KPMG employee who was assisting with unwinding the MF Global UK office, confirmed Sommers' contention. He said, "We know exactly where the money is." So it should now just be a question of getting it back to its rightful owners.

As of this writing, a substantial amount of money has been returned to the MF Global trustees. Repo counterparties have returned between $50 and $55 million, and $78.66 million has come in from the generally defined "financial products" transactions. In June 2012, CME Group returned $130 million to MF Global, though they are still holding $16.5 million. The Depository Trust & Clearing Corporation and the Fixed Income Clearing Corporation both returned the entirety of MF Global's margin deposit, which totaled over $300 million. JP Morgan has returned approximately $600 million so far, a number composed of $89.2 in customer seg funds and about $518.4 million in MF Global assets.

At an August 2012 senate hearing, Giddens told the assembled senators that he'd managed to obtain about $1 billion in cash; Freeh, for his part, assured the senators that every MF Global customer would be getting their money back. Right now, the only question looming is how much money there is still out there to be claimed, and which institutions are holding on to it. But that's not it. There's also the question of ownership of the outstanding assets, and like everything involved with this story, that's not an easily answered question. It will be one the courts have to decide.

That missing money is a significant sum, but its ownership is complicated. JP Morgan, for example, is owed $900 million from MF Global for the "revolver" loan they provided. The margin money they pried from MF Global during its last week can be used to pay that debt down, but technically any money they received that came from the MF Global seg accounts must be returned to MF Global. So any margin deposits transferred to JP Morgan from MF Global's seg funds can't be kept to pay down the $900 million.

Things get a little murkier when you consider how MF Global moved the funds from the client accounts to pay JP Morgan. They first took money from the seg accounts and deposited it into the MF Global house account. At that point, is it MF Global's money or is it still seg fund money? Regardless, given that it's money owed to JP Morgan through the bankruptcy, who gets it in the end? If it's determined to be MF Global's money, then it goes to JP Morgan. If, however, it is classified as seg fund money, then it will revert back to the customers. Until that decision is made, JP Morgan is still holding money to offset the $900 million they're owed.

In a final legal twist, the fact that Edith O'Brien refused to sign the letter from JP Morgan is further complicating the issue. Had she signed it, the issue would be closed. The money would be considered MF Global-owned, and it would go directly to JP Morgan. But since she refused to sign it, there is no paper trail to figure out where the money originated.

MF Global had also sent money over to the London office. Approximately $1.1 billion was across the pond, about $600 million in capital and the $500 million in the form of the "liquidity buffer" and over $650 million in funds sent as margin money to LCH.Clearnet for the RTM margin calls. After the liquidation of the RTM positions and taking into account the losses suffered as a result of selling them before maturity, there was still money left in the MF Global UK coffers to pay the money due its creditors.

Giddens, after examining the books of both offices, came to the conclusion that MF Global was due approximately $742 million from the London office; that figure represents almost half of the missing $1.6 billion in total client funds still missing. While it might seem like a simple procedure to get money wired from the London office back to the U.S. – it certainly wasn't that hard to send when MF Global had still been operational – the UK bankruptcy laws are very different from those in the U.S., and the London office has its own trustee overseeing the unwinding and liquidation of the UK-based assets. Giddens tried for many months, to no avail, to negotiate with the London trustee to get the money back. After a trial was slated for April 2013 to determine if the money will stay in the UK or go back to the U.S., the MF Global UK trustee agreed to return between $500 million and $600 million to the U.S.

One way or another, the former clients of MF Global will get their money back. As one former executive said, "The money did not disappear; it still exists, it's just misplaced." While not the most comforting thing you might ever hear from a financial executive, it is reassuring, at least, to know that the money does exist, and it will eventually find its way back to the people from whom it was taken. The task at hand is finding the money, which has been scattered to various counterparties and clearing banks, as well as the MF Global offices in London. But rough estimates indicate that between the cash currently on hand with the bankruptcy trustees combined with the money in the London office and the money still held at JP Morgan, it is more than enough to pay back all the missing seg funds.

In the end, the crimes committed at MF Global really didn't change the course of financial history in any profound sort of way. They didn't bring on the company's bankruptcy; rather, they were committed because of the impending bankruptcy. It was a last-ditch effort by desperate people trying to save their company from what was, in the cold light of day, all but dead. At best, the use of customer seg funds kept the dying firm on life support for another day or two – three at most – but the ending was the exact same as it would have been had the seg funds been left alone.

Whoever is finally brought up on charges as a result of the seg fund fraud really didn't get much bang for their buck. Three days on the financial equivalent of life support, in exchange for what is possibly a lengthy prison term. Judges typically don't look favorably on financial executives who use their clients' money to cover their own mistakes. If nothing else, the prison term will serve as a warning for others out there who might be contemplating doing the same thing.

It's always easy to say what someone else should have done. But until you're in their seat, sitting at their desk, with your name on the door – it's hard to know exactly how you'd react. There are plenty of people out there serving prison time for their professional misdeeds who stand in judgment in the business pages of the newspaper. Some have been convicted of embezzlement, others of tax evasion. Some have been convicted of outright stealing from their shareholders, while others are in prison for lying about their investment returns. All of these people are serving prison time for participating in different crimes. But regardless of the crime or the sentence, all of them seem to have at least one thing in common: none of them has come out publicly to say that the action was worth the punishment.

CHAPTER EIGHTEEN

After

The Old State House in Boston, Massachusetts, was the equivalent of the modern-day White House in Washington, D.C. Situated at the intersection of Washington and State Streets, the Old State House once served as the headquarters of the British Parliamentary representatives who were stationed in the Colonies and housed both the Parliamentary courts and the Council Chamber of the Royal Governor.

Back then, the building did not command the same reverence that the White House does today; it stood as a representation of resentment amongst the colonists, specifically in regard to the tight-fisted rules and tax policies imposed by the British crown. The most notable clash before the Revolution was the infamous Boston Tea Party to protest taxes levied on tea in 1773, but a lesser-known event occurred three years earlier and despite the fact that the earlier event is less talked about in popular culture, its sentiments were bred by the same resentments, and its ramifications were equally significant.

As a result of the Townshend Acts, American colonists were forced to pay tariffs on a variety of items imported from England, including paper, glass, paint, and lead – all important items in the economies of the fledgling colonies – as well as the ubiquitous tea favored by those who had traveled west from England.

Taxes on those imports were met with the expected anger on the part of the colonists; an anger that simmered, lacking only an immediate catalyst to send it boiling over the edge. Then, on March 5, 1770 a young wigmaker's apprentice publicly accused a British officer of not paying his bill by yelling at the officer as he walked away from the shop. A British private, who happened to be standing guard outside the Old State House, ordered the apprentice to show more respect to his superiors, which led to an exchange of insults. The British private then hit the young apprentice on the side of the head with the butt of his musket, and the ensuing commotion drew an increasingly large crowd of angry citizens.

Other British soldiers came to the private's defense, and the group loaded their weapons. Snowballs and other foreign objects came flying at the heads of the soldiers, one of whom was hit and knocked to the ground. Once he regained his feet and his composure, he fired into the crowd. Then, some other soldiers fired a volley and when it finally ended, 11 of the assembled townspeople had been shot. Three died instantly, and three more died later as a result of the wounds they'd sustained. The incident came to be known as the Boston Massacre.

The soldiers were brought to trial and attorney John Adams was asked to defend them. Despite the fact that local sentiments were firmly against the wellbeing of the soldiers, Adams felt that the troops deserved a defense, and he agreed to do so. In his argument to the court, Adams argued that the troops had acted in their own self-defense, saying, "Facts are stubborn things; and whatever may be our wishes, our inclinations, or the dictates of our passions, they cannot alter the state of facts and evidence."

Just as the public remembers the events surrounding the Boston Massacre slightly different from the actual event, so, too, is the perception that surrounds the downfall of MF Global. There are those responsible for bringing on the collapse of the once-proud firm and there are those responsible for the missing customer seg funds. A vast majority of the people who worked at MF Global are innocent and only a handful of the former employees are possibly guilty, but whether anyone will face criminal charges for their actions is another matter. Because of the nuances of the American legal system, it is entirely possible – in fact, one might go so far as to say it's probable – that no one will spend a day in jail for their actions at MF Global.

That is not to say, however, that they won't be punished. A collection of senior management officials from MF Global were served with class-action lawsuits by lawyers representing affected individuals.

Additionally, the trustees overseeing the bankruptcy proceedings have publicly declared that there is evidence to support claims of breach of fiduciary duty and negligence against Jon Corzine, Edith O'Brien, and Henri Steenkamp.

In legalese, "breach of fiduciary duty" is the failure of a person who has a fiduciary role, who acts in a way that is contrary to the best interest of the client. While it might sound as if there is some wiggle room in that definition, violation of a client's trust – for example, by using client funds in unauthorized or illegal ways – definitely meets the criteria for failure to act in a client's best interests under the law.

Again, though, the chances of anyone serving prison time for their malfeasance while at MF Global are slim. As of November 2012, both the Securities and Exchange Commission and the Commodity Futures Trading Commission had not announced whether or not they intend to pursue criminal charges that could result in prison sentences. Criminal charges are considered unlikely at this point. However, the civil penalties are, in many cases, more severe for those found guilty.

The easiest civil charge to prove would be that of "Failure to Supervise," which essentially means that rules were broken because of executives' lack of oversight and supervision. While it might seem a little like a parent-child relationship, brokerage firms have an explicit legal obligation to supervise their employees to ensure they are not violating regulations. Given the actions of at least one MF Global employee – whoever it was that dipped into the seg funds – it's clear that supervision was, at least for a period of time, less than adequate.

Another legal entanglement facing the members of MF Global's senior management team is the concept of "control person," which is a person who is able to use the authority vested in him by his position to help in making decisions regarding the firm's actions. Control persons have, by their very nature of being control persons, employees over whom they exert influence. And whereas at the Nuremburg Trials the "I was just following orders" excuse didn't work, if the orders came down from one or more control persons within MF Global, they'll likely find themselves in legal hot water.

The third and hardest to prove of the potential charges would be that of "aiding and abetting" on the part of senior management. If it can be shown that anyone knew of the violations while they were being committed and helped execute those actions or hide them, then they'd be guilty of "aiding and abetting." But with no concrete paper or electronic trail for investigators to follow, the chances of a conviction on this charge is unlikely.

The MF Global debacle was disastrous enough to get the attention of the United States Congress, which wanted answers about what had happened. The House Financial Services Subcommittee on Oversight and Investigations, chaired by Republican Representative Randy Neugebauer, issued a report in November 2012 that Neugebauer described as "essentially an autopsy of how MF Global came to its ultimate demise and what can be done to prevent similar customer losses in the future."

Given that a Republican member of the House of Representatives was leading the investigation against a former Democratic senator, it might not come as too much of a surprise that the report was scathing, to put it mildly.

Corzine was the prime target of the report's findings. "Choices made by Jon Corzine during his tenure as chairman and CEO sealed MF Global's fate," Neugebauer said, calling Corzine's actions paramount to "dereliction of duty," because "the responsibility for failing to maintain the systems and controls necessary to protect customer funds rests with Corzine."

Regarding the missing seg funds, the report said simply, "As the company struggled to find additional liquidity, company employees identified excess company funds held in customer accounts. However, because they did not have an accurate accounting of the amount of customer funds the company held, they withdrew customer funds as well as company funds."

It's interesting to note that no employee was named specifically, and the collective party line from MF Global management was that the whole thing was just one big unfortunate accounting screw-up. Reading the subcommittee's report, one gets the feeling that the MF Global defense is going to be one similar to that of Ken Lay, the embattled CEO of Enron who told prosecutors that he didn't know what his accountants were doing. Lay's efforts in court got him 24 years in prison.

But guilt or innocence in terms of legal sentencing aren't in the purview of the United States Congress. The subcommittee investigating

MF Global can only issue their findings and opinions based on interviews with those involved. From there, as the report itself points out, "It will be up to regulators and prosecutors to determine whether he or other employees violated any laws."

* * *

Former CEO Jon Corzine, the man with arguably with the biggest target on his back, said that he, as the CEO at the time of the firm's collapse, is ultimately responsible for everything that happened. But when pressed for details, he said, "I simply do not know where the money is or why the accounts haven't been reconciled." So he's willing to accept responsibility for what happened, but he can't explain exactly what it was that happened in the first place.

In an attempt to win at least one of the many public-relations battles Corzine is fighting, a spokesperson said, "All of the firm's significant business decisions were subject to review, debate and approval." While that may be true, the comment has to be taken with a rather large grain of salt. Corzine was notorious for surrounding himself with underlings who agreed with him and his strategies. Can the opinions of those who owe their livelihood to their blind allegiance to Corzine really be taken as indicative of their true feelings? In other words, after those people "reviewed and debated" Corzine's proposals, is it surprising that they always approved them?

In a final ironic twist of the knife that's been stuck into Corzine's side, it is entirely possible that the former CEO will be charged under the Sarbanes-Oxley Law. Enacted in 2002 in response to multiple corporate accounting scandals that had seriously damaged investor confidence, Sarbanes-Oxley created the Public Company Accounting Oversight Board, which was charged with regulating and enforcing rules pertaining to corporate accounting practices.

As a member of the Senate Banking Committee during his time in office, Jon Corzine was intimately involved with the passage of Sarbanes-Oxley, and was a very vocal supporter of the law. It's reminiscent of former New York Governor Eliot Spitzer's promise to crack down on prostitution rings.

During his time in front of the House subcommittee, Corzine did have an opportunity to throw a little blame away from himself and toward Edith O'Brien. Corzine told the committee in regards to the missing seg funds, "I had explicit statements that we were using proper funds, both orally and in writing, to the best of my knowledge. The woman that I spoke to was a Ms. Edith O'Brien."

O'Brien wasn't quite as forthcoming with names. She invoked her Fifth Amendment right against self-incrimination when questioned by the House subcommittee, though she did dispute Corzine's claim that she had ever assured him that the transfer of $175 million was proper. In March 2012, she declined to answer investigators' questions, instead trying to broker a deal that would garner her immunity from prosecution. She went so far as to refuse to cooperate at all unless she was granted that immunity; prosecutors were undecided as of December 2012 whether or not they would agree to her request.

* * *

In October 2012, the Virginia Retirement System and Province of Alberta, Canada filed a lawsuit against Jon Corzine and other MF Global executives, as well as banks including JP Morgan and Goldman Sachs. The suit alleges that the plaintiffs knowingly inflated their ability to manage risks, in addition to obscuring the risks associated with the RTM trades, and "improperly accounting for deferred-tax assets."

In response, Corzine and his attorneys stated that the lawsuit was basically accusing him of not being able to see into the future. There was no securities fraud, Corzine argued, and the allegations were merely saying that he'd mismanaged the company because he'd been too optimistic and unable to predict that MF Global's credit rating would be downgraded and lead to a liquidity crisis.

Another lawsuit, this one aimed at the accounting firm of PriceWaterhouseCoopers, alleged that the firm failed to adequately audit MF Global's internal controls. It further alleged that those responsible for auditing MF Global should have realized that the internal controls for guarding the sacred customer seg funds weren't adequate enough to ensure those funds' safety. In response,

PriceWaterhouseCoopers said that their final audit of MF Global in March 2011 was done "in accordance with professional standards."

The bevy of pending litigation notwithstanding, the major impact on the financial world as a whole as a result of MF Global's collapse was that wrought on the futures industry. Understandably, consumer confidence in the industry plummeted after the revelation that MF Global had somehow misplaced – or even misused – client funds, and so far resulted in a 10% drop in total customer seg funds on deposit from 2011 to 2012, the year after MF Global's collapse.

Another result of the MF Global fiasco is that futures clients tend to be minimizing the amount of cash that they keep at smaller futures brokers – firms like MF Global – preferring instead to keep their money at larger banks that they deem more reputable. Banks like JP Morgan and Goldman Sachs are benefitting from this windfall, whereas smaller firms are feeling the financial pinch associated with smaller deposit numbers.

More importantly, though, is an industry-wide ripple effect that is the by-product of new understandings of rules for futures brokers. For starters, people are paying much closer attention to the seemingly endless list of regulations governing the industry and the MF Global bankruptcy has increased awareness of the impact of bankruptcies for futures commodity brokers across the country,

The main rationale is a change in thinking about customer funds. Prior to the MF Global collapse, conventional thinking assumed that in the event a futures broker went bankrupt, the customer accounts would be safely transferred first to another firm then to the original owners. But the unwinding of MF Global has proven to be such a complex undertaking that the thinking has changed. That unfortunate event has shown that any missing funds must be accounted for by trustees and liquidators – with funds being transferred piecemeal as they become available – and final settlement of customer accounts can be held up for years.

The MF Global bankruptcy has also been used as a political tool. Headlines of "missing" customer funds totaling $1.6 billion for weeks and months have made it easier for people to further their own agendas. Regulators are no longer meeting with the same resistance they had in the past when trying to force through new regulation. Republicans in

Congress have also targeted Corzine's own past as a Democratic senator and blame regulators for not doing their jobs adequately, going so far as to suggest a merger between the Securities and Exchange Commission and the Commodity Futures Trading Commission.

The CFTC didn't wait long to pass new rules following the collapse; with all the public outrage, they wanted to show an attempt to correct the problems swiftly and decisively. One of the new rules that came directly from MF Global's bankruptcy was one regarding internal repo trades. No longer are futures brokers and broker-dealers housed within the same firm allowed to participate in repo transactions with one another. Additionally, foreign sovereign bonds are no longer allowed to be used in customer seg funds, and the balance of customer seg funds must now be reported daily to federal regulators.

The truth regarding those rules, however, is that they were regulations the organization had been seeking to pass for some time, but had always met resistance within the futures industry. The MF Global bankruptcy served as a catalyst to get them accepted by the larger financial world, but they had no real impact on preventing another MF Global seg fund violations, just as the Peregrine Financial Group collapse and missing seg funds demonstrated just seven months later.

Approximately one year after the bankruptcy declaration, there was a list of additional regulations that were submitted by the CFTC for public comment on October 23, 2012. Those proposals included eliminating the Alternative Method, as well as calling for a requirement that firms hold additional amounts of their own funds in seg accounts as a cushion against margin deficiencies. Another proposed rule would require pre-approval by management prior to the removal of more than 25% of excess seg funds deposited at a firm, as well as providing access for the Commodity Futures Trading Commission and other regulators to view the seg funds held at the clearing banks.

With the new rules – those proposed and those already enacted – there is hope that customer confidence will eventually be restored. But in reality, there were many regulations already in place to prevent what happened at MF Global and those regulations obviously failed. Randy Neugebauer didn't hold back in his condemnation of those responsible for what he saw as a systemic failure. "We don't need additional regulation," he said. "We need regulators actually doing their job."

And while it's easy to suggest that Neugebauer was simply posturing for his constituency, his remarks do have some validity. The House subcommittee investigating the collapse issued a report following their analysis of the findings, and pointed out that "both agencies focused on their respective jurisdictional interests and not the firm as whole" and that "there is no record of meaningful communication between the SEC and the CFTC until the week before the company's bankruptcy. When these regulators finally tried to coordinate, it was disorganized and haphazard." Among the cited examples of this lack of communication was the fact that the CFTC did not inform anyone at the SEC that MF Global personnel were using the controversial Alternative Method of accounting.

* * *

The major players in the MF Global scandal are still among us, and many of them are still operating in the financial world. Jon Corzine is rumored to be starting a hedge fund of his own, which might strike some as a comical attempt at a professional reset, given his last few years at MF Global. Many in the financial world expect that he won't have any trouble raising money, including one such person – Anthony Scaramucci, the founder of the hedge fund SkyBridge Capital – who said, "Yes, I trust Jon Corzine and think if he starts a fund, he will make money and be very successful."

Brad Abelow, the former global chief operating officer for MF Global, stayed on with the firm after the bankruptcy until November 2012. He took a relatively titanic pay cut, however, going from a million dollars a year to a mere $60,000. He apparently felt a sense of duty to the firm's former customers, as he worked to help unwind the firm and clean up the mess that had been created.

Jon Bass served as global head of institutional sales while at MF Global. After the collapse, Bass landed squarely on his own two feet. He took over as head of U.S. fixed income at BNP Paribas in October 2012. Christopher Belhumeur, who served as the head of structured mortgage trading at MF Global, moved to Royal Bank of Canada in January 2012 to serve as that institution's head trader.

Many other major players have yet to rejoin the workforce, though given the success of many former MF Global executives in their hunt for gainful employment, it is unlikely they will remain on the rolls of the unemployed for long. They are, after all, some of the brightest minds in the financial world, and whatever sins were committed at MF Global by a handful of people, many remain highly productive traders and salespeople.

As for the MF Global office in London, the trustee overseeing the unwinding of that operation was unable to find a buyer for the futures and options divisions, as well as for the brokerage and the commodity futures division. Despite opening up the lines of business to auction, there were no bids put forth. The metals division – which employed approximately 50 people – was sold to FC Stone International, the UK subsidiary of a U.S.-based futures broker. The remaining client positions held in the London office were liquidated or transferred to accounts at other futures brokers, with the exception of some options that were deemed too far out of the money to warrant transfer.

This whole story began with the spinning off of MF Global from its larger parent company, ED&F Man, forming the three distinctly separate firms. Man Group PLC became the money management company; ED&F Man International, which later became Man Financial, became the futures broker. The firm that retained the original name, ED&F Man, continued to operate for all these years as a physical commodities broker, and recently entered the futures brokerage and fixed-income businesses by attracting many former Man Financial personnel.

Peter McCarthy led a group to ED&F Man to start the financial markets business, and his group numbers about 150, drawn from both the MF Global London and New York offices. Included in that distinguished group are Stephen Hawksworth, the head of European markets; Donald Galante, the chief investment officer; Nick Masico, a senior vice president who heads up the repo desk; and Terry Stroud, the chief financial officer. In a sense, those who have returned to ED&F Man have stayed "in the family" and returned to the company from which they started.

Approximately 2,600 former MF Global employees have had their lives disrupted. Many are good people and managed successful businesses at the firm. The MF Global story illustrates how the misdeeds of a few people in control of a business can impact a company and destroy the business. The facts of the matter point to bad decisions managing the business and bad decisions – possibly criminal decisions – in the use of customer funds. With any luck, a better understanding of the events, the collapse itself, and what went wrong can someday break the cycle of similar financial misdeeds

* * *

John Adams took it upon himself to defend those who the popular voice called indefensible. Despite the sentiment against him, he did what he could to provide the British soldiers with the best possible legal defense he could muster. In the end, six of the eight soldiers brought to trial were acquitted, with the remaining two receiving reduced sentences.

Adams argued that the facts of the case – like facts in general – were "stubborn," and despite the overwhelming anti-British feelings that permeated the region, those feelings could not "alter the state of facts and evidence." But inevitably, all the facts will one day come to light. And when they do, it will be imperative that the world treats them as the immutable truths that they are. In that same vein, however, it is incumbent on the world to rely on the words of another statesman, Senator Patrick Moynihan: "Everyone is entitled to his own opinions, but not to his own facts."

For sales, editorial information, subsidiary rights information
or a catalog, please write or phone or e-mail
Brick Tower Press
1230 Park Avenue, 9a
New York, NY 10128, US
Sales: 1-800-68-BRICK
Tel: 212-427-7139
www.BrickTowerPress.com
email: bricktower@aol.com

www.Ingram.com

For sales in the UK and Europe please contact our distributor,
Gazelle Book Services
Falcon House, Queens Square
Lancaster, LA1 1RN, UK
Tel: (01524) 68765 Fax: (01524) 63232
stef@gazellebooks.co.uk

CPSIA information can be obtained at www.ICGtesting.com
Printed in the USA
BVOW03s2135291013

334995BV00011B/98/P